Advance c

MW01482308

Wendy's unique take on this global problem emerges from a deep personal inquiry into the meaning of a right relationship with the natural world. It was my privilege to supervise her PhD. And it is my delight, as an IPCC Member, to recommend *Creeksong*, her inspirational book about the most significant problem faced by Earth's communities. Wendy's midlife research journey culminates in a courageous call to arms from an inspired elder.

Professor Peter Newman, AO
Co-ordinating Lead Author
International Panel on Climate Change (IPCC)
Professor of Sustainability, Curtin University, Western Australia

Wendy Sarkissian is an unusual one. People like her are rare. I know her from her wonderful contributions as a speaker, debater, and performer at our annual gathering, the Woodford Folk Festival in Queensland, Australia, over many years. At the time I first booked her, I really didn't know her. I should've.

There are many things in the world that Wendy is not. She is not a dancer, but she dances; she's not a singer, but she sings; and she's not a painter, but she's an artist. Mostly and sadly, she's not a salesperson. Really, she's terrible at that. If she was good at that she would have to let go of a humility that makes her so beautiful. If she did, she would be a household name. I doubt she could handle that. Wendy, on the surface, is not outwardly talented. I'd say she's probably not a good cook.

So why am I writing this? It's because as I got to know Wendy, I discovered magic. Someone very special: a gift to this world. She carries in her very being a wisdom so rare. That she has completed her *Creeksong* memoir gladdens me because she has a story everyone should hear.

Bill Hauritz, AM
Founder & Festival Director
Woodford Folk Festival, Australia

This extraordinary memoir is at last published! I've been a close friend of Wendy's for 50 years, watching and helping a little as her stories have come to life. This book transports us into Wendy's development with remarkable depth and understanding, and the images and writing are remarkable. I've always been well along the materialist spectrum from Wendy's spiritual insights, though, like anyone, I have my own spiritual life. Wendy's writing gives us all bright access into her numinous world. I strongly recommend that those of a skeptical, "mainstream" bent read it. Not least, for her courage, thoughtfulness, and grounding on an earth in danger— lessons for us all. And it's a very good story. This book takes us along a life of continuing transformation, through landscapes painted in many colors, by a writer with a fearless mind and a boundless heart.

Emeritus Professor David Wilmoth
Director, Learning Cities International

Creeksong is a personal journey of discovery and enlightenment. Urban Wendy moves from the constraints of life as an academic wife to become a brilliant student and then a highly successful community planner and consultant. Then she sadly realizes that ecology and environmental ethics are missing in many important decisions affecting life on Earth. She faces many challenges in her solo year in "the bush," living in an alternate community on the edge of tropical Darwin and learning to become environmentally literate.

There, in surroundings teeming with wildlife, mosquito swarms, unusual plants, and the ever present fear of wildfire, she encounters six distinct seasons (well known to First Nations inhabitants). *Creeksong* is a gripping story of Wendy's growing understanding of and relationship with nature, interspersed with the unique characters in the remote and crazy world of the Australian Top End. This inspirational book sends a strong message about the urgent need for humans to re-connect and value nature to rectify the assaults on the very essence of the Earth that sustains human life.

Joc Schmiechen, M Env Studies
wilderness guide and rock art researcher
School of Humanities, Flinders University, Adelaide

Wendy Sarkissian's memoir is a deeply personal and enchanting journey that weaves together reflections and experiences, philosophies and spiritual beliefs, and the threads of reverence for Nature with righteous anger against poor planning, the indifferent violence of modernist suburbanization, and the existential threat of climate change. It reassures us about how the kindness of friends and companions can nurture us and help us find peace and solace in troubled times.

Jason Byrne, PhD
Professor of Human Geography and Planning
University of Tasmania

This award-winning planner's story is engrossing and humbling, revealing and instructive, candid and raw—like no other I have ever read. Sarkissian' s journey interweaves grief and forgiveness, fire and water, reverence and abuse, terror and discovery, spirituality and eroticism, our Earth Mother and actual mother(s), thrown as they have been in the face of climate crisis. We can all be grateful for the insight and unflinching candor of the gift of this book.

John Forester, PhD
Professor of City and Regional Planning
Cornell University, and long-time student
of planners' and mediators' practices

Moving seamlessly between a suspenseful narrative and scientific facts, *Creeksong* shows us the real costs of climate change. Sarkissian also demonstrates the courage it takes to love deeply and to work with urgency to heal mother earth.

Louise Nayer
educator and author of *Burned: A Memoir*,
an Oprah Great Read

Creeksong is a courageous and moving tribute to life, death, healing, and the natural world. It is, at heart, an initiatory journey of a woman, weaving a tale that spans decades and continents, and captures the innocence and hopefulness of a child, the passion of a woman, and the wise humility of an elder.

Yollana Shore
Executive Coach, Awakening Leadership, Australia

Earth is a tiny planet. I met Wendy first in California when we attended an anti-nuclear protest. We stayed in touch over the years, which became decades, then a new millennium. Wendy has a rare ability to capture the micro-detail of a landscape, tap deep into the minds she meets, and channel her energy into effective outrage at the abuse of the Only One Earth and its peoples. Our pathways continued to intersect. When I read Wendy's account, it's as if I am there again, breathing in the intensely personal, intensely political life we lived together. Thank you, Wendy. You are one of the Oracles creating the global noosphere, which will address the global problems we have created collectively. This book is a portal into that world in the making.

Peter Hayes, PhD
Co-founder, Friends of the Earth
Australia/International, MacArthur Fellow
Director, Nautilus Institute

Wendy Sarkissian was a leader in community engagement in Australia for half a century. Now, in *Creeksong*, she blends her passion for community engagement with her spirituality and a deep love of Nature in a hard-hitting, timely book. Wendy's heartfelt reflections on the culpability of planning practice make her book a must-read for anyone working in the spheres of planning and community engagement. Her infinite wisdom continues to inspire me.

Becky Hirst, FRSA
author of *For the Love of Community Engagement*

Creeksong is remarkable. Spun from the life of a leading feminist, planner, and eco-activist, this book is charming, wise, and surprising. Best of all, it is life-affirming as it helps us face dark clouds ahead.

Aidan Davison, PhD
Associate Professor of human geography
and environmental studies, University of Tasmania

Light a red candle for courage–terror essential–inside the inside of *Creeksong's* ephemeral wadi–macro lens on fire ecology–*I am the only being in this forest that does not know its place*–cyclone advice–through tantric opening and beauty and fear and grief–one woman's authentic transformation–redefine ideas about intelligence, relationship, trust, healing, ecology–a path of hidden waters as everything changes.

Dr. Jane Munro
poet and educator, author of *Blue Sonoma*,
winner of the Griffin Poetry Prize 2015.
janemunro.com/

Creeksong

ONE WOMAN SINGS
THE CLIMATE BLUES

A MEMOIR

Books by Wendy Sarkissian

*Stay Close: How to Heal from Grief and Keep
Connected with One Who Has Died*
Ebook: https://amzn.to/2CR6q29/
See www.stay-close.com/

*Creative Community Engagement: Transformative
Engagement Methods for Working at the Edge*
With Dianna Hurford and Christine Wenman.

*Kitchen Table Sustainability: Practical Recipes for
Community Engagement with Sustainability*
With Nancy Hofer, Yollana Shore, Steph
Vajda, and Cathy Wilkinson.

*SpeakOut: The Step-by-Step Guide to
SpeakOuts and Community Workshops*
With Wiwik Bunjamin-Mau. Also with Andrea
Cook, Kelvin Walsh, and Steph Vajda.

*Housing as If People Mattered: Illustrated Site Planning
Guidelines for Medium-Density Family Housing*
With Clare Cooper Marcus.

Social Mix: The Bournville Experience
With Warwick Heine.

Content Warning

This book contains material related to sexual abuse,
mental illness and intergenerational trauma.

Creeksong

ONE WOMAN SINGS THE CLIMATE BLUES

A MEMOIR

Wendy Sarkissian

Tellwell Talent
www.tellwell.ca

ISBN
978-0-2288-8930-4 (Paperback)
978-0-2288-8931-1 (eBook)
978-1-77256-228-6 (audiobook)

Dedication

This book celebrates the blessed memory
of deep ecologist Karl-Heinz Langheinrich.
Written from, with, and for the Earth,
it honors
lifetimes of courageous, life-affirming contributions
by Joanna Macy, PhD, and John Seed, OAM.

*I*n January 1985, John Seed co-facilitates Joanna's Australian "Despair and Empowerment" ritual in Lennox Head, New South Wales. Paired with John in the "Learning to See Each Other" ritual, I look into his eyes. My eyes fill with tears as I witness depths of despair and pain reflecting his years of intense activism for environmental causes. And, astonishingly, I witness hope and joy.

Joanna directs us: *Open your awareness to the gifts and strengths and the potentialities in this being …. Behind those eyes are unmeasured reserves of courage and intelligence …. In this person are gifts for the healing of our world. In him are powers that can redound to the joy of all beings.*

My pain mirrored in John's eyes reminds me that I am not alone. I, too, am a member of All Beings. I promise to join their work.

At last, here is my book, the child of my promise-keeping to Karl, Joanna, and John.

Table of Contents

Foreword

Eldersong
by Chellis Glendinning

*T*he task of the elder, according to psychoanalyst Erik Erikson, is to review one's life in depth and, in so doing, to integrate its many events, trials, undertakings, and experimentations with the aim of accepting them all… accomplishments and failures alike. As an elder myself, I have been amazed to watch as my psyche presents to me—via dreams and remembrances—the many people, places, and moments of history I have known. Even more astounding has been witnessing friends who in all their days have never shown a reflective moment suddenly scratching out autobiographies, editing video collages of their lives, and gathering photo albums. The urge to understand, accept, and integrate appears to be embedded in our very being.

Creeksong is described as a "memoir." The word derives from the French *mémoire*, meaning reminiscence or memory.

Various qualities have been associated in studies of literature to such a piece of writing. First, a memoir is a true story and, *ergo*, is built upon facts—albeit facts as filtered through the author's experience or perception. Second, it is different from autobiography that covers a person's entire life; rather, it presents a focus, a theme, perhaps a slice of time or a specific sequence of events.

Another quality of a memoir is that it reveals some kind or degree of transformation in the author's perceptions, understanding of life, manner of living, or dedication. Lastly, literary studies require that, in a true memoir, the writer's inner world reflects a universal truth that the reader will identify and recognize as part of her or his experience. "Memoir can't be all scene, it can't be all stories. What does it all *mean*?" clarifies author Rachael Hanel.

And so, here comes Wendy Sarkissian at age 80, and what a tale she has to tell. Hers has been a life that ranges from a confusing childhood to an enviably successful career, from a mentorship with a radical ecologist to a liberating personal healing. The story begins in her family-of-origin and so may appear to belong in the category of autobiography. Yet, the text contains a very specific theme: how the author found her way through a long labyrinth to become her own self. In Sarkissian's case, such a focus demands the "slice" of life that includes *all* the years she has lived.

By her own words, the book is an "eco-feminist memoir"—and how refreshing and relevant is such a handle in a world gone mad with nuclear threats, ongoing wars, racially motivated violence, increasing ecological breakdowns and disasters, and rampant global diseases! Eco-feminism has been recognized as one of the more creative philosophies of these times. It encompasses a bringing together of political activism with analytical thought springing from the observation that the various objects of historical domination—women, people of color, rebels, free spirits, and nature itself—are one and the same and spring from the same source of patriarchal insecurity. Too, eco-feminism is a way of thinking/living that invites humans to revitalize our relationship to the creatures and cycles of the natural world.

For Sarkissian, it becomes a reunion that has long been knocked out of knowing/feeling by the survival demands of mass technological society. Such a remembrance requires her fresh awakening to all living beings—from trees and beasties to her own inner self—and a resulting review of her political priorities. It is a rebirth that digs deep into her soul and, ever so wisely, requests that she be healed of the negativity she has long carried regarding her family history.

As she describes it, "I found the courage to come home."

Here I would like to venture to add one unmentioned quality that defines a memoir. Please try this on: the reader will be changed on some fundamental level, perhaps opened to new possibilities—and this is the very feature that stands out in Sarkissian's book. Through hardship and determination, usually guided only by honesty and intuition, she fulfills the integrated personality's task of individuation. According to Carl Jung's analytical psychology, such is a psychic process whereby one evolves until one finds completeness, what many refer to as "one's true self."

In *Creeksong,* this vibrant elder has shown how she managed to achieve such a slippery goal, all the while never evading the bravery necessary to reveal the stumbles and slipups along the way. If the reader has placed one toe upon such a path—or wishes to—this book may well propel one forward.

And that is its meaning.

Chellis Glendinning

Chellis Glendinning is a psychologist specializing in recuperation from trauma. She has authored 10 books, including her most recent: *In the Company of Rebels: A Generational Memoir of Bohemians, Deep Heads, and History Makers* (2019) and a novel, *Objetos,* published in Bolivia in Spanish. She lives in an antique house in Chuquisaca, Bolivia.

I moved in the direction...

I moved in the direction of my deeper Self's desires.
The path knew I was coming.
I ran free, barefoot, touching the Earth.
I sat in the damp, black Earth.
I ate my Shadow.
Earth and Sky claimed me.
For the first time in my life, I howled.
I made my life come alive again.
I found the courage to come home.

Our Climate Emergency

Prayer

We pray for the fragile ecology
of the heart and the mind.
The sense of meaning
So finely assembled and balanced and so
easily overturned. The careful, ongoing
construction of LOVE.

As painful and exhausting as the struggle for truth
and as easily abandoned.

Hard fought and won
are the shifting sands of this sacred ground,
this ecology.

Easy to desecrate and difficult to defend,
this vulnerable joy, this exposed faith,
this precious order. This sanity.

We shall be careful.
With others and with ourselves.
Amen.

Michael Leunig, 1993

No Place to Hide

Highway 7, southern British Columbia, east of Agassiz, November 14, 2021

"Oh, Chris, I'm so sorry you must drive through such terrible weather. We should have left earlier. But I loved our side trip to Hope. And I thought we might outrun this rain. But we're in it now, all right. This is the worst rain I've ever, *ever* seen."

"Can't talk right now, Wadi. Gotta keep my eyes on the road—what I can see of it."

"Well, I've got a final birthday treat for you, darlin'. I saved it for our trip back to Vancouver. I've been corresponding with a young musician and songwriter in Melbourne named Dominic Brinkley. He wrote a song called 'Climate Blues' in 2020.

Dominic Brinkley

"I've fallen in love with his song. Dom's got a real social conscience. He's worked out that governments (like his in Australia and ours here in Canada) have been ignoring climate change for decades, Chris. I'm with Dom. *I'm* singing the 'Climate Blues.' He's my new hero. "And he's worried about how Boomers like us have trashed the planet for his generation. Here, let me play his song for you."

"Climate Blues"
by Dominic Brinkley

He takes a look at the places that he's been
Yes, he's kinda lucky, but he's still not living the dream
He's been told to make the switch from grey to green
But he just don't see the forest from the suburban trees

You see, it's all about economic growth,
And retiring boomers' investment homes;
let's go and walk in the store-bought park down by the road

I take a look at the recent election results

OUR CLIMATE EMERGENCY

So many youth still don't give a shit about their vote
It kinda gets me down, but I'm a little bit the same
And why vote green when your vote's just gonna be in vain?

"Oh, God. Watch it, Wendy! It's chasing us. Oh, God! God! No! The mud, the mud…"

★★★

High ground.
We're safe now.
Outran the devil—that mudslide.

We skid to a halt in a slush of snow and wet gravel somewhere on the edge of Highway 7, above the Fraser River. The last signpost read "Ruby Creek." The GPS says we're 75 miles from Vancouver.

We're both screaming at the car radio that tells us:

Torrential rain expected to continue.
All local rainfall records broken.

Widespread flooding.

Over one thousand people forced from their homes. Hundreds more stranded.

Emergency crews out in force.

Mudslides on Highway 7 between Agassiz and Hope.

Abbotsford Police close Trans-Canada Highway #1.

High winds, devastation, evacuations, polluted drinking water, a dozen human deaths, thousands of farm animals dead…

"Ohhh, fucking hell! I'm so scared. Ohhh, God help us!"

I wrench the car door open and stumble to the guardrail to throw up.

Gasping, I turn to look back. I glimpse the blue snake of Highway 7 disappearing under a slurry of mud, debris, rocks, signs, fencing, massive logs, and branches. Strewn across the highway that's now impassable.

"Ohhh, this is *too* much. *Too* much! I thought I'd seen everything, with that car crash six years ago—plunging a hundred feet into a river! And watching my husband drown there. And now *this*! Jesus, this is *too* much. *This* scared the living shit out of me! Thankfully, nobody died. Thank God Chris is an experienced driver."

Chris leans against the guardrail and rocks back and forth, his head down, moaning between pursed lips.

"Oh, Wadi. I couldn't see a thing. I was sure that mudslide would catch us, that we wouldn't make it out alive!"

Chris pulls his coat over me, and we shiver together in the rain. We sigh. We hug. We breathe. Back in the car, we thank God for our close escape. For the gift of our lives.

When we reach Vancouver, there's water everywhere. But nothing like Highway 7.

With a tinge of gallows humor, someone later calls it "the longest swimming pool in British Columbia."

What is this? The Apocalypse?

OUR CLIMATE EMERGENCY

After a summer of record-high temperatures and forest fires, now we're getting record rainfall.

Can we be safe anywhere?

Is there no place to hide?

The radio helps us make sense of our terrifying experience. Nowadays, everything meteorological is more intense and lasts longer. Some regions in B.C. received more rain in 36 hours than they usually get in all of November. The cause? An *atmospheric river*: a narrow corridor, hundreds of miles long, that carries enormous amounts of water vapor over oceans from the tropics to temperate regions like western Canada. When it makes landfall, it dumps prodigious amounts of rain.

Climate change is the culprit again.

Just like Dom Brinkley, we're singing the "Climate Blues." Again.

On our slow journey back to Vancouver, I reflect on recent events. Before the floods, the town of Lytton, only 60 miles north of here, broke Canada's all-time temperature record: 49.6° C (121.3° F). It was the hottest place in Canada for three days running. The next day, the whole town burned to the ground. Throughout the province, more than 1,600 wildfires burned, charring forests and hillsides, followed by flooding and mudslides. Then autumn brought rain and flooding.

Climate crises aren't limited to North America, of course. In Australia, my adopted home, the same areas that suffered through drought and horrific bushfires in 2019 and 2020, later experienced massive amounts of rainfall. And then floods and cyclones. In 2020, I watch horrified on TV as the edge of a mammoth blaze burns along the perimeter of a beach in Mallacoota, a Victorian seaside town. Under a black sky that turns blood-red, 4,000 people cower in the red ocean. Some hold screaming children above their heads.

And last summer, as rivers of smoke from distant wildfires flowed into Vancouver, nearly 700 people died during British Columbia's unprecedented *heat dome.* A 200 percent increase over the previous year. Most were low-income seniors living alone in older apartment buildings without air conditioning. Our most vulnerable population group. Dying alone, maybe never even recognizing the signs of heat stroke.

Exhausted from driving through pelting rain, Chris gets to work when we reach his place. Feeds Oscar, feeds me, lights his red candle (for courage), and makes a pot of herbal tea. Then he guides me to a spot on the couch with a view of the garden. Spring is still months away, but the patio glistens, and the bamboo's slender leaves tremble under the raindrops. He leans across and gently wraps his mother's soft green woven shawl around my shoulders. I press my cheek into it and inhale the scent of happiness. This is Barbara's last weaving. *Mother is at home.*

I motion Oscar to my lap and let out a long sigh. He sighs back, the gentle rattle of a contented, elderly cat. I brush his soft, grey fur and feel connected again to my life-changing experience, my midlife climate change adventure in the tropical Australian bush. Three decades ago. Meeting the Earth Mother and promising to serve her…. I raise my left hand to touch my heart.

"Let's listen to a bit more of Dom's song, Chris. We cut off by that mudslide."

The time is now, was 10 years ago,
And the times keep changin', so why stay old?
We live in a country that is so shut off,
And the fires keep burning, man, when will they stop?
Cause the time is now; ain't no longer down the road
And if you speak on out, people look at ya cold

Will anything change here, before I die?
Wanna pass something good on before I kiss the sky...

"Dom is in his twenties. He's telling us *the time is now.* But people look at him coldly when he speaks out. And he's worried about what will happen before he kisses the sky. What about *us*? We're three times his age! I could kiss the sky any moment now!

"Oh, Chris, when I was a graduate student in the early nineties, global warming felt so 'out there.' I worried, for sure. And after I graduated, I spent a massive amount of my professional life working on climate change and environmental protection.

"But I never imagined climate change could *kill* me."

"Well, it nearly did today, Wadi. That's the truth. Let's get moving and finish your book, okay? We need to tell your story before it's too late."

I turn to him. His face is lined with weariness and concern.

"Yes. I agree, Chris. I'm on it."

Things are desperate.

*What **can** I do? What can one person do in such a climate crisis? What can one older woman do? Am I too old to make a difference? Does **anyone** know how to make a difference?*

When I was a young activist, we marched. We chanted, *Think global, act local.* We agitated to *prevent* climate change's negative impacts. Now I am reduced to *adapting.*

And I know that the real work of climate change is not talk. It's action. Hopeful action. Sure, I face limits. *And* I need to set my sights high. And I *must* rekindle my hopefulness. *Right here, right now,* I must show up. I'm old. *And* I'm a climate activist. So, I must turn my back on fear and embrace *active hope.*

And when I look inside my heart, *hope* is exactly what I find.

"Chris, I have a new idea. Working title: *One Earth Moment.* I remember being a community engagement planner. So, I'm suggesting that whenever we hold workshops or meetings, we begin our process by *listening before we speak.* Just stop and listen to what is important. And then we take *One Earth Moment.* Take time to do three simple things.

"First, we acknowledge the climate emergency. Out loud. No more pussy-footing around. Second, we accept that all human activity has implications for the health of the Earth. Again, we make this a fierce and unconditional condition. Anthropogenic climate change is what we're facing. We created it and now we must face it and address it. And third, we agree to cooperate to support the Earth. So, everything we do in whatever process or project we're working on must support the healing of the Earth.

"For decades, we've acknowledged the traditional custodians of the land on which we meet. When we use my approach, our *One Earth Moment* will come first. We won't take a single step until we pay respect to the source of all life on Earth."

I turn again to my sweetheart. He nods, snuggles up to me, and pulls the shawl around his shoulders.

"You know, Chris, I was born a planner. When I was a child, I asked small questions. Like: Why was my elementary school an hour's walk up a steep, muddy, rough, unlit trail? Why was everything around me so badly planned—or unplanned? I was small then, so my focus was small, local. Now I have *global* questions. *And* I'm that same curious person.

"'Scaredy' was my word then. Today, climate change nearly killed us, Chris. But I've had scaredier days. Six years ago, with an inch of air to spare, some divine power saved me from drowning so I could do something good for the Earth. And thirty years ago, I made a big promise to the Earth Mother. Now, I'm going to keep it. I'm nearly 80 and I'm not going to be cowed by the taunts and dismissiveness of the gendered ageism I see all around me. Not for one minute!

"*One Earth Moment* is my new activism. I've got projects galore. The heat dome, my cool room idea, and deep, wide-ranging and inclusive community engagement around climate change issues… I may be old, but *right here, right now*, I'm standing up and speaking up for the Earth."

Part 1
The Innocence

Six and Three-Quarters Years Old / Our Big Road Trip /
Meeting My Armenian Family in San Francisco

Six and Three-Quarters Years Old

Lindsay, Ontario, October 1949

Who are these people who say they're my parents?

How would my *real* parents do such a terrible thing and ruin my life? I must be adopted. I knew it all along. How come I have blue eyes and blond hair, and everyone else in my family has brown eyes and dark or red hair?

This new thing is the biggest disappointment of my whole life. It's just not fair. I waited a whole extra year to start school because I was born in January. I'm six and three-quarters, and I'm finally starting elementary school. That's really, *really* bad. The other kids learned printing in kindergarten, but I couldn't go, so my teacher tries to teach me printing, but I don't want to learn that. Printing is for children. I want to write joined-up letters right away because it's the grown-up thing to do, and I want to be a grown-up.

And now these people who say they're my parents say we have to move to Vancouver. And I have to leave all my friends

I just made at school. I'll probably never make any new friends again in my whole life. And I have to leave my beautiful teacher, Mrs. McKenzie. There are probably no other good teachers in the entire world. Mrs. McKenzie teaches me a new word when I discuss things with her, and it lifts my spirits. That word is *stability*. Life is orderly and stable at school, and I feel more comfortable there than at home. I like stability—being away from the ups and downs of home.

I'm *so* disappointed about this change. *And* things are not going right in my family. I am a worrywart already. Every day I worry about how I am going to grow up when nobody even notices me or my problems. But the moment I get to school, I work out that getting an education might be my secret. I don't know anybody with an education; my parents don't have one, and my daddy feels really bad about that. He's pretty smart, but he couldn't have an education because scaredy things happened when his daddy drove his car into a train and got obliterated. (That's my new word: *obliterated*: "uh" + "BLIT" + "uh" + "rayt" + "id.")

That was pretty much the end for my daddy. I'm not scared of being hit by a train or stuff. It's more that my family is sort of lost. I can't explain it. But I worry about it a lot.

Still, I am so excited to start elementary school that I almost wet my pants. My school is small and old, but I am okay with that. It's historical. It is two stories tall, with red brick walls and rows of big, square, grey stones at the bottom of its walls, a flagpole out front, and some big maple trees out back. I can walk there in five minutes along the sidewalk from our house on Melbourne Street. My school's old name was South Ward School. Now it's called King Albert Public School, after the King of Belgium. He was an example of

THE INNOCENCE

bravery, loyalty, and hard work: a perfect person to name our school after.

I love my teacher, Mrs. McKenzie. She has a really, *really* sweet face and beautiful soft blond hair that she ties up in a bun and holds together with some silvery bobby pins. And little curls slip out all around her pale face and her neck that has tiny blue veins in it. And the seams in her nylon stockings are always perfectly straight. I feel comforted and loved by Mrs. McKenzie. If this is what an education feels like, I know I will be perfectly fine getting educated.

Then I get the bad news: we have to move a million miles away so my daddy can get a better job. I love my daddy (he really *is* my daddy, and I am pretty sure I'm not adopted), but his better job is not here, in Lindsay, Ontario, where it should be. It's in Vancouver (wherever that is).

Daddy comes home from a business trip to Western Canada. He stayed at his favorite hotel in downtown Vancouver, the *Georgia* (where he has *contacts*). And he found us a new house and gave people money so nobody else could buy *our* new house. We are moving there soon. Daddy reads me some brochures he got about Norgate Park. Our new house is called "ranch-style." It is one story tall (not like ours here in Lindsay, Ontario), and it has three bedrooms.

Six and Three-Quarters Years Old

The brochures have pictures of happy families in brand-new houses near some water across a big bridge with big pointy mountains in the background. Daddy says 125 families will be living there by the time we arrive.

The brochures also say that our new house will have "every modern device for better living." Already, the community is "bright, cheerful, convenient, friendly, progressive, and has a small-town friendliness." That's a lot to take in. I will be safe from fast-moving traffic because a strip of park goes from our new house to the school. Pretty soon, they will build a brand-new shopping area with a playground where mothers can leave their children while they do the family's shopping. That will be practically next door, so Mummy can walk there. The houses will be built from materials that come from a respected local timber merchant. And they did everything to make sure that everyone has a good view of the pointy mountains. I am impressed.

Daddy tells me how he found our new house.

"Wadi, you will not believe this. It was magic. I was selling watches door-to-door in North Vancouver, and I saw trucks going in and out where there were some tall trees. And I said to myself, 'That little Wadi of mine loves trees, so I'd better check out those new houses that are getting built there.' And pretty soon a man is showing me some new houses beside the forest with the tall trees. I liked the one across the street from that forest. They gave me a choice of streets (they call them *crescents* there), so I chose Oakwood Crescent because Oakwood is our next-door town to Lindsay."

My daddy is always into magic.

THE INNOCENCE

"Wadi, you will have an experience that no six-and-three-quarters-year-old will ever have. We will drive across the States to San Francisco and up the coast to Vancouver. We will drive through dozens of states, and every state will be different. We will drive through prairies, and deserts, and lots of mountains, and eventually, we'll get to San Francisco."

I listen carefully, but I'm not totally convinced. But it means so much to my parents. Hopefully, I can get back to school pretty fast.

But I cheer up when I hear what Mummy has to say about moving:

"I love Daddy's news! This move will be *really* good for us, Wadi."

We're standing together at the kitchen table, and Mummy beams as we fold the pillowcases in the special way Nana taught us. "When Daddy has a better job selling Oyster watches, life will be better for us. You wait and see."

Mummy also wants to move. *She* wants a new start, too.

So, we are moving. I have to accept that.

Daddy comes to get me at school (after I've been there only a month and a half). We leave on our Big Road Trip the next day. My teacher and I stand on the grey stairs in front of the big green front door with the round window like an upside-down half-moon above it. I am crying. I hold onto my teacher's dress, and when I look up at her, I see she has tears, too.

Six and Three-Quarters Years Old

"I will do my very best, Mrs. McKenzie," I gasp between my sobs. "I promise."

Mrs. McKenzie leans down and whispers to me: "Wendy, you have something special inside you, and I think you know that. I am sending you on your great journey with confidence that you will have a wonderful life. I know you will be successful."

At that moment, I do not know what I know later. In my life, I will have more supportive teachers, warm colleagues, and beautiful, wise, and compassionate friends. And, when I grow older, loving and attentive lovers and partners. Still, I will never feel the way I feel at that moment with my first teacher. I feel perfect. I am perfect in the eyes of my teacher. And as I am a bit lonely already, that is a huge thing for me. I cry for the rest of the day. I am finally having a taste of an education. And now, I need to change gears and figure out how to manage a new life in Vancouver.

I will never forget the smell of autumn in Ontario. I am a person who *totally* loves trees. I *adore* trees, especially maple trees, because they have big, flat leaves that you can dunk in melted wax when they turn color. In Ontario, people pick up scads of leaves with giant rakes, dump them in wheelbarrows, and then throw them into burners in their backyards. And the air is full of smoke, and it smells so wonderful! All my life, whenever I smell leaves burning, I am back to being six and three-quarters, standing with my lovely teacher on the street lined with maple trees.

This move to Vancouver is a very scaredy time for me, but I also feel excited. I am going to have a new life. I can make a fresh start. Maybe I will be really happy, and that will make

THE INNOCENCE

up for moving and the weird things that sometimes happen in my family.

Before we leave, Daddy gathers us together and explains his plan. I sit on the floor with Dolly and Pretty Bear. My parents (they must be mine, after all) stand because our furniture's gone.

"First," announces Daddy in a MOST SERIOUS VOICE, "we need to move fast because winter's coming, and we don't want to drive through too much snow. The car's heater doesn't work too well, so we need to wear our outdoor clothes in the car. It will be pretty cold in the mornings. Also, we will be driving straight west for the first leg to San Francisco. I don't want to drive into the setting sun. It's too dangerous. So, it will be an early start for us.

"We must be packed up and on the road before 6 am, and we'll stop at a motel before 5:30 at night. Oh, and just to warn you, I will be driving pretty fast. This is not a sightseeing trip," he explains, looking stern.

I try to relax about not doing things right on my first Big Road Trip.

In the car, we sometimes play a singing game we invented. I yell out a word, and Daddy comes up with a song with that word in it. He sings it, and then I learn it by singing along. It's really fun. For example, I might yell, "Shadow!" above the clanking of the car's heater. And Daddy's right onto it with "Me and My Shadow." Or I yell out, "Blue!" And he sings three of our favorite songs, "My Alice Blue Gown," "Am I Blue?" or "My Blue Heaven."

Six and Three-Quarters Years Old

At first, I think this Big Move is all Daddy's idea. But then I hear my parents talking after they think I'm asleep. Things are not going that well for our family. Daddy was a wireless radio operator in the Royal Canadian Air Force in the War. He got wounded in his knee and has a big scar there. He was really upset after the War, but he never talks about it. Except how they accidentally bombed that French village from his plane. Daddy feels so guilty about that. The rest of the War is like a bad dream, he says. He saw men get killed, too, with their blood all over the place. And everything. He thought he'd never see Mummy and me again.

Mummy has been sad and depressed for years and years— since her other baby died when I was about two. All I can remember is her being depressed. But we aren't allowed to talk about the dead baby. The doctor said, "Nobody can ever talk about it. Never. *Ever.*" That dead baby would have been my brother, his name would have been Harootune, and he was dead when he came out from Mummy's tummy. That's so horrible.

Mummy says Harootune died because the doctor was a Catholic. (I guess she has to blame somebody.) My uncle Ron buried Mummy's dead baby in my grandfather's grave in Orillia, Ontario. But nobody ever went there to visit the grave or said a prayer or anything. Mummy and Daddy are both upset that Harootune is dead, and it's a sad thing between them.

My mummy is also getting old. She's 35 and has lots of dreams, but she can't seem to make them happen. She dreams of what she calls "a house on the hill." Mummy also wants to be in the driver's seat of our family, which is funny because she doesn't know how to drive. She wants to be in charge. She explains some sad things to me about her childhood.

THE INNOCENCE

"My daddy died when I was really young, Wadi, but nobody let me cry very much, so I have a lot of old tears stored up inside me. There was like a ban on crying in my family. And it was like I was the 'walking wounded,' out in the cold and not included in everyday family things. I never fit in. And I couldn't figure out why."

Much of the time, Mummy is pretty sad, so I just hang out with Daddy. He is much more approachable. But Daddy drinks a bit, and that brings out his own sadness. It's because his daddy was obliterated quite young, and that broke everybody's heart.

Sometimes Daddy talks to me like I'm a grown-up.

"I want a new start, too, Wadi. And I'm worried that things might not work out in Vancouver. I know it's odd, but sometimes Mummy doesn't know her own mind. I love your Mummy because she is creative and artistic and has poetry in her soul. And she can be very passionate. She could be a great writer or a public speaker—or even an artist. But she needs help. And I don't know how to help her."

When I hear my daddy say this, I feel sad deep inside.

Before we leave, I say a private goodbye to our house in Lindsay, Ontario. I know it's alive and has a soul like a person or a cat. So, I save a piece of chalk and draw a little pink heart on the inside of my bedroom door where nobody could see it. I color inside the lines. And then I gently pat my bedroom door, put my cheek up against it, and tell our house I love it. I thank it for keeping me cozy on cold winter nights.

Six and Three-Quarters Years Old

Our Big Road Trip

$\mathcal{P}$retty soon, we are all sitting in Daddy's pale blue Chevrolet with the beige seat covers, and we're driving to the American border. (Daddy always buys a Chevrolet and prefers blue or green. Once, he bought a Chevrolet that was a "lemon," but he's extremely loyal and would never buy a Buick.) Mummy sits in the back seat. I sit in front with Daddy and tell him I've decided not to step on the alien ground of the United States because that would be unpatriotic.

Daddy smiles at me when I say that.

"Wadi, I am trying to understand your reasoning, but that's simply not practical. You will have to walk with your feet on another country's soil. You will have to eat their food and sleep in their beds. I am not going to carry you across this whole continent. We will all walk on the soil of the United States, and we will be perfectly fine."

"Okay, if you say so, Daddy," I say. I have firm opinions about my sacred, patriotic duty as a Canadian citizen.

The day before we leave, Daddy buys me my most favorite new thing, a jigsaw puzzle of the whole United States. I am excited when I put the first American state (New York) in its place when we get to a place called Buffalo. At the border, a fat man in a grey uniform, a pink face, and bright blue eyes smiles at me.

"Hello, little lady. Welcome to the United States of America. You are now in God's own country. You will be a completely different person after this big adventure with your family. Have a wonderful trip, and travel safely. Y'all come back, y'hear?" he grins.

He waves, and I turn around and wave back as Daddy drives us into a totally different country where I have never been before.

We stay in a little motel near Buffalo because we were a bit late leaving, and everybody is quite exhausted. I fall asleep with my clothes on. The motels we stay in are okay for the rest of our trip. But in the mornings, it's freezing, and we have to pile on all our winter clothes, hats, and scarves until the car warms up. Daddy is always trying to get Mummy to hurry up.

The sun is rising behind us as we head west into the darkness, and it slowly changes everything around us in a magical way. The sky turns a dozen colors of blue with some pink and yellow mixed in. Daddy says Mummy has a good eye for color. She's very poetic about the sky in the morning. "That's *azure* blue," she exclaims and waves her hands dramatically as the whole sky glows in front of us.

The rest of the time, because I sort of slouch back into the seat and doze, I only see bits and pieces of things flying past my window: tall grey cement grain elevators, some metal ones, red barns, the tops of tall, dark trees, some bushy yellow trees, a billboard or two, and telephone poles. It's a lot of the

THE INNOCENCE

same. In some towns with streets and stores, the leaves are still turning, and I spot a maple tree or two.

Daddy says I can eat anything in the restaurants, and Mummy agrees. I have no experience with restaurant dining, so I just choose desserts. I figure I can't go wrong. The Americans have great desserts compared to ours. Especially the pies that sit on the counter on special, shiny silver stands with high clear plastic tops on them. In Canada, we have plain old apple, cherry, and the occasional lemon meringue. American pies are much better, and the slices are way bigger. They have banana cream, blueberry custard, strawberry rhubarb, caramel, pecan pies, sometimes even chiffon pies, and a cream pie from Boston. Their milkshakes are better, too. They give you two straws that stand up straight because the milkshakes have lots more ice cream. One flavor I particularly adore is chocolate mint malted.

I have a favorite diner, too: Stuckey's. They are dotted all along the highway, so a Stuckey's diner automatically appears on the horizon when my tummy begins to rumble for another treat. Their signs say it all: "Pecans—Snack Bar—Candies." Is there anything *else* in life?

My absolute favorite is the Pecan Log Roll. In Lindsay, Ontario, we would never dream of such a treat. The menu lists all the delicious ingredients Mrs. Stuckey uses in her old family recipe: a light, fluffy nougat center (called *Divinity*) with maraschino cherries, dipped in freshly made, buttery caramel, and topped off by hand-rolling it in chopped Georgia pecan pieces. I imagine her making the rolls: all warm and motherly, with a long white apron and curly grey hair.

Daddy explains that we are not visiting Georgia. But I put that state in my puzzle anyway, in honor of the Pecan Log Roll.

Because our trip is a bit boring and I sleep a lot, I don't pay much attention to every geographical feature. But one day, Daddy calls me to wake up immediately because something is about to happen that will change my life forever. I believe in magic from an early age, and so does my daddy, so I immediately sit up and look. The road we're on is approaching a gigantic bridge. It doesn't go up very high, but it's long and stretches over a wide, muddy river that is not moving very fast. Daddy pulls the car over because he doesn't want me to miss this momentous occasion. Then he jumps out, lights a cigarette, and blows the smoke dramatically. He looks really impatient, so I find my shoes and jump out to inspect this river before we drive across the long bridge.

"Wadi," Daddy exclaims with an air of authority as he waves the smoke away, "we are now crossing the Mississippi River. This is a gigantic river. It starts way up in Minnesota near the Canadian border and flows from north to south through like eight separate states. It's a *really* important river for the Americans. Lots of boats go up and down it, and it goes way, *waaaayy* down south to the Gulf of Mexico. It's the engine of American transport and commerce and the biggest, most wonderful river you'll ever see in your entire life. It's as important as the Nile. (In case you didn't know, Wadi, the Nile is in Egypt.)"

I stare at the river. There are heaps of reeds growing at the edge. The water looks like chocolate milk, and it isn't very beautiful. But "beautiful" is not what we're after. Daddy explains that this is a *Significant River*. It even has locks and dams on it.

This whole trip, I am trying to be hopeful. This is the start of our new life as a family. Vancouver will be a wonderful new home for us, with everything a family needs to be happy.

THE INNOCENCE

Meeting My Armenian Family in San Francisco

I trust that, although the sower does not see it,
yet the seed is growing.

Rev. Harootune Sarkissian, Nicosia, Cyprus, 1890.

*T*he Golden Gate Bridge is the last big thing on our Big Road Trip. I'm shocked that it's not golden. It's orange. And there is fog all around it. But I *am* impressed because it's my first ever suspension bridge. Daddy says North Vancouver has its own, and we will drive back and forth across it.

I totally disapprove of this side trip to San Francisco. I figure we could go there another time. I need to get back to school, but nobody seems to care about that but me. We are going to visit Daddy's two Armenian aunts, Hosannah and Rachel, who have the same last name as ours. Daddy's daddy died really young, so he needs all the family he can get.

We're sitting in the last diner on this leg of our trip. I've overdosed on Pecan Rolls, so I'm having a vanilla milkshake. Then Daddy leans across the Formica table, takes my hand, and gives me his more-than-serious look. He speaks slowly: "When you meet your aunts, Wadi, please remember they had a tough life. They lived with my family in Canada for a while, so I know their story."

Later that day, as the sun is setting, Daddy drives up a giant hill to the very, very top. He has to change gears a couple of times, and our Chevrolet is groaning by the time we get there. I hold my breath all the way up that hill. I'm leaning out my window to try to see the house numbers…

Finally, Daddy spots number 1169 on the wall of a building.

"Found it, Wadi." He lets out a shout.

I'm scared and excited at the same time. As we're walking up to the front door, I feel very shy, so I stand behind my daddy, sort of hiding. I expect to meet two sad people who were wrecked by their tough life.

We hear footsteps on the stairs, and then I glimpse two old women through the glass front door. They look like twins. Aunt Rachel and Hosannah welcome us into their home and their hearts. They hold our hands in their two hands and kiss us on both cheeks. The older sister, Hosannah, says to me, "Little Wendy, you are the light of my eye." All this is strange and wonderful to me.

THE INNOCENCE

The sisters have lots of room for us, and we're so happy after all those little motels.

Rachel and Hosannah live in a tall, skinny, blue house that's three stories high with no front yard or back yard. Not at all like Lindsay, Ontario, where everyone has front and back yards. I never saw tall houses like that before—all squished up and nearly touching each other. Their house has six giant white columns at the front with a golden stripe around the top of each of them. Their front door is made of glass—of all things—and then you climb up 20 steep stairs to the part of the building where they live. It's called an apartment. Other people live in the same building, and sometimes we hear them laugh.

The other houses are painted in bright colors—like yellow and orange. We would never have that in Lindsay, Ontario. And some houses (Daddy calls them "Spanish Mission" style) have curvy bits and things that look like crowns and trees sticking on their walls. It's weird!

We're right in the middle of a big city, but I can see low mountains a long way away. And their street is really wide and chopped in half. It has grass growing down the middle of it. And smack in the middle, they have a kind of tree that Daddy says is a palm tree. I never saw such a funny tree. It does not have leaves like the maple trees in Lindsay, Ontario. I get scratchy things all over my sweater when I hug that tree.

1169 Dolores Street, Noe Valley, San Francisco

And they have fog. I never saw that before, either. Every morning it rolls in from the ocean and lasts for hours. And it's really cold when it's foggy. And their neighborhood is called something like "No Valley." And we can walk about four blocks down the other side of Dolores Street—a really steep hill—as steep as the one we came up—to a little square with a children's playground near the stores and the dry cleaner. They have ice cream there, too.

My Armenian aunts are really different from my Ontario relatives, who are pretty white and ordinary. Hosannah and Rachel are *exotic*. When I grow up, I want to be *exotic* like them. They speak softly and have heavy accents. Their English is perfect. But they speak more from their throats than we do.

THE INNOCENCE

Sort of breathier. And they pronounce their words slowly and carefully, as if each word really matters. When they say, "Thank you," they often say *merci* in French.

"It's just a thing we Armenians do," Rachel explains.

Their house is a bit dark inside. It has heavy curtains with some velvety bits and dark, old-fashioned furniture called antiques. They have lots of paintings in golden frames on the walls. And the floors are shiny, yellowy wood, not like our beige wall-to-wall carpet in Lindsay, Ontario. They have lots of Turkish rugs in different colors and sizes. (Mummy says their tastes are *eclectic*. I love that new word, /ɪklɛktɪk). And they play Armenian songs on their record player. They're really slow and sad, and my daddy almost cries once when we listen to them.

Rachel and Hosannah are both over 70. Their eyes are pretty wrinkly, and they are bent over a little bit, Hosannah a bit more than Rachel. They walk sort of slow but are also pretty perky. Both are short, like my daddy, and, like him, they have curved noses and slightly bushy eyebrows. They have dark eyes and wavy white hair tied up in tight buns. They wear black dresses most of the time. Hosannah, the older one, is a bit shy, plainer, and old-fashioned. But sometimes, she can act quite young. She has a little trouble with her eyes, I think.

Aunt Rachel is lots of fun. She wears bright red lipstick and acts like a young girl.

They say they are soulmates, and sometimes they stand arm-in-arm and smile and giggle. Sometimes they just giggle like children. I'm a giggler, too, so pretty soon, I'm giggling! In Spanish, Dolores Street means *The Street of Sorrows*. But to me, it's *The Street of Giggles*!

Meeting My Armenian Family in San Francisco

I can't believe these women who had such tough lives have so much joy. Aunt Rachel says she can see herself in me, and I think we look similar. I promise I will act like Aunt Rachel when I get old. I introduce them to Dolly and Pretty Bear and tell them some stories about them, and we all get along fine. (I want to put them at ease because they don't have their own children.)

Daddy thought the sisters moved to California to be near other Armenians. But Aunt Rachel says, nope, they wanted a bit of adventure, and they were not ready to retire. They wanted a new start, so they bought this house, got good jobs as nurses, and advanced their careers. They wanted something different, sort of an escape. And they were a bit tired of being so "Armenian," so they moved to California to get away from themselves.

Daddy also thought they might be sad because they never got married. Nope, again. My aunts tell me they were both happy to have careers helping people. They did not miss having husbands and children. Rachel was a pediatric nurse. I guess that's why she's so good with children.

Aunt Rachel tells me a lot about *their* daddy. His name was Harootune, like my brother, who was dead when he came out of Mummy's tummy. He was a minister: a wise, kindly man with a big heart. He knew lots of stuff and helped lots of people. When he was dying, all his family sat beside him in his bedroom and sang his favorite Armenian hymns. And he was singing, too.

They have a picture of him in a black frame on a table in their living room. I look at it really closely, and I can see from the look in his eyes that he saw lots of sad things in his life.

THE INNOCENCE

Rev. Harootune Sarkissian, about 1910

My daddy interrupts in a shaky voice: "I had a son who died before he was born, and his name was Harootune. We named him after your father. He would be about four years old by now."

Aunt Hosannah cries then.

Except for some sad parts about the Armenian Genocide, the sisters keep smiling and telling us they're so happy we came to visit them. Their hometown is Aintab, a village in Turkey. Aintab is terrific because it is the world's capital for baklava. I had never had baklava before. It has walnuts and honey in it. I already love honey, and now I love walnuts.

At the sisters' house, we drink hot tea in glasses without milk or sugar. Hosannah pours it from a brass thing with a handle and a hot spout. And they always have snacks like nuts and fruit. And we have meals that are different from anything I ever ate before. Not like in Lindsay, Ontario, where we hardly ever had meals at our house. And they teach me how to make a special kind of pizza with ground meat and spices. It's called lahmajoun. It's the Armenian national dish. We roll it up and squeeze lemon juice on it. It's my first pizza, and it's delicious.

I spend most of my time with Aunt Rachel. She's good with children, so I decide to discuss a few personal matters with her. I sit on her lap, and she rocks me in her arms. I feel so cozy there.

"I want a good life when I grow up," I whisper. "I want to make a difference and care for people." I hang my head and confess: "I have a big heart, and Daddy says I have to be careful not to overdo things. I have big dreams, and sometimes they get in the way." And I kind of hint that I don't think my parents are managing too well. I explain to Rachel: "It's like they're floating on an ocean of confusion. Like they don't know where they're going."

I can tell Rachel has heard these sorts of things before. She has heard everything, and nothing frightens her. She cuddles me back against her chest and says, "I want to talk to you about trees, Wendy. Because you feel close to trees, it would be good if you could find a forest. And then spend as much time there as possible. I mean a *lot* of time. Is that something you could do? I have no idea if there are trees or a forest near where you're moving in North Vancouver."

I jump up because I am so excited. "Oh, Aunt Rachel," I blurt out. "I have magic news! Daddy said there is a forest with big trees right across the street from our new house."

We agree it's magic news. It's wonderful having an adult to share things with.

THE INNOCENCE

I hug Rachel, climb out of her lap, and go to my room to discuss these new ideas with Dolly and Pretty Bear. I pray to God in the sky that there *will* be a forest in North Vancouver.

One foggy morning, Aunt Hosannah asks if I'd like to take a look around the neighborhood. I love walking, and we work out an easy way to walk and have a conversation at the same time. Hosannah holds my hand, and it's the coziest feeling. I look up, and she looks down, and our eyes meet, and we're sort of on the same level. We walk to the little playground in the square on 24th Street. We walk *verrry* slowly because it's a steep, steep hill, and we have to take baby steps so we don't trip and fall down.

I don't know who is holding onto who!

When we finally reach 24th Street, I play on the swing, and Hosannah rests on a bench in the sunshine. Later we have ice cream cones.

I can tell Hosannah has been saving up something to say to me. While we sit together, she turns to me and takes my hands in hers.

"Wendy, it's been wonderful meeting you. I want to explain something. Sometimes I can sort of see into people. So, I imagine your parents might worry about how things will work in Vancouver. It might be difficult for them to find their way, and they might struggle to work out how to do things. This is a big move for them.

"So, I want to tell you something that might help *you* find *your* way. Wendy, you come from a long line of brave and caring people. My father, Harootune (your great-grandfather), didn't know how to do anything but care for people. And you have his blood inside you. Oh, Wendy, you are at the beginning of a precious human life. I hope you will grow to be an old woman. And I am confident that helping others will come naturally to you. You only need to do three things. Follow your heart. Understand that you are part of a great family. And carry the message of hopefulness from one generation to the next.

"Please remember this day, Wendy. The two of us walking hand in hand in the sunshine. And remember that you are a member of a great Armenian family. You will feel me holding your hand just as I am doing now. And you will hear my voice asking you to carry *my* hopefulness forward in *your* life just by doing the best you can. Every time you do your best, my hopefulness will grow inside you. And it will become *your* hopefulness. If you keep your hopefulness alive and follow your heart, you will know what God expects you to do. Your duty."

When Hosannah says those things, I feel something move inside my heart. Quite high up near my throat, actually. Like squirming inside me, like she's sending something into my body. And when I look up, she has a distant look, sort of magical, and not at all scaredy. Hosannah whispers, "I will always be just a touch away, Wendy."

When she wipes her eyes on the sleeve of her black coat, I reach up and hug her really tight. And I whisper, "I promise to do what you say, Aunt Hosannah. *I will do the best I can.*"

Hosannah smiles, squeezes my hand, and hugs me back. And she asks, "Do you know what my name means, Wendy?"

I do not.

THE INNOCENCE

"Well," says Hosannah, raising her eyes as though she's looking for an idea in the sky, "my name is like *please* and *thank you* rolled into one. It's a call to God for help. And it's thanking Him for helping. So, when things get hard for you, little Wendy, you can whisper my name. Just say *Hosannah*, and you will be calling out to God and thanking Him. And when you do that, wherever I am, *I* will hear you and help you.

"Wendy, please listen while I tell you one more thing. The blood that runs in your veins is special. Its name is *courage*. You and I both have brave blood. We Armenians often say, 'The blood of the martyrs runs in our veins' when we meet. In your case, you can imagine *my* blood inside you, helping you."

Then I tell Hosannah about a big secret that has worried me for years. I think I'm adopted because I have blond hair and blue eyes. If I'm adopted, I do not have her special blood with the courage in it.

But Hosannah disagrees. *Totally.*

"No, Wendy, many Armenians—especially in northern Turkey—have blond hair and blue eyes. One of my cousins looked exactly like you. You *are* Armenian, Wendy. I am positive about that! Put that idea out of your mind forever, my dear."

And I do. I say *merci* in her singsong way of speaking. And we laugh together.

Meanwhile, Daddy is getting anxious because he's afraid there will be a lot of snow when we get close to Canada. We have to drive through steep mountain passes along narrow, winding roads. So, we pack up our car for the last leg of our Big Road Trip.

Just before we leave, as I get Dolly and Pretty Bear settled into the back seat, I notice Aunt Hosannah handing Daddy a brown envelope. Then she hugs him really tight.

"Gordon, I put in two thousand more than we discussed because you will need help with that new house, my dear nephew."

After we have big goodbye hugs and lots of tears, we pile into our car. Through the car window, Rachel hands me packets of baklava and lahmajoun wrapped in aluminum foil. I press one against my cheek, and it's still warm.

I wave goodbye to the two sisters standing arm in arm outside their tall, blue house. And a bit later, I turn my head and wave goodbye to my first suspension bridge as the Golden Gate Bridge slowly slips into a soft blanket of fog.

The most beautiful thing about my first Big Road Trip is meeting my two great-aunts. I look up into their dark, shining eyes, and I know we have the same blood of courage in our bodies. We stand up for what we believe. We care about other people. And we sow the good things in ourselves.

Rachel and Hosannah barely escape being obliterated. They see lots of people killed. In Marash in 1920, a stray Turkish bullet kills their beautiful sister, Leah Poladian, in her home, leaving her seven children without a mother. They see houses on fire and burned to the ground with women and children in them and piles of children burned alive. Smoke and ash and blood everywhere.

THE INNOCENCE

In 1896, Turkish soldiers lock their daddy, Rev. Harootune, in prison in Aintab. He is 78! They say they will kill him unless he says he hates his God. (He won't do it.) Armenian people from his church congregation sneak around *really* quietly when it's very dark and the moon goes behind big clouds. They have crowbars and stuff, and they come to the back of the prison in the darkness, and they pry open a back door, really, *really* quietly. They untie Harootune and lead him out of the prison, and they all run away in the night. The family meets up somehow, and they all get on a bus or something, and they climb onto a boat, and they all sail to a big island called Cyprus. It's hundreds of miles away across a giant sea called the Mediterranean.

Harootune is the kind of minister who wants people to know Jesus personally—like a friend. Even though his church is a bit different, Americans in a church in Cyprus welcome him, and he gets to be a minister again. By now, he's really old, and nobody can believe this old man (who can't even speak the local language) is building new churches and telling everyone good stories about his God. And Harootune takes good care of his wife and his family, and they all live safely on that island for seven years.

And now, *many* years later, on the other side of the world, Harootune's two daughters are full of life and hope. I do not know about God or much about anything yet. But I know life and hope when I see them. I want them in *my* life.

Finally, we cross the Canadian border and arrive in Vancouver.

That is the biggest disappointment of my whole life.

Meeting My Armenian Family in San Francisco

Part 2
The Wounding

The Capilano River / Rain / Norgate Park / Lost in the Forest /
Starving for Something Else / Singing the Blues / The Powwow

The Capilano River

I can't wait to see the Lions Gate Bridge when we reach Vancouver. It's smaller than the Golden Gate Bridge, but I am okay with that. We're neighbors—the bridge and I—and I can easily walk over it to a great big park in Vancouver called Stanley Park.

What is really exciting is what's on the far side of the bridge. It's still light when we arrive, and I have that feeling I've been here before. I'm coming home. And just as we come to the end of the bridge, I see something magical on my side.

"Daddy, Daddy," I yell. "There's a river at our place. We got a river!"

Daddy is pretty tired, but he manages a smile.

"It's the Capilano River, Doll. It comes down from really high up that big mountain ahead of us, and the melting snow makes it flow. Yes, it will be our river, Wadi, for sure."

So, I'm pretty happy. There's a forest across the street from our house. And we have a river. At six and three-quarters, that's an excellent start to my new life.

Now all I need is a school.

We stay at the Ranch Motel and Trailer Park beside that river for a few days because our house isn't quite ready yet. The river is really muddy, but it's my new river, so I walk down to the bank and introduce myself. I know we're going to be friends. Now that I've met the Mississippi, I love rivers.

The very next day, Daddy drives us a short distance to our new house. He is so proud and excited because he is a responsible husband and father.

Our new house *is* disappointing. It's not ready for us by a long shot! It's sitting in a sea of mud, and it's still got ladders, cans of paint, dirty old cloths and rags, and mess all over the place. Nobody could move into this house right now.

THE WOUNDING

Mummy stands on a wooden plank that stretches over the mud. She stares at the house and shakes her head. Then she starts to cry: "Ohhh, no! Why am I here? What have I done? All wrong. All wrong." My tummy feels sick when I hear this. Later, I discuss it with Dolly and Pretty Bear, and we agree that this new plan *must* work. We want Mummy to love her new house, herself, and all of us. And then we can all be happy together.

Mummy hates what she sees in front of her: the mud covering our front and back yards and a house painted in colors that she despises: orange, dark green, and a kind of dark purple. So, Daddy immediately organizes a man to repaint the house inside and out. (In March next year, Daddy reads from the newspaper that "Bold Use of Color is Norgate Park Feature." The Norgate builder used a "veritable rainbow of color.")

Too bad it doesn't work for Mummy.

Before long, our stuff arrives in a big white truck, and the man finishes painting the house in pale colors that Mummy likes. And pretty soon, we're sleeping in our old beds again. A few things got broken, like three Spode side plates and the gravy boat. Mummy cries because it's hard to get that exact design these days.

I like our house because it's new and I have my own bedroom. And Daddy does not have to go on another road trip until after Christmas. Looking back, I can see it's lucky we arrived when we did. We just say goodbye to the men in the white truck when everything begins to fall apart.

That's when the rains start.

The Capilano River

Rain

Yes, it rains a lot in Canada's Evergreen Playground.
At least you don't have to shovel it.

Daddy (who grew up in snowy Saskatchewan)

$\mathcal{M}$y daddy is not one hundred percent honest about the rain (or maybe he just doesn't know). He does not tell us that the Fraser River flooded the year before we arrive. They closed every beach in Vancouver because they were scared people would get typhoid, which is a very dangerous disease that kills people.

We decide I could wait another week before I start school. I am desperate to start, and I'm pretty disappointed when I discover that the school is such a long way away. And I'm pretty scared about walking there alone. It's up a steep, muddy hill. (I hope I find some new friends.)

Then it starts raining.

I mean *raining*.

Like all day.

Every day.

Weeks and weeks later, when it stops raining for a few days, Daddy and I race off to the hardware store to get some wood. We put down more planks going from the road to our front door. Our Norgate Park roads are made of dirt and gravel, and we don't have sidewalks like we had in Lindsey, Ontario.

Mummy says we must have the newspaper delivered because they do that in the better families. So, Daddy reads to me about the rain, especially what's happening with my new river. It rains every day for 65 days. North Vancouver air is mixing with warm wet air from California. I have relatives in California, but I think they should keep their warm air to themselves because it makes big clouds that hit our pointy mountains. Then the rain pours down on our heads.

And my new special river turns out to be a real problem. At the end of November, the Capilano River breaks its banks and floods all over the place. I'm not happy. It's really *scaredy*. I especially hate the newspaper's scaredy language. Before the big rains, local people called it "our pint-sized, placid Capilano River." Now, the newspaper writers go nuts and write stuff like this: *River Danger, the runaway Capilano, raging waters, the rushing Capilano, the rampaging Capilano River, a fury of nature, a furious mountain river…*

Then a *really* scaredy thing happens. My river, chock full of giant stones and trees and logs and stuff, smashes smack dab into the Capilano Bridge that joins North and West Vancouver. And it washes the bridge away.

THE WOUNDING

Bingo.

No bridge.

Washed away.

Even *more* scaredy is that some broken bits of steel and wood are still dangling in midair. Everybody is petrified.

And scaredy things are happening up our pointy mountain, too. Swollen streams overflow their banks, and culverts (they are big ditches, I think) flood all over the place and wash out some roads and bridges. And Seymour Creek (it's somewhere up there, too) breaks *its* banks and drowns lots of houses. And so does Mosquito Creek. West Vancouver's new Capilano Pipeline (that everybody said was *totally* safe) breaks open and spews water everywhere.

Daddy reads me newspaper reports of heroic rescues, but there are tragedies, too. A tugboat overturns, and six people drown. A man drowns in the river up the mountain, trying to save his brother. The stormy seas stop the ferries from going to West Vancouver, so people there are completely stranded.

Daddy explains. Because Canada is a modern democracy, 35 Army reservists from the 6th Field Company bravely build two temporary bridges. They are helped by 56 sappers (soldiers who build things). Our army is there to help citizens in need. And they work together all night under a gigantic searchlight that is so bright it's got 80 million candles!

Under that searchlight, volunteers from the Red Cross mobile canteen give hot coffee and sandwiches to the men.

Daddy reads me a really scaredy story about a woman who is pregnant with her fourth child, and she is actually in labor, like she's about to have her actual baby right there and then. She walks across the broken bridge, and an ambulance takes her to the hospital, and she has her baby right away, and it doesn't die. Or anything.

They have to do everything super-fast, too, so we even have women helping with sandbagging. Which is *amazing*. And they get gigantic bulldozers to go out into all that sand and mud in the middle of a bunch of log jams to try to get the river's channel to go back where it belongs. You can't have a river just running all over the place, you know. Giant Army trucks must bring in scads of equipment and bulldozers, and the soldiers build two bridges called Bailey Bridges. And each one weighs 52 tons! And then, with the bulldozers and more trucks, they make new roads on both sides to connect with the two new bridges. Then they take down the dangling bits.

It's a lot of work for all concerned, and I am genuinely impressed.

But I am not impressed by my river. It turns out to be a big disappointment.

★★★

When my river washes the bridge away, Mummy gets *very* sad. It's like *she* is the bridge. I hear her crying in her new bedroom. She says she's landed in the eye of a storm and now there's chaos all around her.

THE WOUNDING

And for some reason, Mummy expected Vancouver to be like California. Not cold and grey and rainy, but warm and bright and sunny. And she can't believe she left her mother, two brothers and two sisters, and all her friends back in Orillia, Ontario. She knows she's got no chance of going back to Ontario. Not any time soon, anyway. Nothing is any good any longer... Mummy still feels sick, her breasts still hurt, and she's ashamed of the long scars and how they arc flattened out and hanging down instead of perked up like before...

And my poor daddy. He feels so helpless. When he's playing solitaire on our new white kitchen table with the clever fold-up ironing board above it, I hear him whispering under his breath, "I just don't know what to do. I don't know how to help my wife."

★★★

It *was* really scaredy, but my first big rainstorm also fills me with great respect for rivers. Like I do with forests, I know rivers will be important in my life. I try to make friends with it again. Listening to the river is easy, and I often walk through the forest and sit beside my river. Just listening to its song.

My river sings to me.

Years later, people living on the North Shore still ask, "Where were you when the Bridge went out?"

Of course, the storm destroys our front and back yards. Daddy has to go on his business trip, so it takes months before we can clean that up. I am sloshing around in my galoshes and getting mud everywhere. I hate messes! I wait impatiently for Daddy to return from his first big trip so we can fix our yards.

Norgate Park

All of us carry within us a picture of the terrain that was learned roughly between the ages of six and nine... revisualizing that place with its smells and textures, walking through it again in your imagination, has a grounding and settling effect.

Gary Snyder, 1990

In 1949, when I move to Norgate Park at age six and three-quarters (and a little bit more), there are no trees there. And it's as flat as a pancake. Once upon a time, Norgate Park was a big, tall forest, but they killed all the trees to build Capilano Air Park. That project flops, and a young developer buys the land and builds houses there from 1948 to 1952. Our new house is one of them.

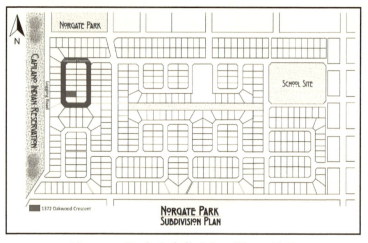

Norgate Park Subdivision Plan, 1952

Our house is in Stage 2, and it's like all the other houses. Only some are reversed and have different windows and different colored paint on them.

All the same and made to look different...

Norgate Park

All the lots are 100 feet by 60 feet. In 1949, Norgate Park has houses. That's it. No stores, no school, no bus, no community center, and no places to play except the baseball diamond with the bleachers and the abandoned sawmill until they tear it down.

My mother can't understand why nothing is there in our neighborhood. How can that be? And it sure doesn't match what they said in those brochures we read.

Norgate Park is noisy and smelly, too. Not like where the "better families" live (I guess that's up the mountain where it's quiet, not smelly, the air is fresher, and they have wraparound views of the harbor). Poor people like us live south of Marine Drive, down here on the flats. The waterfront sawmill is noisy. They say it uses bad chemicals. The creosoting plant belches out black smoke, and the fish plant on the barge stinks. The smoke from the beehive sawdust burner makes our air foggy, so we hear those depressing foghorns every morning. Our smelly ditches often overflow, and so do our septic tanks. We don't get sewers until 1963.

Norgate Park is a bit of a mess, actually.

As soon as we can after we arrive, we find my elementary school and get me enrolled. I'm so worried I'll be behind, but I quickly catch up. I go to Capilano Elementary School for grades one and two, I make two new friends, Joanie Fowler and Jeanie Pearson. Joanie and I walk to Jeanie's house on Bowser Avenue. Then the three of us clamber up a raggedy, slippery path called "the Chicken Walk." The walk there is horrible. Absolutely horrible. I despise every inch of it. I'd call it a *climb*, not a *walk*. The journey takes about an hour from my house. I hate being wet and sweaty when I get to school.

THE WOUNDING

I'm always asking whose idea this is. I keep asking, "Where is our own school for Norgate Park's children?" Were they just pretending when they wrote that stuff about our school in those brochures? A few streets down the road from our house, there's some land with a sign that says a school is coming, but we wait for them to build it…

And that old Capilano school up the slippery hill is *totally* falling down. The sign in the hall says it was built in 1924. That's *really* ancient in my world.

What the old school does have are great *trees*. The schoolyard is a forest. I love that. Every day I play there among the trees at lunch and recess.

I keep grumbling about the Chicken Walk, but I want to go to school more than anything else. I am desperate to learn. Norgate kids can't stay after school and play with the other children who live nearby, especially in winter when it gets dark so early. We have to slither back home in the rain.

Sometimes I discuss how upset I am with Aunt Rachel in my thoughts. It works, and pretty soon, I hear her telling me that very same thing: "Just do the best you can, dearest Wendy." I try. But sometimes, I get upset.

I blame other adults, not my parents, for the mess with the school. My dad reads me a newspaper article about adults having a great big argument about how to chop up the school districts in North Vancouver. In the meetings, the adults yell at each other about how to get enough money to pay for the Capilano schools. (That's *our* schools.) Dad says that somebody at that meeting called our schools "a perfect disgrace for a progressive community."

I want to go to one of those meetings with all the adults and yell a lot about how Norgate Park children are not getting the education we deserve when we need it. And we need it when we first move in. (Not a hundred years later when we're dead.) I keep asking myself, "Why am *I* the only one who worries? Why am I so *different* from the other children? Why do I *care* so much?" (Daddy says it's not good at this age and stage of my development.)

And why do I *hurt* so much?

In September 1951, our new Norgate Park Elementary School finally opens, but only for the first four grades.

I am nearly nine, and I am not impressed.

Oakwood Crescent, about 1952

THE WOUNDING

Trees in the Squamish Nation forest in the background

Still, I love riding my bike to school and not having to climb up that horrible hill. But I can only go to our new school for grades three and four because they haven't finished building it. Back I trudge—with Joanie and Jeanie—to ancient Capilano Elementary, climbing that hill for two more sweaty years. I worry I am not getting a high-quality education. I did not go to kindergarten, I started school late because of my bad birthday, and now I need to catch up. When I am an adult, I promise that all projects under my control will be much better planned.

Not long after we arrive in Vancouver, Daddy tells me he has some news. He sits me down on the couch beside him and holds my hand.

"Dear little Wadi, this is so sad, and I already cried about it. Yesterday, your dear Aunt Hosannah died in her sleep."

Daddy cries again, and I hug him. We knew it was coming, but I am really sad. So, I sit on my bed with Dolly and Pretty Bear and tell them how kind Hosannah was and the good things she told me to keep my spirits up. Sometimes she used her Armenian ways of talking. Once, she said to me in her singsong way: "Let me take your pain." And she always held my hands in hers when she kissed me on both cheeks. And now she is dead.

I remember to say Hosannah's name as a prayer: "please" and "thank you" to God. I am so glad I met her and Rachel. Dolly, Pretty Bear, and I say a prayer so that Hosannah can go straight to heaven and be peaceful there. (I am sure she's in heaven already.) And over the years, when things get tough for me, I often feel Aunt Hosannah near me and hear her soft voice comforting me. I whisper the prayer that is her name. I know she will never leave me. We have the sort of connection that lasts forever.

Only a few months later, Daddy comes to me again with that look. This time it's Aunt Rachel. I hoped she'd live longer, but she loved her sister so much that maybe she just had to go to heaven to be with her. They were like twins in their souls. I pray for Rachel, too, and I remember her bright red lipstick and how much she loved to sing.

★★★

Since I was very young, I have been fascinated by housing. Drawing in books was strictly banned, but my two A. A. Milne books, *Winnie-the-Pooh* and *Now We Are Six* (that I got when I was three and five), are full of drawings of me with pigtails and houses with chimneys, front yards, and front stairs. Big, bright suns are shining on them. Housing is in my blood.

Me and my houses in a landscape, about 1946–1948

So, I totally love the "housing" education I am getting right outside my front door. All around our house, five separate construction crews are building our new suburb in the most organized way. (Compared to life at our house, where nothing is organized.) I spend most of my time with Crew 1. They make the houses grow from the ground up by installing heating under the floors. They plunk the copper tubing right into the wet cement. It's like they pour in the fruitcake batter (the cement), add the nuts and fruit (the copper tubing), plop, and then it hardens. Magically, all that buried copper will heat a house—for about $170 a year. "Radiant heating," they call it. It sounds like a lot of money, so I ask.

"That's an excellent rate, Wendy, a very fair price," one of the builders tells me. "And there's more," he says. "You can turn the heat in individual rooms on and off at will."

That sounds very modern to me.

Later my daddy shows me newspaper advertisements that explain how families can have "radiant *living*" at Norgate Park. It sounds so hopeful, and I am into hopeful. That new-style heating makes everybody's floors nice and warm. And we have natural gas, too, so no more noisy radiators that bang and clang, like in the old days. Just safe, warm floors for happy children to play on. I love the entire house-building process—one orderly step followed by the next. I love order.

I make friends with two workmen on Crew 1: Norm and Gordon Norby. I remember Gordon because that's my daddy's name. He explains we can't have basements like other people because of the Capilano River. So, we have concrete slabs. When I don't understand, he pulls up a big shiny white can with a lid on it, says I can sit down on it, and then he draws a picture on a piece of drywall with a thick, square pencil he sharpens with a knife.

Gordon says, "The water table is extremely high in Norgate Park because our river changed its course from the ancient days. Your basements would flood if you had them."

Listening to Gordon talk about ancient rivers, I work out that rivers are alive. Gordon explains that Norgate Park is not the ideal place for a housing subdivision: "It's the estuary of that ancient river—all flattened out."

I love the sound of that word, so Gordon prints it for me, and then we both practice speaking it: ˈɛstjʊəri. No wonder the Capilano River flooded and threatens to continue flooding until they build the Cleveland Dam in 1954. The river belongs here. We are living in the middle of the river's home, in its ˈɛstjʊəri.

One crew sets up a cutting and assembly plant in an airport hangar a few blocks away on Pemberton Avenue, so I ride my bike to check on their progress. Inside the building, they give me a stool in a corner. I watch them build all sorts of things: framing timbers, roof trusses, interior walls, storage cupboards, kitchen counters and cabinets, built-in dining room cabinets, built-in bedroom closets, a pull-out chopping board—even a hideaway kitchen table with a miniature ironing board that you pull down over it. We have one at our house. It's a brilliant design.

Steve, the foreman, likes to answer my questions: "Our fabrication work here is the best modern machinery can produce, Wendy."

They build 500 ranch-style houses in Norgate Park in batches of 50 because that is the most efficient. My dad reads me the advertisements. The houses cost $9,000 if you have

THE WOUNDING

cash or $1,800 down, and you can make monthly payments of exactly $46.85 for 15 years.

"We based our house designs on the best available research from all over North America," Gordon tells me. I love that! I adore the idea that the developer did all that research and traveled all around and stuff just to get things right at Norgate Park. He sounds so orderly to me.

Gordon explains a bit more: "The layout of each house is fully engineered."

He runs his hand over a newly sanded dining room cupboard, waiting for a home.

"Engineering" means you don't have to walk far to answer the door or use the bathroom.

Gordon is on a roll now: "All the houses have different roofs, window styles, steps, and colors. People can choose their color scheme inside and out. And every house has a carport with a shed at the back."

Once I see Mr. Norm Hullah, the developer. He is only 30, and they tell me he's already one of Canada's first builder-developers. He traveled all over Canada and the United States, looking at how people build houses in large housing projects. Not far from my house, I watch Mr. Hullah visit his workmen, checking that they are on schedule. Later, he's talking to a bunch of people gathered there. "We are passing on the savings to the buyer with our mass buying, precision factory assembly-line production, and modern construction methods."

Norgate Park

Boy, am I impressed! I love the plans and drawings, lots of equipment, *fabrication*, technology, the whir of the saws, the smell of the sawdust, and everything fitting together in a neat, logical, and predictable way.

I don't see any women working on the job, but I still decide to become a builder when I grow up.

I also dream about the families who will soon be living in those new houses. I pray for their peace and contentment, happiness, and security. I wish them long and happy lives without too many disappointments. I wish them hopefulness.

All this talk about rivers with Gordon changes my feelings about Norgate Park. To me, now, it's part of a river that changed course in the ancient days. But my dad doesn't understand that. To him, it isn't even land, exactly. Our yard is *property,* real estate. And he *owns* it. When they are making our lawn, Dad and Mr. Murphy, our new next-door neighbor, dig six jeep loads of river stones out of our two back yards and dump them in what is to become my school friend Carole Gill's front yard when the last 50 houses in Stage 16 get built. (To be fair, there weren't even any roads there when Dad and Mr. Murphy dumped their river stones.) Carole tells me that her dad is terribly upset that he ended up with heaps more stones than any of his neighbors. But Dad doesn't have the heart to tell Carole's dad where his stones came from. And he is always very nice to Carole, out of guilt, I guess.

I have terrific friends in Norgate Park. Diane (who becomes Tammi when she's old enough to change her name) lives next door for our first year at Norgate Park, and we are best friends forever. Joanie lives on Tatlow Street, and Jeanie lives on Bowser. But us Norgate kids have nothing to do and nowhere to go in *our* suburb.

To me, the Capilano River is a big boundary. Like Marine Drive, it separates us from the richer people in nicer houses in neighborhoods without creosote smoke, fog, and rotten fish smells. Richer people live in West Vancouver and up the hill above us. But we have the best stands of old Douglas fir and red cedar. And we have pointy mountains, the best snow, and our snow stays longer because our mountains are half again as tall as theirs. And our snow is deeper, and it slides down the mountains in white ribbons through the green forests. It's just beautiful.

West Vancouver has a flattened-out, boring old mountain with a little round pimple called Hollyburn that gets a little snow. But it's not nearly as good for sledding as our Mt. Seymour. So, in the mountain department, we're the best. And just before we move here, Grouse Mountain gets the world's first double chairlift. And we have bigger pointy mountains *behind* our pointy mountains with snow that lasts and lasts.

And sometimes, on sunny days, we can see Mt. Baker in Washington. It has *perennial* snow.

My favorite thing is standing in our front yard on a winter morning when there is frost on the grass. I turn to the north and look to see light snow, like icing sugar, on our pointy mountains. I love the way individual trees stick up through the snow.

Lost in the Forest

No two leaves are the same to Raven.
No two branches are the same to Wren.
If what a tree or a branch does is lost on you,
You are surely lost. Stand still. The forest knows
Where you are. You must let it find you.

David Wagoner, 1978

Our parents ban all of us kids from playing in the forest, but like children everywhere, we play there. We also fish in the river. (That's banned, too.) I am a nervous child, so I stay pretty close to the forest's edge. But one day, I get lost when I'm there alone. I am about eight, and I think I know my way around. But forests can be dark, scaredy places, and my forest is really, really big *and* dark.

Getting lost scares me half to death. I lose my familiar landmarks, it's getting darker, and everything looks the same in all directions. There are no homey sounds. The river doesn't make much noise, there are no roads nearby with any traffic, and the Norgate backyards are too far away to hear voices.

I wander for hours. My body is shaking with fear. I will die in my special forest: the place that protects me from my mother and the sadness of my life. That can't be what's happening to me!

I'm sobbing, and snot is running down my face. I feel desperate. No place to turn. Nobody to turn to. Lost! It's nearly dark when I work out that I'm walking in circles, so I sit down on a mossy log to collect myself. I try to breathe. I wipe my nose and eyes on my jacket. I beg the forest for help. It starts to rain, but the forest canopy is so dense at the top that it's dry underneath. But the hammering sound of the rain, the long shadows, and the darkness creeping in make me feel worse. Make me feel really scaredy.

THE WOUNDING

I try to breathe deeply. I wipe my eyes again on my jacket sleeve and sit there, begging for help. This forest is my real home and my comfort, so I hate it when a scaredy feeling fills me up inside. Trees are where I take my problems, and the forest is where I feel whole. So it's really scaredy getting lost in my forest. Is this how my short life is going to end?

Suddenly, I hear sounds. I gasp, then make myself quiet. I jump up so I can listen better. Two men are yelling about a broken bicycle. I know only one place those men can be: the Logging Road.

The voices are far away, but fortunately, they keep yelling, so I head off in that direction. I thank God and whoever is watching over me. I will be saved, after all. I won't die a lonely death from starvation. Or maybe I'd be eaten by a bear or a mountain lion…

Soon, I recognize familiar things: Mid-Fairyland, the rope swing, and the fallen log by the old yellow cedar tree. I am safe now. I can breathe now. I quickly scrabble through the forest to the Logging Road.

It is completely dark when I reach home. And the rain is coming down in buckets. I mean buckets. I am sobbing, soaked, muddy, exhausted, and *soooo* hungry. And incredibly relieved I am not dead.

The porch light isn't on, so I burst through the back door into the kitchen.

"I'm safe!" I sob. "It's fine. Don't worry anymore. I was lost, but now I'm found. I'm back safely. I found my way all by myself. I'm safe and sound!"

"I hope you weren't too worried," I call out, standing on the doormat, careful not to muddy the kitchen floor.

Silence.

"I'm safe," I say again, slower and in a softer voice, now mostly to myself. I sit on a kitchen chair, pull off my muddy galoshes, and prop them beside the furnace. I hang my wet jacket over the clothesline by the back door.

I walk around the corner and peer into the living room. Music is playing on the radio. Twinkle is curled up asleep by the fireplace. Mother is sitting in the big yellow chair, reading *Maclean's* magazine, and eating a grilled cheese sandwich. She doesn't even turn to look at me. My dad is away on a trip.

Yep, I say to myself. This is how it is here. Welcome to my life. But at least I'm not dead.

I find a towel, dry my hair, and change into my pajamas.

There isn't any dinner, so I make myself a sandwich with Kraft cheese slices. The white bread curls up at the edges, but I don't care. It's food, and I'm starving.

And I wonder: what would life be like in a family where people noticed you?

THE WOUNDING

Starving for Something Else

*The greatest burden a child must bear
is the unlived life of the parents.*

Carl Jung

$\mathcal{B}$y the time I'm 11 or 12, I work out that Norgate Park is one of the most boring places on earth. Except for some exciting moments in the early years when mountain lions crawl down from the pointy mountain and rummage in our garbage cans at night, waking everybody up. The fathers are frightened. I bet they want to be brave and chase the mountain lions away, but not one father ever does. They lock their doors and pray that the wild animals will go home, and eventually, they do. But I know they can't really go home because the loggers chopped down their green world and spread grey stuff all over it.

The mountain lions died of homesickness. I *know* that. I pray for them.

I also have a kind of homesickness. Like the mountain lions, I am longing for a *real* homeland. I am dying because 1372 Oakwood Crescent is my prison, not my home.

Our move to Vancouver turned out to be *One. Big. Disappointment.*

I love my dad, but he's never home. He goes away for three months at a time, selling watches and jewelry all over Western Canada, staying in hotels, and displaying his items in sample rooms. I think he has a lot of fun on the road with different people, maybe other women even, and Mother is jealous of that. And when he returns, they argue and yell a lot. Mother often screams that Dad drinks too much. She says he also gambles, and that's why we never have any money to pay the mortgage, and the bank manager rings every week. We don't have enough money for the orthodontist for braces for my crooked teeth.

I hate these arguments and am so embarrassed that the neighbors might hear our family secrets. So, I get a chair and run around to all the windows. I climb up and shut them tight. Life is bad enough at our house without everybody else knowing about it. (Later I read in a book by John Bradshaw that "families are as sick as their secrets.")

Our life and our failures are all Dad's fault, Mother says. He is a fun-loving sort of a guy, a bit like a child, actually. He loves a party with everybody singing around the piano. I love that, too. And to be honest, living with Mother, I don't think *all* the wrong things in our family could be Dad's fault.

When Dad is away on a business trip, our house is usually a mess, with some terrible thing thawing beside the sink

THE WOUNDING

destined to become my dinner. (If I'll eat it.) I refuse to accept that our family has to be so different. Other children's parents call them home for dinner. Some even have whistles their children recognize if they are playing in the forest or some distance from home. I come home when the other children leave for their dinners. And then I need to figure out what to do.

I come in through the back door, ducking under the wet sheets and towels hanging in the kitchen. Other families have a dryer, but we can't afford one yet. So we get used to damp laundry because it rains two days out of three in *Canada's Evergreen Playground.* (I do like the clean smell of the wet laundry.)

Mother hears the screen door slam and calls to me from her bedroom. She's always in that room that smells like tears. (Day and night.) I never actually walk into the bedroom. I open the door a few inches and stand there.

And then it goes something like this: "Wendy, I'm glad you're home. I've had a really difficult day, and I won't be getting up now. I'm just going to stay here and rest."

"What's for dinner, Mother? I'm really hungry. I was cleaning the blackboards at school and missed the last bus. So, I had to walk home. It's bucketing rain and *really* cold outside, and my galoshes are leaking. I didn't have lunch, and now I'm starving."

"Darling, you'll be really happy to know I've already started a lovely, *lovely* dinner for you. It's going to be a lovely,

lovely beef and kidney stew. All you need to do is just finish it off. I've already started it."

This seems unimaginable. I'm still waiting for a *lovely dinner* prepared by my mother. (She bakes an excellent apple pie once a year, but growing kids can't live on apple pies!) So I quietly close the bedroom door and walk back to the kitchen. The stovetop is grimy with baked-on food on the burners. A small, battered aluminum saucepan contains a few inches of a thick boiling liquid. It looks terrible and smells bad—not like food. On the top of the liquid, a few scraps of wrinkled plastic wrap are swimming in a grey, frothy scum. I turn off the burner and set the saucepan on the drainboard.

I guess this was another crisis-ridden day in a long procession of Mother's sadnesses. No wonder her bedroom smells of tears.

We've lived on Oakwood Crescent for about five years now. And already our house is wearing out. The kitchen looks dirty and dingy, though nobody ever cooks there except me when I do home ec projects. Everything is covered with grease. The floor has black streaks on it. (And all this with a cleaning woman, Mrs. Miller, who comes for a full day every two weeks.) It just doesn't make sense.

I feel like an archaeologist examining the mess scattered on the drainboard. I work out the origin of the scummy liquid. Mother threw two items from the freezer compartment into the saucepan: a plastic-wrapped package of beef kidneys (not yet cleaned and full of gristle and fat) and cubes of beef, also wrapped, sitting on a cardboard base. She added a bay leaf, an onion, and a few cups of water.

THE WOUNDING

I'm supposed to cut off the kidneys' fat and gristle, rinse off the cardboard scum and the plastic wrap, and combine the kidneys with the hard grey beef cubes. That will be my dinner.

I stare at the tangled, greasy grey froth. How can this be my dinner? I open the back door, brave gusts of sideways slanting rain, make it to the driveway, and throw the whole mess into the garbage can. I slam the metal lid like a pronouncement: "Enough!"

A grumble is growing in my tummy.

I wander back to the bedroom and tap on the door. I open it a crack and say something like this: "Mother, honestly, that mess on the stove is not *food*. It is absolutely disgusting. Nobody on earth could eat that. I threw it in the garbage can outside. Why don't you just get out of bed and cook us dinner like the other mothers do?"

I jump back, knocked by her anger: "Wendy, you are the most ungrateful child I've ever met. Not only are you totally rude and insolent, but you are also totally ungrateful. Shame on you, Wendy! Shame! That is your dinner. That is a dinner your father bought for you with his hard-earned money. I cooked it for you. And now you are going to eat it. And if you *don't* eat it, there will be severe punishment when your father gets home. And your allowance will be docked for two weeks. Do you understand? That is your *dinner*. *Your* dinner, Wendy. *Eat it*, Wendy!"

Her scream ends in a long sigh that turns into a stream of sobbing that continues for hours.

Starving for Something Else

I walk back to the bad-smelling kitchen. I check the fridge. It's a disaster of rotting vegetables in the crisper, open cans, dried-up processed cheese slices, and jars of expired Cheez Whiz. I close the door. Then, curtained by damp sheets and towels, I kneel in a dark space beside the low cupboard where we keep the food Dad bought at the supermarket. Three shelves of processed food. All neatly lined up: cans of Heinz pork and beans, spaghetti, tuna fish, salmon, and something called Finnan Haddie. Some sliced green beans. And several boxes of Kraft Dinner.

I select a small can of salmon.

I wash the dishes and the can opener sitting in the sink and open the can. Then I put on my outdoor clothes and some dry shoes and go outside. Inside the garden shed, I sit on a folding chair. It feels comforting. Like many homeowners, we have tools, a lawn mower, and pruning shears. I feel almost normal sitting in the shed, even though I am a bit cold. I take a deep breath, shiver, and draw my jacket around me.

I slowly eat my salmon. At times like this, I wonder why I am me and not someone else. Well, this is me. This is my life. I'm on a long road to freedom. But I am not going to starve. Not for food, anyway.

THE WOUNDING

Singing the Blues

I'm not much of a reader and don't have many books. But I have *A Tree Grows in Brooklyn,* and reading it makes me feel brave and hopeful. I remember Mary Rommely, who was poor and had a hard life, telling young Francie (an American girl) that education is the path to success. That lines up with my plan to escape from my family as soon as possible. That book also has stuff in it about *imagination.* Like this bit when Mary says:

The child must have a valuable thing which is called imagination. The child must have a secret world in which live things that never were. It is necessary that she believe. She must start out by believing in things, not of this world. Then when the world becomes too ugly for living in, the child can reach back and live in her imagination.

There's lots of stuff in that book about a tree called *Ailanthus,* the *Tree of Heaven.* It grows in places in Brooklyn where nothing else will grow. It never grows where the "better families" live. I work out that *I* am that tree. I don't have much, and I need what that tree has. Later, I learn another word about that tree: *endurance.* But mainly, that book teaches me about imagination.

My dad is filled with imagination. He's not that practical, but he's a great dreamer. I get my dreaming from him, for sure. When Dad is home, I love to sit on the piano bench beside him and sing songs from the green loose-leaf binder he bought from a porter on the Canadian Pacific Railway. I try to catch the loose sheets as they flutter to the floor when their holes tear because the binder is too full. I learn to sing the words by tasting them. After my many years on the piano bench, my ears are tuned to songs.

Singing is the best thing in my whole life. I love singing "You Go to My Head" and belting out the words like Sarah Vaughan. Dad and I practice seriously—like we are going on stage any day. Mostly, we learn the Blues: "Darn that Dream," "Me and My Shadow," "Am I Blue?" Our absolutely favorite song is "Singing the Blues," a song more of *my* generation. I'm thirteen now and have records of my own. Dad says it's about a broken *heart*. To me, it's about the end of the world:

There's nothin' left for me to do

But cry-why-why-why over you (cry over you).

I often worry about the end of the world. It's funny because I am quite an optimistic person. But I also have this sort of dread inside me.

Dad and I have a secret we never discuss: we *both* have the Blues! Dad explains that the Blues are for everyone everywhere, including us. These laments are about feeling sad, discouraged, or melancholy because of hard times, broken hearts, or plain old depression. The sound of the piano and Dad humming (he is a bit shy about his singing) opens my heart to the big sadness that lives there. It really gets to me if a song is complicated and about sadness.

THE WOUNDING

One song we practice a lot is "You Go to My Head." Billie Holiday sings it on our record, with Oscar Peterson playing the piano. Dad says it's in a minor key and something called a progression (I think). It's a sophisticated song because the melody has a whole bunch of repeated notes. I memorize it: ... *I'm certain ... that this heart ... of mine ... hasn't .... a ghost ... of a chance... in this .... craaaa-zy ... romance...*

Though I love singing with my dad, that's not my *real* life. My life is in my forest, where I work on my courage so I can escape from my family. I can see the top of my forest's tallest trees from our living room window. To get there, I just run along a path between two fences. It's 120 steps long. By the time I reach the Logging Road, I am a new person. I am free. I sing in my outside voice, and my forest always sings, too.

The path to the Logging Road that separated Norgate Park from the Squamish Nation Reserve #5

When I run through that "in-between" place (just like Francie does in my book), I remember my imagination and change deep inside. When I reach the Logging Road, I stop hunching over and looking down. I look up at the tops of the tallest trees.

The Logging Road separates Norgate Park from the Reservation. It's not really a road anymore. It's a wide, muddy track bashed up by thousands of monster trucks hauling huge, swaying logs from the pointy mountains to the sawmill on our waterfront for years and years. All our parents are so scared that a truck's chain might snap and send dozens of massive logs bouncing down the road, killing their children.

The Logging Road, 1949

But that never happens.

Eventually, the logging trucks stop coming (because all the trees on the pointy mountain got killed). Then we can play safely all along the Logging Road.

All us Norgate kids play in the forest. It's the natural thing to do. We need privacy. *I* need privacy because I am on

THE WOUNDING

a mission to keep myself together, grow up fast, become an adult, and escape. Even on the darkest winter days, my forest never disappoints me. The afternoon light slants through the dark trees, sort of yellowy and lemony green. It shines on fallen logs and stones, and some of them glow like magic. God lives in those glowing spots, and I spend a lot of time near them.

The light also makes stripes—like somebody took a giant brush and painted thick yellow lines sideways across the tree trunks. That magic happens every single sunny day.

I try to get Mother to come to the forest, but she never does. The forest has bugs in it, and she hates bugs.

In my forest, I sometimes hear a voice above the foghorns, the seaplanes, and the whistle and clatter of the train. It's an ancient voice, and it's not human. It's like it's more-than-human. I always listen because whatever is behind or inside that voice wants my love, wants me to care about it. It makes a sort of song, a bit whispery, but loud enough so I can hear the good things it says. It sounds like a grandmother, cuddling and soothing me in her lap and singing songs about hope. That voice always calls me by my personal name, *Wadi*. And that makes me feel incredibly special and hopeful. I know I will help that voice, and it will help me. Give and take. My hopeful feeling feels like happiness.

One magical day, long after the trucks stop crashing down our Logging Road, the fog lifts after approximately 90 days of rain. Then we discover a gigantic puddle. I mean *gigantic!* And that summer, a pair of Mallard ducks make our puddle their summer home. I can easily spot the daddy, with his glossy, green head and a white stripe between it and his purply brown breast. The mummy is nothing to look at, a mottled orange-brown.

Singing the Blues

Anyway, every day, while the puddle is full, I walk over, carrying some bread crusts but keeping a polite distance. I call out to the ducks:

Hello, there, both of you, ducks. Welcome. My name is Wendy. But you can call me Wadi if you want. That's my personal name.

Welcome, welcome, my new family. Welcome. I'm so glad you're here.

Maybe you could have duck babies here, and I could help you care for them.

Please stay forever and be my new family forever, okay?

I do not mind that my new family is not human.

In the early years, I play in the forest with the other Norgate children in "Mid-Fairyland." I don't remember how it got that name. Maybe because it is in the middle of the forest or at the core of it? Anyway, it's a magic land where fairies live. A dreaming place and a real place at the same time. For me, it's where I feel safe, protected and cared for. And it has a hidden beauty that only us kids understand.

There we have a rope swing with a wooden seat. And we invent our own society, with a King and a Queen, other royalty, and a strict code of conduct. And we always respect individual rights and privacy. Years later, Tammi-who-was-Diane remembers Mid-Fairyland:

Oh, Wendy, you were our brave Valkyrie and so much a leader of our forest adventuring. You showed the other children how to love the forest and to be brave there. Your forest leadership encouraged me and my brother, Dave, to grow up loving Nature. You made the

THE WOUNDING

forest come alive for us, and trees have been an important part of our lives ever since.

It's good to hear that I made the forest come alive for the other kids. Because the forest helps me come alive to myself. When Tammi, Dave, and I were children, my forest was my *everything*: my protection, my community, a safe place where I could hide, a place where I could sing out loud all the time, a magical, hopeful and joyful place, and a reliable place that never rejected me. And when I was a child, I needed something hopeful in my life.

Back in the grey world beyond my forest, I keep my eyes down under my tartan headscarf because I don't want people to see how ashamed I am. I learn that from Mother. If I look down and sort of hunch over, I can keep her stabbing eyes from piercing my soul. As I walk, I look down at my scuffed brown Oxford shoes and my pinky-white socks accidentally washed with a red pullover. I look at the blacktop and watch where it cracks when it gets cold. Then I place my foot firmly on every crack, remembering a nursery rhyme that makes sense:

Step on a crack,
You'll break your mother's back
Step on a line,
You'll break your father's spine.
Step in a ditch,
Your mother's nose will itch.

I often stay late at school to clean blackboards, do little jobs, and discuss things with my teachers. They like me, and I'm a good student, especially in English and poetry. I'm good at memorizing poems. (Teachers love that.) Unfortunately, staying late at school sometimes means walking home in the dark.

When I go to Capilano Elementary School in the early years, it's down that horrible, slippery Chicken Walk. That is *scaredy*.

For the first four years in Norgate Park, we have muddy, dirt roads. Then we have blacktop. Beside it are deep ditches with tall yellowy-green weeds waving out of muddy brown water. I walk close to the ditch because I'm afraid I won't get off the road fast enough when a car comes. I can't figure out why the streetlights and the sidewalks end at Sowden Street, where our suburb begins.

Why should they end there? Our suburb is brand new. Don't *we* need streetlights and sidewalks like *other* people? Even if we are poor, children still deserve to walk safely.

As I slosh slowly along the road, I make up little songs to cast a spell of protection around me. I sing one special (magic) song when nobody can hear me:

Ah, oh, I'm doing my duty. I'm doing the best that I can.
Ah, oh, I'm doing my duty. I'm doing the best that I can.

Sometimes, when I sing, *Ah, oh, I'm doing the best that I can*, I time my singing to match the foghorns: *Hoooo, Hoooo, Hmmm, Hmmm.*

When I'm singing this song, I often hear Aunt Rachel's soft, lilting Armenian voice singing along with me. That feels really cozy.

I have a secret I never share. I have to protect my inside part to help society later in *The Crisis*. I have no idea what *The Crisis* will be. Or when. For now, I concentrate on my *protection*.

THE WOUNDING

First, I use a spell. It is simple enough, and it works. Anything in reverse will stop the evil that lurks everywhere in everyday things, especially at home.

Here's an example. When my parents force me to go to church, the sermon and the Bible readings feel dangerous, so I *Count* backward, starting at 500. I invented that myself. After the church service, safe and released, I scuttle away with my head down. I'm happy that I can't remember a single word anybody said. I use this spell in church until I am about 11.

I always *Count* when Mother screams at me. When she does the most scaredy things and *Humiliates Me in Public,* I *Count* backward very fast. I *Count* other things, too, always backward. When I get sent to my room for being insolent, I punish everyone by sleeping with my head at the bottom of my bed. It's hard to breathe there, but it feels like a powerful spell. My mother is in a storm of madness much of the time. Later, I learn a little about what makes her crazy, but that doesn't help me when I'm young.

We never have regular meals, bedtimes, or *anything* except when Dad is home a few times a year. Then we have meals. He always packs my lunch (his scrambled egg sandwiches are beyond yucky by lunchtime). We drive together to the supermarket and bring back big brown full paper bags. Dad loves to drive, so he takes us on picnics in the forest up the Pointy Mountain. We drive everywhere, sometimes even to Horseshoe Bay, to look at the ferries. In winter, he takes us sledding on big cardboard boxes from the supermarket that he flattens into sleds. Mother is a spoilsport and never comes on our excursions, but Dad loves fun so much that nothing could spoil his enthusiasm.

For some reason, I love planning, timetables, and calendars. I mark every day, every month, and every year on my calendar as milestones on my road to freedom. And every year, I discover a miracle along the Logging Road that reminds me of my progress. Blackberries grow there in late August before the maple leaves begin to change color. My dependable blackberries teach me to trust life's natural cycles. First: white and pale pink flowers. I know it's going to be good. Then: hard green berries become blackberries. The actual blackberries are enormous, glossy, juicy, and delicious. In late summer, all of us Norgate kids are running around, grabbing handfuls of berries, and dumping them into plastic ice cream containers and colanders that are soon brimming with sweet berries. Purple mouths. Stains all over our skin and clothes. Other mothers make berry pies and dark, glistening jam in glass jars, melting wax on top. My home ec teacher teaches me how to make blackberry jam.

We go to school with Chief Simon Baker's children, who come from a family of nine. They live in a big house on Marine Drive that their dad is always busy extending. I do not know then that they are the first Native children to attend public schools in British Columbia. Their dad, the Chief, pays special money so they can go to school with us and not to a residential school. That seems ridiculous. The Baker kids are just kids like us, and all the other kids go to school for free. They are members of the Squamish Nation, and my forest will be theirs forever. I am okay with them having their forest. I'm just grateful to be free to visit, climb among the mossy, fallen logs, and let its magic seep into me.

I would never harm their forest.

THE WOUNDING

The Powwow

The Capilano Indian Reservation, where the extended Baker family and other Squamish people live, is out of bounds to us kids, except for the part of the forest near the Logging Road. But once a year, the Squamish people invite White people to their annual powwow. It's a seasonal festival.

It's May and pretty warm when I enter the magical world of the powwow. It's so different from life in Norgate Park.

First, we hear the drummers and singers start. About 10 men are sitting in a circle with a huge round drum in the middle. And all of them are drumming together, hitting the drum with all their might. And then one drummer (he's wearing a red hat) raises his stick, and he's sort of in charge for a while. It's so cooperative: the drumming. I love it!

We watch the Squamish dancers high-stepping in traditional costumes decorated with eagle feathers. Most of them wear high boots, and some wear moccasins. Some are wearing red and white blankets with lots of buttons sewn on them. And some have big bunches of feathers tied on their backs that look like wings! Or bunches that look like tails. Those dancers look like birds to me!

And everyone is singing, too.

We wonder if we should clap. And then we *all* do. Like **spon tan eous ly**. We clap in time with the drums. It's magic!

After we watch some more dancing and listen to more singing and drumming, Chief Simon Baker puts on *his* feather headdress. He walks into our circle to welcome us. He's got yellow boots on. A bunch of us White Norgate kids (all Norgate kids are White, actually) sit cross-legged at the front. Our parents stand behind us, just looking the tiniest bit uncomfortable.

Daddy told me a bit about Chief Baker before I went to the powwow. His Indian name is "Khot-la-cha." That means "Man with the Kind Heart." He works as a longshoreman. Chief Baker has smiley, crinkly eyes we can see behind his round glasses.

Chief Baker bends down to us children (and we can see up-close the feathers on his head), and he explains things to us in a really big voice: "Welcome, children. You are all welcome here today. *Everyone* is welcome here in this forest. Just to explain our dress today, especially the dancers' dress, each feather is a symbol of life. And together, the feathers represent the whole of life and how it continues forever. Our powwow is about dreaming and curing the sick. Welcome again, everyone!"

I sit cross-legged on the soft earth. This is good for me because I can dream and pray a little (in private, not out loud). I watch my prayers rise with the cedar smoke high above the forest's tallest trees. When I pray, I always pray for peace. Peace for everyone, including myself. I want the dreaming that Chief Baker tells us about.

THE WOUNDING

The delicious food they give us for free is an excellent part of the powwow! They have a barbecue with a gigantic fire pit dug into the earth and rows of huge, sizzling sockeye salmon hanging like pickets on a fence. And the Squamish women serve us big pieces of salmon with baked potatoes and corn on the cob with scads of butter. It is delicious.

One of the Squamish women takes me aside and whispers that she wants to chat a bit. I don't know why she chose me, but I go anyway, and we sit together on a big log. Her name is Nancy. She tells me that this forest is a *wild spirit place*. She says my spirit will be safe and renewed when I go there. She has a sort of singsongy voice, and these words feel really soothing to me. I listen to every word.

So, on some days, I walk back early from school and spend a couple of hours in Mid-Fairyland, sitting on the fallen log, leaning back against the old cedar tree. As I listen to the rainsong drumming in the top branches, I inspect the pale, velvety fungus that sticks to the sides of the cedar tree and the fuzzy, curled-up fern shoots covered with tiny hairs.

And I dream.

And when I dream, I feel the soft, green arms of the forest moving in close around me, wrapping me, and protecting my personal wild spirit.

For me, it's always the same in my safe forest nest. Even when it snows—I'm always safe and dry inside. And my forest's song makes my heart go all soft. I feel strong then, and I sing my brave songs in my outdoor voice. I belt out my songs to the forest because I know it loves to hear my strong singing.

When I get older, I am teaching architecture students and I do this exercise with them as part of an "Environmental

Autobiography." I draw my childhood home and my forest. In my drawing, my house and Norgate Park are all grey and filled with violence, sudden shocks, and *Hate.* But my forest is holding me, and a small, frightened creature is there with me (maybe it's my cat). My roots go deep into the rich earth, and the forest's green hands wrap around me. The tall trees protect me from the rain and from my mother.

When my forest sings, it sounds like the voice of a kind old woman, a whisper I hear above raindrops drumming on the high cedar branches. It's holding me and telling me not to be afraid.

In another drawing I make about the same time, the forest sings to me, "I will protect you." I always sing back to the forest: "Thank you. I needed it."

Part 3

Growing Up

Escape from Norgate Park

*A*fter 14 years of plotting my escape from Norgate Park, I do it in style. I don't have much to work with. No money, contacts, and hardly any family, but I have a few lucky breaks. When I am 18, I'm in a television competition on Channel 12 in Bellingham, Washington, just south of the border. It is called *Project 12*.

High school students interview foreign dignitaries and are graded on questioning content, presentation, and depth of interview. Over five months in early 1961, I appear on several interview panels. I come in second. (I imagine it's because of my looks. The other contestants are certified geeks, and I am pretty.)

The prize is a week in Ottawa or Washington, DC, all expenses paid. I want to see the bright lights (anybody can visit boring old Ottawa, Ontario), so I choose the United States Capitol.

En route to Washington, DC, August 1961

In the lobby of the Roger Smith Hotel, on a balmy evening in mid-August 1961, I meet a student spending his summer working for his Republican congressman. The congressman's office hosts the teenage winners, and he's assigned this young man as my guide for a week. The TV station sent a letter that included a note: "P.S. The boys at the station say this one's a living doll."

I step out of the elevator and see him lounging there in a brown leather armchair. He's wearing a blue seersucker suit. His blue eyes are shining.

I gasp. He is the one.

I never lived at all
Until the thrill of that moment when
My heart stood still

What a beautiful man! I am 18, and he is 20. He is tall, dark, and handsome and about to enter his junior year at Yale, where he subsequently graduates third in his class. To this day, he remembers me calling him my "prize." (I certainly thought that of him.)

I am swept up in a whirlwind summer romance for 10 days. We go canoeing on the Potomac River, walk hand in hand along the riverbank, linger over candlelit dinners, and visit the Lincoln Memorial at sunset… I'm enthralled. Sidewalk cafés are prohibited in Vancouver, so I am excited to eat in one. We drink iced tea and eat French onion soup and lobster (wearing tie-on paper bibs) at Bassin's Café on the corner of 14th Street and Pennsylvania Avenue.

I am completely enchanted.

I have few clothes, but blessedly I brought the right things for a hot, sticky Washington summer, and, for a shy teenager, I feel comfortable and confident. My high heels hurt, but I do not complain.

By the time I return to Vancouver, I've pretty much netted myself a fiancé. His family lives in Washington State, only 85 miles from Vancouver.

Keeping Myself Tidy for What Lay Ahead

I do many courageous (and some foolhardy) things to achieve my escape from Norgate Park. And I am still a child of the fifties with almost no sense of self—*or* my boundaries. I am not yet a person in my own right. So I am highly nervous when I first visit my sweetheart's family. His father is a gynecologist in a small Washington town. His mother, only 36 when I first meet her, is pretty spaced out. I learn later she's addicted to prescription drugs. Later still, I understand why.

I am on the launch pad of my journey to join a "better family" with good prospects. And, at first glance, this one certainly looks okay. I want to rise above my humble origins. So far, so good. Nice, educated people, a nice house, good car, dishwasher, and a good professional job.

Check.

Well, almost.

On my first visit, my sweetheart's maternal grandmother, Norma Garlick, corners me on the back deck. She's not quite five feet tall, but somehow, she towers over me. Her steely eyes drill into me. Her tone is shrill and demanding: "Wendy, you are about to join a Race of Giants. Are you aware of that? You must know this: *everything* we do in this family is excellent. Top-notch. This is my warning to you, Wendy. We will expect a lot from you."

Charming.

I ignore her warning and my prospective father-in-law's creepiness. I accept my sweetheart's addicted mother. I am on a mission, willing to join the Giants' team (though they hardly resemble the *Friendly Giant* I knew from childhood TV).

On my second visit, we announce our engagement. I am pretty, bright, and pursuing an education. So far, no impediments. (Canadian is not *ideal*, but it's acceptable.) But can I carry on the better family's dynasty and contribute to the Race of Giants? Who knows?

And who could imagine that an innocent girl of nineteen would permit her prospective father-in-law to examine her sexual organs? We drive to his medical office, and he ushers me into the examination room. No nurse is present. I'm terrified. He asks me to undress and lie on the crisp paper on the examination table. Then, without speaking further, he briskly guides my feet into the stirrups. I'm horrified with embarrassment and shame. Then he pulls a metal thing from a drawer. I gasp. It looks like a duck.

"Now you're going to feel a little pressure, Wendy," he mumbles, not even looking at me. He inserts the metal thing into me. Just like that. It's more than a little pressure, and I hate it. I feel like I'm being invaded.

That's it. We go back for dinner. We never discuss it. I feel I have no choice, and it's the right thing to do. My fiancé is brilliant. I guess the family needs reassurance that his wife can have his babies.

Imagine that. I do not ask.

Looking back, I doubt my fiancé even notices what happens to me. I am entirely numb during and after that humiliating experience. Frozen. And too ashamed to tell anyone. I don't have anyone to tell, in any case. And I don't know any better.

Years later, I reflect that nobody suggested an examination of my fiancé's sexual organs.

(Nearly 20 years after that event, I watch on TV as Diana Spencer marries Prince Charles. I'm appalled that she submitted to a gynecological examination to confirm her virginity. Her uncle, Lord Fermoy, announces to a press conference: "Diana, I can assure you, has never had a lover." Poor Diana. Just like me, she has no language for it. She stammers: "I knew I had to keep myself tidy for what lay ahead." At that time, I wonder again about *my* bizarre experience. Was it my virginity they were confirming? Or my fertility?)

In 1962, pronounced "fit-to-travel," I prepare to marry my catch. I manage to convince my Vancouver doctor to prescribe the recently approved Pill. (*That* is a courageous move.)

Ironically, I am *not* fit and fail to deliver on my assignment.

Keeping Myself Tidy for What Lay Ahead

Going to the Chapel

Yale University's "freedom-riding" Chaplain, William Sloane Coffin, Jr., marries us in Yale's Dwight Memorial Chapel days after the Yale graduation in June 1963. My father gives me away. (In the photos, he looks relieved.) I wear my maternal grandmother's cream satin wedding gown and a veil I make myself. (I dye the fabric in tea to create an "antique" look.) By all accounts, I achieve a remarkable escape.

Despite my naïveté, I *do* love this man. He does make my heart stand still. He is handsome, intelligent, kind, funny, and hugely supportive of my getting educated. It takes courage to move to the United States and marry a man I barely know. But somehow, I pull it off. I don't feel anything resembling passion. Shy and inexperienced, I am in love with love. Like a bride entering an arranged marriage, I pray that passion will come once we get to know each other.

With my prize, I prepare to build a New Life.

I know I am making an irrevocable decision. On my solo journey, I establish the pattern of putting as much distance as possible between myself and my abusive mother.

Nearly six decades later, my now ex-husband confides a secret about our courtship. He believed this "bubbly little person" (me) would make "a pretty good companion to a rising politician." Now I wonder if he ever loved me. Like me, he was bent on a "solution" to his problem. Both his parents had severe mental health issues. We were two young people doing our best to escape the wreckage of our childhoods.

In Connecticut, from 1963 to 1967, I am a "Yale Wife." I observe the excesses of male privilege and discover a passion for community planning. I study hard, work two jobs, and earn two arts and education degrees. I write a master's thesis in literature.

Then I spend a delightful year in London, my head in the Public Record Office's newspaper archives, supporting my husband's PhD research about missionaries in southern Africa. I type my detailed notes for him. Then I accompany him while he undertakes doctoral research throughout Europe and for three months in South Africa. In the Pietermaritzburg newspaper archives, I read every newspaper published in Natal and Zululand between 1830 and 1865. I type my detailed notes for him.

My husband easily secures an excellent tenure-track job at Adelaide University, and soon we are settled in Australia. I type his PhD dissertation. I find a job and study part-time to become an urban planner. I join a women's group and start reading books by feminist authors. I try to navigate this exciting new terrain while being an academic's wife with all that entails. I have lots of medical problems culminating in a hysterectomy at 31. He gets his doctorate and easily secures tenure. We buy a beautiful heritage house in a classy neighborhood.

He leaves me, moves in with and later marries his lover, and they have two perfect children who graduate with honors from Cambridge and Harvard. I finish *my* thesis, patch up my broken heart, campaign for better public housing and women's rights, learn more about feminism, and have a few lovers. I'm terribly bitter toward my ex. I try to heal, forgive us, and move on, but my grief and anger persist. By early 1978, I have not recovered from the pain of losing my husband and all the trappings of married life. My healing needs more.

Deeply distressed that I missed a critical developmental stage (my youth) by marrying so young, I decide to back up and pass through my youth again. At 35.

But in 1976, well before that, I embark on the first stage of a journey that transforms my life.

GUNUMELENG SEASON 1976
THE OUTBACK
Mid-October to late December 24°-37°C

Gunumeleng, the thundering time that precedes the monsoon rains, usually occurs from mid-October to late December.

White people call it the Build Up, but local Aboriginal people call it Gunumeleng, the first of the two suicide seasons. Heat and humidity continue in this time of the first rains. Massive cumulus clouds and oppressive heat give way to spectacular, fast-moving, easterly electrical storms across the afternoon sky.

As the rain starts, the frogs croak at night. The land begins to turn from brown to green. Green plums, white apples, red apples, and blackberries ripen.

Camp Concern

... coming to terms with the night is an act of trust: the decision to accept the night, not floodlit but in its own soft darkness, to be still within it and let it present itself, not peopling it with the shadows of our fears but accepting it as it comes to us .... Only where humans dare douse their lights and be still with the night can it happen.

Erazim Kohák, 1984

$\mathcal{I}$ will never forget the day I met him. In Adelaide, August 1976, at the Australian Planning Institute conference, aptly named "Where are We Going?"

"G'day, the name's Mica," a tall creature announces during the conference's morning tea break. I'm loading slides for my lecture later that day.

"You'd be Wendy. Is that right? Folks at the Environment Center tell me you're a good woman, and I should talk to you. Understand you're working on housing or something like that. Want some coffee?"

I smell this man before I hear his voice. I raise my eyes from the slide projector to inspect a tanned, damaged face, bright blue eyes, a mustache, and a long mousy beard. A tall, lanky bushman emitting a fragrance of tobacco and woodsmoke from a distant fire. He's my age, maybe 10 years older, wearing dark blue denim pants, a denim shirt and jacket, and heavy black boots. He holds a torn brown felt hat in long, nicotine-stained fingers.

Mica, 1976

Mica's morning speech takes the planning conference by storm with a simple message: *the city is not a living habitat.* With an air of controlled desperation, he advocates his case in workshops and speeches, distributing photocopies of his tracts on an astonishing array of topics: uranium mining, the environmental revolution, "Fourth World thought" in Australia, children's housing, legalization of marijuana, politics, and liberty. Australia is about to commit itself to an open-cut uranium mine in sacred and ecologically significant country in the Northern Territory. To Mica, this constitutes an unprecedented national emergency.

Before an audience of hundreds of planners, he pleads, "The survival of life depends on city people like you understanding the limits of the consciousness you have picked up in the city and the ecological impacts of your sensory deprivation."

Mica stays a week in Adelaide. Most of that time, I share Mica with my teaching partner, Doug, an architect, who's my closest male friend. Doug's in his late fifties, and he and Mica really hit it off. Mica can't believe how many fruits, vegetables, and trees Doug manages to grow in his tiny inner-city Permaculture garden. Mostly, the three of us talk about uranium mining. I learn we must leave it in the ground. Says Mica, "People can't see it, can't smell it, taste it... so they don't believe in it (even though it emits radiation)."

Occasionally, I'll glance up to notice Mica looking at me. I wonder what else he might teach me. I am ready to learn. I am in my mid-thirties. Catapulted from a passionless marriage, I am making the most of my bad luck, experimenting and enjoying the pleasures of the youth I missed by marrying young. I am having an exciting political time, too. It's the mid-seventies. We are marching in Adelaide's streets. Promoting the Women's Movement, gay rights, and housing rights, *Everybody's* rights. And now: campaigning against uranium mining. I'm highly active, struggling to explore avenues to help poor women access good, safe housing. I'm making speeches, writing, and teaching about housing.

Decades later, my ex-husband remarks that he never witnessed any evidence of my activism in the 14 years we were together. Then I realize something important: my activism didn't flower until he left me. (How familiar is that story!)

In any case, I successfully sublimate my fear, pain, vulnerability, and loneliness in my work.

Until Mica comes along.

One bright winter morning, we are sitting in a North Adelaide café. Mica makes his move. "Wendy," he exclaims. He puts down his newspaper, leans forward, and grabs my hand in both of his.

"You must visit the Top End, Wendy. To see the problem for yourself, mate. To widen your horizons."

I do not move my hand. I sit there, staring into those blue eyes. And I'm nodding.

Later, I learn that Mica had another life before he became a self-styled "environmental conscientious objector." He changed his name only the year before I met him. He was a senior clerk in the federal public service in Darwin and was married with three children, no less. His mother is a teacher-librarian. He's eccentric, self-educated, and literate. He has no respect for authority. Mica lives in a tent in an isolated rural location and sleeps with his dog, de-worming both occasionally. Bathing does not feature in his lifestyle.

GROWING UP

I've never encountered anyone vaguely resembling Mica before.

During this time, I am writing sad, lonely poems that chronicle my attempts to live as a single woman after fourteen years with *The Rational Man*. I was a virgin when I married, so I have lots to learn. After *The Rational Man* moves in with his lover, I consider telling the world I just arrived in Australia after fifteen years in Africa. I want to forget it all. Especially my married life.

The release of the Eagles' 1973 hit, "Desperado," coincides with the breakup of my marriage. It's my song: *You better let somebody love you before it's too late.*

At 33, I'm terrified it's too late.

I explore my desperate feelings in my poems, sharpen my outline, and draw boundaries around my new identity. I discover new lovers, massage, candles and roses, and breakfast in bed. I send roses to the first man who initiates me into that delight. I'm in London, and he is a young journalist with the *Financial Guardian*. Even eating what I want when I want is liberating. I become a vegetarian. I deeply engage in becoming myself.

While I pursue my self-improvement project with a vengeance, I am struggling with my *professional* identity. I have hard edges, and because of my public persona as a feminist activist, people think they know me. And I hate the one-dimensional person they think they know. They (and I) cannot imagine a man ever loving this harsh, armored woman.

One poem I write at that time explains that deep inside, I am *not* the confident woman people see. I am nothing but needy:

> *need helping*
> *need holding*
> *need touching*
> *need loving*
> *need tasting*
> *smelling feeling crying laughing*
> *need being.*
>
> *so lonely*
> *so angry*
> *so eager*
> *so frightened*
> *still trying.*

Mica expresses little curiosity about my identity crisis. My *ecological* consciousness is all that interests him. That's always his bottom line. He despises my slot on a fortnightly ABC radio program where I carry on about "bad kitchens I have known." He's also worried about my previous job, planning schools in new suburban areas. He explains that suburbia is part of the problem, not the solution. Automobile dependence is killing the Earth. (I say I know all about suburbia. I am just trying to help the lonely, isolated women marooned there.)

One day, we are sitting at the table in my tiny back courtyard. It's nearly spring, and the jasmine is flowering, climbing up the lattice and filling the tiny urban space with its heavy, tantalizing scent.

Mica puts down his mug of coffee and fixes me with his "Ancient Mariner" stare.

"Your radio work is just not important, Wendy. A complete waste of time. You're rearranging the deck chairs on the *Titanic*. A woman of your influence should be addressing much more urgent global issues—like climate change. If we don't fix this climate crisis, you'll have no planet to put the kitchens on. You need to rethink your priorities, girl."

I stare back. I thought I was making a difference with my radio work. Educating the public about housing. Not in *his* opinion.

His task, he decides, is to guide me on the path to ecological literacy. But never for one second does Mica suggest that my transition will be painless. For him, a shift to a new environmental consciousness will force me to confront what he calls "the burden of awareness." "Awareness is a lonely and poorly understood personal crisis, a desperate place," he writes in 1976. The prophetic quality of his words lingers with me.

Over time, I begin to discover Mica's purpose in my life, reaffirming those insights into my old age. Mica represents unhealed aspects of myself that I disown. I need to reclaim them. He's my Hermes, the thief and trickster, messenger of the Gods, my guide to the underworld: a disheveled and eccentric soul guide. And he is also a guardian figure— watching over me as I journey in unfamiliar realms. In 1976, Mica arrives precisely when I am desperate for transformation.

Two weeks after the planning conference ends and Mica returns to the Northern Territory, the September weather is just beginning to get warm. Jasmine scent envelops me as I step outside to collect my mail. I sit at the oak table in my North Adelaide kitchen and stare at the neat printing on an envelope. At that moment, I couldn't imagine how one letter would forever alter my life's trajectory.

Mica's letter reiterates his invitation: "Your intention to visit and find out what is happening is well received. You will be welcome." He's spoken about my intended visit to solar power people in Darwin. They are planning to build a demonstration low-energy village at Humpty Doo. Design students in Brisbane are drawing up plans for it right now.

If anyone tried to tell me that, fifteen years later, I'd live in that same solar village with those same people, I would violently disagree. Not me. Not the tropical forest. And certainly not with Mica, however intriguing he is.

I make another strong coffee and sit back at my kitchen table. I reread Mica's letter. Several times I fold it and put it back into the envelope, only to open it and reread it.

What am I doing?

And what am I waiting for?

I'm so tempted. So eager to learn and grow. So wounded. And so terrified. I look down at Mica's letter in my hand. It's shaking. Something is happening—happening *to* me. And *through* me. Forces I do not know or understand are demanding that I change.

But how?

And how can this eccentric messenger help with my healing?

I write an evasive reply to Mica. I've made plans to spend a few months in London writing a book about urban happiness. I have no intention of visiting him. But apparently, nothing can dampen his enthusiasm.

A month later, another typed message arrives—this time with directions.

I can fly from Adelaide to Darwin. From there, the road trip will take half a day. Mica has no car and makes no offer to meet me. There is no public transit. I must hitch a ride. Me! I've never hitchhiked in my life. Mica directs me to get off at the 170 km marker on the Arnhem Highway, walk west for about 150 meters, then south down a dirt track for 1,510 of his paces. That will deliver me to the "Welcome Tree" beside an outside kitchen on the lakeshore. He advises me to *coo-ee* loudly, sit down, and wait for the shy natives to greet me.

As to amenities, Mica advises that a "sand bed" awaits me at his house, called *Sunshower*. He recommends bringing light bedding, a mosquito net (for the *sweltering* nights and savage mozzies), a sleeping mat, and light, mosquito-proof clothing. I must bring food and drink for both of us for a week. The whole experience sounds terrifying and intimidating. I'm not the camping type. I feel vulnerable even *thinking* about this adventure. I've never even put up a tent by myself. Or made a campfire.

I'm the furthest thing from a bush person you could get. My idea of a good time is an almond croissant and a cappuccino in an air-conditioned café. I'm not physically strong or fit. In my job, I use my mind, not my body. I'm not afraid of spiders or snakes, but I hate getting sweaty and dirty. I love hot showers and clean sheets.

I'm 33, for fucksake. I *know* these things about myself!

Nevertheless, I made a promise, and I keep it. I can fit it in before the London trip. My teaching has finished for the academic year, so I really have no excuse. By this time, Doug has fallen in love with Mica's ideas, and he believes that transformation is in the cards for Wendy. So, he strongly encourages me. He is fully aware that ecology is the subversive science. He reckons he just has to get me started, and then, as the Aussies say, "She'll be right."

Doug lends me the necessary gear and coaches me to reframe the adventure. I am simply going camping in the outback with a new friend. I swallow my fear and pack a pile of unfamiliar stuff into Doug's backpack. My mouth is dry, and my heart is pounding as I wait to board the plane. What would my mother say? What if Mica is an ax murderer? Did I pack the right things? Then I hear Doug's laconic reassurance. "No worries. You'll be right, Wendy. Break a leg, mate."

I know nothing about the Northern Territory except that Cyclone Tracy destroyed most of its capital, Darwin, a couple of years earlier. I've never been there, never wanted to visit the "ends of the Earth." But I steel myself and fly into that strange northern city (that's more like a small town). As I step out of the airport, a wall of hot, humid air strikes me. It's a shock after Adelaide's dry climate.

I've never been to such a foreign place.

I have one friend in Darwin, and he's up for a bit of an adventure, so I pay for his gas to drive me to Camp Concern. I am horrified by how long it takes in his un-airconditioned Jeep. It's *so* hot. And I'm astonished by the massive Arnhem Highway: 124 miles of two-lane, wide, flat, newly paved highway—from Darwin to the Ranger uranium mine. Mica later explains that this massive investment in infrastructure reflects the miners' confidence in thousands of truck journeys to and from the Ranger mine. (They are right.)

Fire and evidence of fire are everywhere. Flat, charred, barren land stretches as far as I can see. Small fires smolder everywhere. What's all this fire about, anyway?

By late afternoon, we've found the track to Camp Concern. Neal and I are hot and exhausted, but I'm excited to begin my new adventure. After trudging what I imagine are 1,510 of Mica's long strides from the highway, we arrive. And there, in the dirt, leaning back against a big tree, sits Mica, naked, with Tom, also naked. They are currently the only residents of this anti-uranium demonstration camp.

"Hello, Mica," I say formally, struggling out of my backpack and setting it down in the dust. I mop my forehead with my bandana.

Neal steps forward to greet them. I hang back. They chat for a while the way Australian men often do. It's almost a foreign language. Darwin's population halved after Cyclone Tracy two years ago, so everybody knows everybody. Finally, Mica looks up at me and nods. He sits there smoking. I avert my eyes from his genitals as my mind registers the longest testicles I have ever seen.

Camp Concern

"G'day, Wendy," he replies without getting up. "Good to see you. Bring anything cold to drink?"

After we say goodbye to Neal, I begin to work out where I am. But the guiding philosophy and the specifics of Camp Concern take a while to dawn on me. I'm visiting a radical, residential, anti-uranium camp. Mica and Tom (and 2,000 others who will visit until 1979) are protesting the building of a uranium mine in a sacred World Heritage Park, Kakadu National Park (20,000 square kilometers, one-third the size of Tasmania). Naomi, the only other permanent resident, is away in Darwin. These activists are "sitting in" to show their commitment to protecting the land, the culture, and, critically, precious and delicate tidal waterways and river systems from what they view as inevitable (and massive) devastation by open pit uranium mining. They believe their peaceful, non-violent demonstration is bearing witness to the first stage of that devastation.

(They are right about that. Over decades, the uranium mine's tailings dam leaked hundreds of thousands of liters of wastewater daily, polluting groundwater with heavy metals, toxic chemicals, and radioactive substances, such as radium and uranium. Contamination of wetlands and wildlife poisoned local water and food sources. Then, 30 years later, nuclear-risks.org reports that cancer incidence among Kakadu's Aboriginal population increased 90% more than expected.)

Their courage to persist in such harsh conditions gains them legendary status among environmentalists in the urban South. Mica later explains that *just being there* was a political statement for him.

Although this is the tropics, it's not like any tropics I've experienced (like the Everglades in Florida). It's the Wet-Dry tropics. So, it rains for only part of the year, and it's hot and dry the rest of the year. For interest, I pull Doug's camping thermometer out of the backpack. That first afternoon, it registers a high of 42 degrees C (107.6 degrees F).

I've never been anywhere like this before. The land is desolate, hot, and bare, a savannah grassland with skinny gum (eucalyptus) trees (mostly woollybutts and stringybarks) scattered about. Many stand no taller than I am. An unrelenting tropical sun glints off metallic, burnished earth. I can't walk barefoot for more than a few seconds. It's the driest, hottest place I've ever seen. Bushfires scorched the trunks of most of the larger trees. (Mica says smaller trees and shrubs burn up in a bushfire.)

Mica is at pains to describe this unfamiliar climate. It's all about seasons. As much as 1,300 mm of rain will fall in the next few months once the annual rains arrive. Camp Concern is located in the *Thunderstorm Bioregion*, a land of dramatic seasonality. This region's traditional owners identify six seasons, defined by the skies, rainfall, plants, and animals.

Mica is eager to teach me about the *Aboriginal* seasons.

"Here, we have a much more complex calendar than White people's two seasons for the Top End: the Dry Season (April to October) and the Wet Season or tropical summer (November to March). The transitions between seasons are marked by subtle variations in the weather, the plants in flower, and the bush foods that are most abundant. In November, we're at the end of Build Up season (*Gurrung*), a transitional time between the Dry and the Wet."

As I wrap my mind around *six* seasons, Mica hits me with another curve ball: "I work on 365 seasons. Oh, yeah. Because every day's different. Every day's a different season." Nevertheless, I soon realize that November, the *suicide season*, is the worst time to visit the Top End. (Thanks, Mica.)

One Flower Lake is my first billabong. I recognize the word from "Waltzing Matilda," the Australian song about the swagman. It's a large pond (Mica says it's about the size of a soccer field) that fills only in *Gurrung* season after substantial rain. We're between seasons right now, so water is still in it. But the deepest spot is only a few feet deep. Mica gave the billabong its name. He says it's the victim of the impacts of feral water buffalo: gigantic animals introduced in the mid-Nineteenth Century to supply meat to northern settlements. Grazing on aquatic grasses, wetland plants, and pandanus fronds, these giant beings devastate the local ecology by wallowing for much of the day and muddying the billabongs. Few flowers bloom there because they need clear water to thrive. However, this tiny human settlement dramatically improved the billabong's life after only a year because the camp dogs keep the buffalo away.

Several noisy white waterbirds are sitting on the lily pads, eyeing me. More birds will come with the rains, Mica says.

Mica is proud of his house, but to my mind, *Sunshower* is little more than a stained Army tent pitched over a rough frame of wooden poles. Under the canvas, the upper floor is recycled wood from a house demolished by Cyclone Tracy. The ground floor is sand. Mica sleeps upstairs under a mosquito net. I smile when I spot a feature cherished by the librarian's son: two metal filing cabinets under the house. That's the library: Mica's highest priority.

GROWING UP

Sunshower: **Mica's house at Camp Concern, 1976**

Mica says he thought a lot about where to build his house, aiming for breeze capture and an all-around view so he could be "master of all he surveys." He designed it for starlight, too: "to consider the effects of silhouettes in the forest." All I can see is a makeshift lean-to.

After a few false starts with Mica standing by but not offering to help, I blow up my air mattress, plop it on the sand, and tie my mosquito net to poles under his house. Then I inquire about the amenities.

"Amenities! Hah! City girl!"

There is no toilet, no running water, and no electricity.

"Washing? Forget that!" A sponge bath by the muddy edge of the billabong.

Mica instructed me to bring a trowel and toilet paper. I can pee wherever I like, but to shit, I must dig a small hole as far as I can get from the billabong. Pissing and shitting are major territorial issues in the inter-species warfare between the buffalo and us, who Mica calls "the apes." Perhaps in retaliation for apes pissing in its "territory," one buffalo recently dropped a gigantic mound of dung on the "dining table" (the sand under Mica's house).

My days at Camp Concern are bewildering and revelatory. I'm visiting an isolated landscape that feels hostile, barren, and alien. The heat and humidity defy description: it's the oppressive suicide season. The annual rains are late, and the air is stifling under cloudy skies. But the night sky reveals a vast array of luminous stars when the clouds disappear. I struggle to keep from being drawn up into the sky, terrified I'll disappear forever into the powerful magnetism of its spangled resonance.

The following morning, I tell Mica about my experience with the stars. He's ready for me. He explains that in Australia's tropical north, stars shine with great brilliance and luminosity in a vast, pristine night sky unimpeded by the landscape. Each star has a different color and intensity. Red stars! All over Australia, Aboriginal people believe that in the Creation, what are now stars and planets were once men, women, and other animals. Following some mishap on Earth, they flew up to the sky. A shooting star is a spirit canoe carrying a dead person's soul to the new land.

In the Southern Cross and the Pointers constellations, some Aboriginal people see a white gum tree with two sulfur-crested cockatoos approaching. Later, I read that Australian Aboriginal people never saw stars when they looked up at the night sky. They saw only their ancestors sitting by campfires on their celestial journey. *And their eyes met.* For me, this Aboriginal story captures something about *inseparability.* Living humans and the spirits of dead ones can and do co-exist. And humans and Nature can be one as well, connecting over time and space. I am grateful for this insight.

For me, visiting Camp Concern is like an ecology seminar with a tinge of romance and the planet's most appalling food. We eat canned fish and boiled white rice. Mica drinks warm beer from a cache of cans buried at the muddy edge of One Flower Lake. His candlelit lectures on groundwater pollution in the Alligator River system and what to do if a buffalo charges are intimidating and confusing. I role-play, and we have hilarious moments as I pretend to climb a straggly tree to escape a charging water buffalo.

Mica is the buffalo.

"Run, Wendy! Run for your life!!" yells Tom.

Mica gestures wildly, jumps up and down, his fingers on his head for horns, and makes scaredy noises. I race away from him and attack the most robust tree I can find. Then Tom helps me pull my feet up to get a perch on the lowest branches. Mica prowls around, growling. It's pretty hilarious, and it's serious work.

And Mica didn't exaggerate about the mosquitoes. They are gigantic. I am their dream of a plump, juicy morsel brimming with city sugar, fresh milk, and cheesecake.

I am a long way from home. I'm accustomed to order, cleanliness, and predictability. I tidy and dust my desk daily. And here I am, in the harshest place imaginable. I hardly recognize myself. I wonder: *Could I get used to living like this?*

The answer is a firm "no."

I brought a tape recorder and later transcribe some of our conversations. There's lots of singing, with both Tom and Mica playing guitar. They share a love of bluegrass music and repeatedly sing "Mr. Tambourine Man." Like a mantra. I record some of Tom's beautiful guitar picking.

Partly to justify such a visit during the academic term, I pretend I'm reporting to these environmental activists about the UN Habitat Forum conference I attended in Vancouver a few months earlier. I listened to distinguished elders like Margaret Mead (age 75), Buckminster Fuller (also 75), and Mother Teresa (age 66) inspire huge audiences about activism, feminism, and environmental reform. That Forum changed the course of my life forever.

When I get started, I have so much to share with my new friends:

"Habitat Forum was like an island of suspended reality. As I passed through the gates, I felt anything was possible, including conversations about the most radical ideas. The whole context was designed to support the flourishing of the human spirit. It was a crucible experience. Nobody could attend Habitat and not be affected. Everything I wanted to do (or learn about) was in one place.

"Just as an example, I could attend a *Sand Play for All Ages* therapy workshop, listen to Bucky Fuller, learn about the Findhorn community, experience Transcendental Meditation, hear Margaret Mead's wisdom, help establish the Women and Environments International Network, visit amazing bookstores... And everywhere, I experienced examples of alternative energy and other 'green' innovations. Habitat was a cocoon of creativity. I was ready for it and profoundly affected by it."

Later, I figure out that explaining my Habitat adventure to Mica and Tom helped me make sense of my newfound environmental consciousness. Although they were, in one sense, a world away, Mica and Tom "got it" and helped me make sense of that powerful experience. As the two men listen to my stories, I start to relax and not feel so nervous. Maybe I'm not so alien, after all.

I also regale them with contemporary Adelaide tales of changing from an activist in hippie dress to a power-dressing bureaucrat for the board meetings I attend. They listen politely. Mica tries to contextualize things for Tom: "Wendy's been into the same sort of planning lane that I have."

We talk endlessly about the principles Mica used to design and build his simple shack. On housing, Mica and I can easily relate. I sit by the campfire with Tom and Mica and gaze at Mica's house, silhouetted in the moonlight. For him, views are everything, so he tried to achieve a 360° view of the billabong from his bed. He failed because the low "walls" of the tent roof blocked part of it.

Slowly, I realize how incredibly complex and dangerous this project was for Tom and Mica (the only permanent residents). They had no electricity, equipment, or vehicles. The 10 ft. by 10 ft. plywood floor came from a Darwin cyclone recycling center, and friends hauled it on a trailer and dropped it in the parking lot. Then Mica faced a terrible dilemma. How to get this massive thing to his house site without damaging any trees? So, the two men dragged it 500 meters through the forest. But that was only part of the trip. Next, holding onto it and swimming, he floated the floor across the billabong.

"We got the floor across the lake, and people helped pull it out of the water. Then we had to wait to get labor together. Because it was so hot, I left shifting the floor until late in the day. We took the tent off the ridge pole, put the floor on, and threw the tent back on.

"Then I found four people to tie it with wire to the ridge pole. At first, it didn't work because I hadn't allowed for the uprights' height in my measurements. When it nearly got up, with Tom and I standing on the floor, we couldn't hold it anymore. And it wasn't vertical enough for the people below to take its weight. So, we made a quick decision and pushed it right over the top. And it fell down.

"Then I took off all the wire, took it apart, and put it back up piece-by-piece. Later, I braced up the north ridge post. But my plan didn't quite work out, and it's on a lean. And there was this bit of temporary bracing at the south end. Because it'd been there so long, I decided it was an 'affectation.' So, I took it away, walked away 50 feet, and the whole house started to fall down. I had to put it back quickly. It wasn't an 'affectation,' after all. It made structural sense."

GROWING UP

After that briefing, I turn to regard this ragged structure with new admiration. I marvel at their ingenuity. I have a funny feeling that what I'm learning here will serve me somehow in the future…

At 33, Mica's spent all his adult life in the Australian conservation movement, including several years on the Australian Conservation Foundation Council. He eagerly explains that he and Camp Concern are "a one-person Friends of the Earth outpost." The idea for Camp Concern arose when Mica worked with Peter Hayes, who later gained an international reputation and the coveted American MacArthur Fellowship (the "Genius Grant") for his nongovernmental advocacy work.

In 1974, Peter and Mica reviewed international information about the peaceful use of uranium. Mica found it a horrifying experience. They collated six filing cabinet drawers of research material and reported their findings in the first Friends of the Earth tabloid publication on uranium mining and nuclear power in 1974: *A Slow Burn*. Both credit that work with strengthening their activism.

Mica says he moved to the *Determination* stage of the stages of change model after he and Peter investigated the dangers of uranium:

> *We were at the last stage of preparing "A Slow Burn." We had half a column set aside for the subject of plutonium. It was getting late. And I looked at Peter, and Peter looked at me, and we looked at the clock. And we agreed to wait until the sun rose before we wrote about plutonium. We couldn't do it in the dark. We needed the sunshine. For me, not so much for Peter, it was just too horrible. By far the most disturbing material I read was about the toxicity of plutonium. I didn't know much about plutonium before that.*

Mica then explains that he was so frightened by plutonium because it's alpha radiation, a highly ionizing form of radiation, rather than beta or gamma radiation. When they get inside cells, alpha–emitters are extremely hazardous and can cause between 10 and 1,000 times more chromosomal damage than beta or gamma rays.

When our conversation drifts back to Camp Concern, Tom and Mica explain that their project involves being good neighbors. Local Aboriginal people are confused and frightened by the Ranger mine, so these activists try to maintain a peaceful presence to reassure them that at least some White people care about their sacred and fragile country. Relations with local White people are understandably complex. But Tom and Mica delight in reporting that they spent last Christmas with the Ranger, Gordon, and his wife,

Betty, at the South Alligator wildlife ranger station. Gordon drove them back and stayed for a few rums.

I learn that Mica is an amateur ornithologist after hearing him hold forth on birds, specifically waterbirds, cormorants, and whistle ducks. We're sitting in deck chairs at the edge of One Flower Lake. After initially claiming that "the world's full of voyeurs," Mica explains his take on the theory of convergent evolution based on his observations over the past few months. The display of one group of black cormorants triggers the display of another group. Then they buzz the whistle ducks and influence *their* behavior. Mica believes the cormorants' excessive caution rubbed off on the whistle ducks.

It's always like that: our conversation veers off in unexpected directions, supported by a generous supply of weed that materializes out of nowhere.

Surprisingly, on his home territory, Mica is pretty shy— different from the strong, confident, and didactic persona I encountered in Adelaide. He's been living in a remote location for a long time, often alone with only Sam, his dog, for company. On a good day, there might be three or four people living there at Camp Concern. It's a lonely place. On ecology, Mica is a "full bottle" (deeply knowledgeable) and can spot a eucalyptus blossom at 300 feet, identify every birdsong, feather, paw, and claw mark, and devise a scenario to accompany every buffalo wallow.

On feelings, he's not that forthcoming. When I'm not looking for a place to pee or shit or racing away from a water buffalo, I wonder: is he interested in me? Like sexually? Romantically? What would it be like to be with a man like this?

This wild man?

In Adelaide, I noticed him noticing me. Here on his home territory: not so much.

On this, my first of two visits a year apart, I stay a week at Camp Concern. Mica and I hitch a ride together to Darwin and spend the night with his friends in a lightweight, wooden tropical house. In the dawn light, he answers one of my questions. Shyly, quietly, we engage in some hesitant lovemaking on a mattress on the floor. The lack of privacy inhibits us, and I feel uncomfortable with his musty smell. *And* I am intrigued.

"You owe me half a fuck," Mica whispers at the boarding gate in Darwin airport, leaning down to pat the top of my head with two fingers in a curious gesture I come to decode as intimate. For nearly four decades, he will laughingly remind me of my debt.

My First Environmental Speech

I fly back from Darwin in a trance. On the plane, I scribble speech notes on small index cards.

The next day I'm scheduled to speak at a women's seminar to celebrate International Women's Year, the start of the United Nations Decade for Women: Equality, Development and Peace. I'm sharing the platform with a local physician, who's a few years older than I am: Dr. Helen Caldicott. She's a prominent environmental activist, and I greatly admire her. Helen goes on to spearhead several global anti-nuclear initiatives that gain Nobel Prizes. I will be in good company.

As I open the door from the airport terminal, I breathe in deeply. Early summer. Hotter than when I left. Hot, dry, Mediterranean air. I've lived here for eight years now. *Home!*

"Can we stop at a 7-11 on the way to North Adelaide, please?" I beg the taxi driver.

It's late, but he finds one on O'Connell Street. I rush in and gather life's essentials: milk, cat food, and cigarettes.

With my key in the door, I stop for a second and breathe again. *Home!* I have eight hours.

And I know how to do this.

I'm relieved to find my neighbor's taken good care of Esther. She purrs her enthusiastic welcome while I get to work. Feed her first and change her litter box. Pull off my hippie clothes and throw them with the towels and bedding into the washing machine on the long, hot cycle. Pile Doug's camping gear by the back door and stash the suitcase in the closet. Step into a hot shower. Shave legs and armpits.

Then I stop to breathe again. As the clear water trickles through my matted hair and down my sunburned face, I realize I'm washing away the unfamiliar and tantalizing fragrances of a distant hearth and a distant man.

Must be done.

I furiously scrub my blackened feet. Then, wrapped in a large towel, I deodorize myself, set up the ironing board on my kitchen table, and run an iron over my grey suit with the shoulder pads.

A night's sleep, feed Esther again, some strong coffee, and I'm ready.

Five minutes on the road, and I'm locking my bicycle outside the Town Hall. Find the room and greet the organizers. Grab my name tag and another coffee. Congratulate the organizer on the great donuts. (Aussies rarely do good donuts.) Pronounce my Armenian last name a few times for my session chair.

Then I face my audience of bright-eyed women. We know each other. I'm a regular on the Adelaide feminist speaking circuit.

My topic is women's access to public housing.

I speak *not one word* about women's access to public housing.

Instead, I formally "come out."

From the participants' body language, I can see that my dramatic speech initially startles them. I explain how in 1973 when I "came out" for women and education, my first feminist speech instantly cost me my public service job. (That was a sharp lesson in sexism. My male boss was in that audience.)

I plant my feet and imagine Earth energy surging up into my body. I take a deep breath.

"Today," I announce, "I'm coming out for the environment."

Puzzled glances greet my announcement.

I soldier on. I summarize my activist stances since that fateful 1973 speech and reveal my dramatic change of consciousness, beginning with the UN-Habitat Forum a few months ago. Then I describe meeting Mica, my visit to Camp Concern, and what it means to him to be an "environmental conscientious objector." He regards the city as not being a habitat but "an environmental hazard that damages all life on Earth."

I draw a link between my talk and my advertised topic: *habitat*. My audience is confused, to say the least. I persist.

I grip the lectern with both hands and pronounce: "I am speaking out today because Mica challenged me to take *personal r*esponsibility for my environmental impacts."

I beg my audience of urban women to stop being antagonistic to Nature and adopt a cooperative attitude. Then I recount the lessons of my recent trip to Camp Concern: "We must work to make the Earth an intentional community, not a haphazard place." I explain the problems with Australia's default "urban bias": urban people and politicians make "environmental" decisions in cities that are not living environments. Here in the city, we really have no idea what we're doing or the consequences.

Pretty soon, I'm shaking and close to tears. I beg my friends and colleagues: "For the survival of all life, we city people *must* understand the limits of our consciousness. We *must* learn about the bush. We *must* take responsibility for our environmental impacts. And, as a matter of urgency, we *must* stop uranium mining in Australia. Immediately."

Finally, I quote Mica: "There can be no peace if we stifle the growth of our friends. Save the Earth."

Silence greets me. Initially. Then the women slowly begin to applaud. Some are crying.

I've come out, all right. My speech cements my credentials as an activist. But only *I* know how much I have changed in a few months.

I turn a corner, and I never look back.

GROWING UP

California

$\mathcal{I}$n February 1978, I change my life. A lot. I walk away from a tenure-track academic job. Give my Adelaide house to a bankrupt friend. Put a few belongings into storage. And fly to California on a one-way ticket. My professor friend, Clare, is on sabbatical. I'm teaching her courses and minding her house. I live in a room in that funky old Berkeley house that I share with four housemates. I've never lived in a share house before, and it's so much fun. I'm 35, but I feel 18! For two blissful years, I embrace the youth I missed. I smoke dope, march, make new friends, delight in a much younger lover, and make love all weekend.

Berkeley in the late seventies is heaven on a stick. I wait for six hours to attend Judy Chicago's "Dinner Party" exhibition. I am excited as I drink in its brilliance, promising myself to be more creative in my life. Peter Hayes (introduced to me by Mica) invites me to accompany him to observe a political action against a nuclear reactor built near a seismic fault near San Diego. The Abalone Alliance holds a blockade at the Diablo Canyon gates. In all, 5,000 people attend the rally, where 487 people are arrested when they cut through the fence to the facility. As I sit in this huge crowd, I feel my environmental consciousness expand and deepen. I belong with these brave people. Their peaceful "sit-in" campaign aligns with what I witnessed two years earlier at Camp Concern. It's all the same cause. Save the Earth!

At Berkeley, I deliver a lecture on how the Camp Concern anti-nuclear protest camp embodies principles of social ecology. Mica mails detailed drawings and notes for my lecture. My landscape architecture students stare in bewilderment. I've introduced a bizarre story from an alien culture into a university course. They don't know what to make of it—or of me!

I teach two lectures a week. That's about all I have time for.

My resume says I am spending two years as a Visiting Scholar at the University of California, teaching, writing chapters for a colleague's book, and co-authoring a book on housing design with another academic. But really, I am just having fun. And I am deepening my environmental consciousness in this hotbed of activism.

Later, I live in San Francisco's Noe Valley neighborhood with my lover, Don. I am happy.

But my work visa is running out. So, in early 1980, with Don, I fly back to Adelaide. Predictably, it's a pale shadow of the liberal paradise I knew in the seventies. I try working as a manager in a local municipality but lack the necessary patience. Don finds an excellent job in Sydney, so we move there. We have nearly a decade of married life, and I learn to be a planning consultant. I love my work. Later, we live in a college town and happily share an academic job for a few years. We start a small publishing company. It's a busy and exciting time.

Don and I separate amicably in 1988. We vow to maintain our loving friendship and succeed admirably to our mutual delight.

I move back to Adelaide, my Australian "home," in 1990. And that's when fate returns Mica, the trickster messenger, to me. Tragically, the Ranger uranium mine has been approved, so he's moved from the isolation of Camp Concern to a new eco-village in a place called, amazingly, Humpty Doo.

This time, both my heart and my mind are aligned with his. We have lots to talk about: uranium mining, the climate emergency, and what "sustainability" means for cities, planners, and the bush. We rekindle our relationship over Christmas in Adelaide.

Part 4

A Midlife Journey

So I say, "Seek initiation." When we enter the self by penetrating with our awareness the deeper zones of mind and body, we see that the wound that has opened in our psyches and on the body of Earth is a continuum of suffering. Self and relationships, self and setting are not separate. They are a "unity in process."

Joan Halifax, 1993

GUDJEWG SEASON 1990-1991
THE ORDINARY WORLD
December to March 24°-34°C

Gudjewg, a season that generally lasts through January and February, is the monsoon season. It is a time of electrifying thunderstorms, heavy rain and flooding, and vivid green landscapes.

Wind and weather come from the northwest, with periods of grey clouds, overcast skies, and cooler temperatures. The change provides great relief after months of the oppressive Build Up season.

Magpie geese nest around the billabongs. Many other animals nest in this season, so it's time to collect eggs.

1. The Yearning

*Drinking the Tears of the Earth / I Am Being Dragged
Along / My Plan to Learn about Ecology*

*In nearly all traditions, sacred psychology assumes that the
deepest yearning in every human soul is to return to its
spiritual source, there to experience communion and even
union with the Beloved.*

Jean Houston, 1992

Drinking the Tears of the Earth

Flax

such a sunlit sky
    the blue of wild flax

sky's pool
    flower after flower
    gone as mornings go
so much blue behind me

Jane Munro, 2006

*I*t's early 1991.

I'm 48.

Teetering.

On the edge.

Of the dark night.

Of my soul.

And it's not really about *me*, either. Desperation about the state of our global environment (specifically the climate crisis) overwhelms me. My urban planning colleagues' indifference throws me into despair. They say climate change has nothing to do with *planning*. I'm losing all sense of camaraderie with my colleagues. I am a leader in a profession where nobody is listening.

In 1971, I was the first woman to study planning in South Australia. For decades, I am the only woman in any professional meeting I attend. I hear my colleagues muttering that I worry too much about ecology, global warming, climate change, sea-level rise, species extinction…. "Can't we just get on with our work and then go to the pub, please, Wendy?" they sadly ask. There are still very few women working in the planning field, and sadly, the professional men lock me out of the conversations that matter.

In 1991, our local and national press is full of talk about Ecologically Sustainable Development (ESD) and the Greenhouse Effect. Basically, climate change. Information about ESD consultations, government Greenhouse Effect conferences, reports, and proceedings bombards me. Environmentalists now insist that we planners insert the letters "ESD" into every planning document. But planners have no idea what that means or how to make a difference. It's "greenwash." We inhabit two entirely separate realms: planning and "the environment."

That year, I speak with a group of Australian planners about ESD, and they say things like this:

I see you quoted saying something rude about cars. My belief is that the car is such a liberating invention that technology will soon

4.1. *THE YEARNING*

make private transport less polluting and accessible to a wider age and physical disability range.

and

Someone (you?) should establish whether local food production is good or bad for ESD. I suspect it's certainly not beneficial and may even be the reverse.

Awareness of climate change is hardly new. The Club of Rome published *Limits to Growth* in 1972, and the United Nations' Brundtland Commission published *Our Common Future* in 1987. It was supposed to unite countries pursuing so-called "sustainable development." I've worried about these matters for years. When *The Rational Man* left me in the mid-seventies, I re-inhabited the green heart of my childhood. That marriage stifled my politics, but I quickly recovered. In 1986, I co-author a book with a timely, "green" title: *Housing as if People Mattered*, riffing off Schumacher's 1974 title, *Small is Beautiful: Economics as if People Mattered*.

For decades, I've been an activist, a "green" planner, and a contrarian. I've been a seeker in many realms. And I've tried to bring insights from my personal life into my professional life. But things are different now. *Now* I face a quandary that is genuinely life-threatening. Not just for *my* life, but for all life on this planet. I ask, how can Australian planners honestly face up to the climate emergency? Why are we avoiding it? How can we learn enough to make a difference? Who can teach me? How can *I* learn enough to make a difference? What's the highest and best use of my skills? Can I make *any* difference at all? Midlife is cooking these questions and issues inside me.

In the seventies, I was known for my *feminist* activism. Once, in late 1977, on national TV, as part of a larger campaign, I ask South Australian women to send their knickers to the Minister for Housing. To show that women "wear the pants" in public housing and must be represented on the state housing authority board. The Minister receives hundreds of pairs of underpants in the mail in an election year. And, in the State election, he loses his seat.

Adelaide *Advertiser*, December 21, 1977

4.I. THE YEARNING

One evening, not long after my TV appearance, I hear a knock on my door. It's past 10 pm, but I sense there's nothing to fear. I welcome two senior Labor Party officials who have been drinking at a nearby pub that closed at 10. I've never met either one, but I know who they are. They are a bit tipsy, perhaps emboldened for their visit to the feminist activist.

We sit at my kitchen table, and I offer a glass of wine.

"Thank you, Wendy," one says, taking a sip. "We are not here, of course, and this visit is not taking place."

"Of course," I say politely. "You are not here. I can see that."

"Thank you again, Wendy," the other one chimes in.

"You were very brave on TV. You put that pontificating bastard in his place at last. Those Letters to the Editor from the women's shelters, the Women's Electoral Lobby, and so forth. They made a real difference. *You* made a difference. Now we will get rid of that arrogant sonofabitch. And we will have you to thank."

That feminist campaign was a huge success, but my prominence was an exception. Generally, I did not stand out because good feminists always work collectively.

For decades, desperate to fit in, I try (and fail) to be "one of the boys."

For example, the boys mock my search for ways to be "ecological" in planning a vast Melbourne suburban housing development, Roxburgh Park, which will eventually house 25,000 people on 1600 acres of what was once productive farmland. In 1989, four of us are sitting in a windowless conference room in a government building in central Melbourne. I've brought a bouquet of flowers for the table. Other than that, it's a harsh, austere environment.

Doug, a senior engineering consultant six years my junior, taunts me in a job interview. The tables are turned, for once, and *I* am on the selection panel. He's a candidate. (If selected, his engineering firm will earn 10 million dollars over 10 years from this project.)

So, I ask Doug: "Can you please explain how your firm plans to be 'ecological' in your civil engineering work for this outer suburb?"

Doug shoots back a reply tinged with mockery: "So, what do *you* want on this suburban housing site, anyway, Wendy? Solar panels on the roofs of 10 thousand houses?"

I jump back like he's struck me.

It's not Doug's *mansplaining*. All women professionals recognize that unique patronizing condescension that keeps women from speaking up. It's much more than that. I *do* want what Doug is trivializing. And I want *more*: solar panels, water-sensitive urban design, Permaculture landscapes, rainwater tanks, higher housing densities, transit-oriented development, permeable surfaces, natural watercourses, and public transit. I want all the ecological elements that fill our fancy sustainability policies. In my view, these civil engineers are tragically out-of-date.

4.1. THE YEARNING

Doug makes such a mess of his pitch for Melbourne's biggest civil engineering job that his colleague, Phil, has to front a follow-up interview. Wise Phil offers a much "greener" perspective on suburban civil engineering. They get the job, of course.

Amazingly, retired engineer Doug confesses in late 2020 that my provocative questions catapulted him onto a new path for the remainder of his professional life. He says, "Phil saved me in that 1989 interview because he understood the science and what you were after." Phil chimes in by email to explain the political and bureaucratic constraints he and other engineering colleagues faced, including the precarious global financial situation at the time.

At age 72, Doug confides that while my questions initially terrified him, they opened him to ecological perspectives that dramatically transformed his engineering practice. He went on to successfully "green" his business. I'm touched to have such a conversation. And Phil, also retired, is now a "green" farmer, deeply into regenerative agriculture. Thirty years ago, I felt that Doug, at 40, was just another out-of-touch, old-school professional. More likely, Doug and his engineering colleagues were cut off from their roots in Nature. Now I regret I misjudged him, and I bless his memory. I'm also delighted that I *did* have an influence on his environmental values.

But in early 1991, these insights are slow in coming. I'm struggling mightily to manage my green heart and my expanding global consciousness. From about 1989, in speeches and workshops, I play with ideas like *The Great Story* and invent role-play scenarios grounded in global evidence. In one event, planners dress up as gods and goddesses to represent key players responsible for (and affected by) Melbourne's arterial roads. Gaia, the Mother of All Life on Earth, is always front and center in these role-play events. Often, I play her myself.

My professional work reflects my desperation to heal my estrangements and find a greater sense of connectedness. Every day, I confront practical and existential dilemmas in my planning work. Like *every* day. Working on a waterfront site for a proposed marina throws me into turmoil. Am I inadvertently colluding in creating environments that will be submerged or subject to devastating storms caused by climate change?

I ask Herb, the consultant hydrologist, who shrugs his shoulders and chuckles at my question: "Don't worry, Wendy. Leave that to us experts. Just focus on locating the childcare center, okay?"

Rising sea levels and the demise of Bangladesh and small Pacific islands invade my dreams. Contradictions and paradoxes fill my days. Is fluorescent lighting better for the Greenhouse Effect? It draws less electricity, the bulbs last longer, and it uses fewer accelerants. Or should we recommend full-spectrum incandescent lighting because of its fewer harmful *health* effects? Do I recommend higher housing densities on the urban fringe? That would bring reduced pollution and energy use by private cars, hopefully, with beneficial impacts in terms of Greenhouse gases. Yes? Or *what*?

And what about the *social* impacts? Is it reasonable to pay more for solar water heaters or photovoltaic cells because they reduce the depletion of fossil fuel resources? Should we ban rainforest timbers from Malaysia and Australia's tall forests for house construction? Or *what*? What are the trade-offs? What's the evidence? What's the best mix of strategies? How can I educate myself about these things? And how ethical is it to carry on about these matters when I have an uneducated "green conscience"?

I keep trying—and failing. In the middle of 1991, over three months, I conduct 26 meetings about housing issues throughout the Northern Territory. We meet with hundreds of tenants in tropical and arid regions, towns, cities, and remote villages. The tenants hate their housing (designs concocted in temperate cities and sent to the desert or the tropics). They are beyond hysterical with rage and frustration. They beg for rainwater tanks. They rage against poor ventilation in sweltering climates. They are furious about the expense of air conditioning. They call the Northern Territory bureaucrats "dinosaurs."

The Northern Territory Government's steering committee rejects every one of my findings and recommendations because of my "green bias." They bury my report. Make it un-happen.

Meanwhile, I notice a frightening new feature in this landscape: the gravy train of industries committed to "making the most out of Greenhouse." Consultants and entrepreneurs confidently imagine banana crops growing in South Australia's vineyards. Some even visualize the tundra yielding rich wheat crops and fruit orchards in Canada! Planners reluctant to climb on the Greenhouse bandwagon are experiencing paralyzing despair or panic. In contrast, others seek refuge in technical solutions. Mostly, they just ignore the problem.

Drinking the Tears of the Earth

Just thinking about these complex issues fills me with dread. I am trying to "confront the future," look at my life more deeply and examine my fear of death and the despair and grief that accompany these fears. For the last few years, I've been up to my ears in grief and personal empowerment workshops. After I've been trained by John Seed and Joanna Macy, I'm conducting Deep Ecology "Council of All Beings" rituals, where participants embody other-than-human-beings. With them, I'm working to shake off my deep-seated anthropocentrism (human-centeredness). I'm reading everything I can get my hands on. And I'm just plain terrified. Other species on this planet are in danger, so *I* am in danger.

Our planet is dying, so I am dying.

I must find ways to act so I can express my grief.

And somehow, I need to keep my hopefulness alive.

I Am Being Dragged Along

At times, it was a struggle to stay aware and responsible in the ordinary world, with the forest exerting an emotional pull inward…

Jean Shinoda Bolen, 1994

*W*e're not only having a global *ecological* crisis. We're having a global *financial* crisis. Sitting in my windowless home office, I try to reframe it. The recession messing with my head and bringing my business to its knees is another of life's seasons. So I'd better get my bearings. Years later, I remember these difficult times when the (official) Global Financial Crisis cripples my business. Then I try to forgive myself.

So much sadness around right now. So much sadness around right now. I recently lost a dear friend, Stephen, who died of AIDS. He was so young. It was so tragic.

By early 1991, I am *beyond* impatient with my woundedness and yearning. My nagging impatience is like a dog biting my ankles. Piss off, impatience! I ask endless questions: how can I free myself of this emptiness and reconnect to my life source? I am starving for something else and have no idea what that is. I feel strongly I am entering into a time of learning about seasons and seasonal changes. But what does that mean now? In real time?

Is this another "coming of age" time for me? At 48? It does feel like a time of transition. I desperately yearn for time alone, time to sink deeply into grown-up questions like, "What have I learned about life from my experience?" and "What truths do I need to face now?" I need solitude. And an opportunity to find my lost hopefulness. I'm running workshops about creativity, shuttling between left and right brain, attunement, alignment, humor, and listening to the softest voices, listening through the ears of others. I just don't believe a word of it any longer.

I need a break.

I read what Jeanne Achterberg says about the trajectory of seekers like me:

She who goes willingly, the Fates will lead;
she who does not go willingly,
the Fates will drag along.

I am going willingly, *and* I am being dragged along. I know I will make my new path by walking it. Occasionally, I glimpse a thin, almost indistinguishable mark in the dust beckoning me. I must find and follow it, carrying my longing and vulnerability forward. I must not excise or bury them. Now, more than ever, I must walk into the darkness of not knowing.

4.1. THE YEARNING

When I feel brave and poetic, my thinking goes something like this. My future beckons to me, as I stand at a threshold, a place of crossing-over, as I prepare to walk into the landscape of my new life. But I am lost. I do not know what or who I will meet or if or how they will restore me. *And* I must leave my old life and make a new path.

Right here, right now.

So I sing my brave songs joyously in my outdoor voice. As I walk around the block, in the supermarket, at home, at my desk. I sing the gentle, sentimental laments my dad taught me. The Blues. The Climate Blues.

Later, I bask in a balmy spring evening. The air offers only a whiff of distant bushfire. Standing in the doorway, I hear a bar-shouldered dove calling from a nearby tree. Its mournful, repeating call awakens something inside me. Is it a memory? Is it beckoning me?

I decide it's time for divination and choose the Norse runes. I have a modern translation by a Harvard scholar. He offers contemporary interpretations of rune casting for people like me, who seek wisdom and guidance to effect positive changes in our lives.

Throughout the day, I sit with a simple question: "How should I proceed?" Over the years, these runes have guided me through problems and helped me predict what might happen with a particular course of action. They work by allowing me to focus my conscious and unconscious mind on the question or issue at hand.

Barefoot, wrapped in my Fijian sarong, I step outside into the tiny courtyard. I love going barefoot so much of the year. For some bizarre reason, my dad insisted we wear shoes indoors. It was his Canadian prairie upbringing, he said. Going barefoot in Australia feels like the ultimate rebellion. (Fifteen years ago, I stopped wearing a bra as another protest statement.)

I light my red candle (for courage) and place it on the glass table. My shoulders relax as I settle in. I lay out the deep violet velvet cloth I trimmed with a gold braid. I draw out my book of Norse runes from my box of sacred items.

I pull up a chair and prepare to seek guidance for my future direction: guidance my everyday, rational mind cannot provide. I open the small cloth bag and pour 24 clay stones onto the velvet cloth. They are about half an inch wide and nearly square. Each is inscribed with a symbolic marking (a glyph or rune). And each stone tells a story. I turn them, so only the blank sides appear, averting my eyes from one I mended with super glue.

Then I frame my question for a three-rune spread: *What do I need to change in my life now to become whole and live a life that will serve this planet?*

These stones are my friends, and I can rely on them. (They say the right stones stick to your fingers.) I draw three in order: one for the *context* of my inquiry, one for an *action* required of me, and one to describe a possible *outcome* of my inquiry.

Carefully, I turn over each stone. I must do this without distraction, because the message is often negative when a rune appears in a reversed position.

A soft breeze swirls scented air around the courtyard as I breathe in the messages. I am now experiencing a time of diligence, stripping away, fertilizing the ground, listening to my inner self, attentiveness, and sensing subtle changes in my bodymind. I may experience the death of friendships, a darkening of the light, and a need to face up to death. I may need to accept that some changes are permanent. I must remain modest, be in the world but not of it, experience the true present, and know myself. I must seek a correct relationship with the Self.

I exhale the big lesson. *Right here, right now*, the Universe is demanding that I change and grow. I must expect a great awakener, elemental natural powers, disruption, and "radical discontinuity." I must release the old and embrace the new.

Later, as I sit with my question, grief trumps false optimism. I acknowledge my grief and I promise to heal it. I say the words: *I need to change my life.* My understanding of life is changing dramatically because, at some level, I know a new naïveté awaits me. In my new state, I might be able to reintegrate parts of me that have been pulled apart. I have options. I can escape this life and find freedom—and a new way of living.

Above all, I must have compassion for myself. Matthew Fox knows about this: "The only way to learn compassion is through your heart; you have to back up and pass through your own pain."

I know I'm broken. Maybe I need to break open even more. Maybe an unexpected mentor will appear to guide this yearning soul? I'd better remain open.

Well, where are you, mentor?

Maybe my mentor is Mica, my hippie friend? Hmmm.

I Am Being Dragged Along

My Plan to Learn about Ecology

I call this consciousness estrangement because its essence is that we do not see ourselves as part of the world. We are strangers to nature, to other human beings, to parts of ourselves. We see the world as made up of separate, isolated, nonliving parts that have no inherent value.

Starhawk, 1982

I keep thinking about the message of the runes (and a hundred other signs that seem to arrive daily).

My first idea is to close my business and write a book about how people like engineer Doug should get their ecological act together, become literate about ecology and the current (and predictable) global crises, and act like more ecologically responsible professionals. Fortunately, a professor friend suggests a wiser strategy: I will apply for a PhD scholarship to fund my inquiries. Mica has already imagined a similar approach.

A few months later, I become a PhD student. I find a supervisor and enroll in the Environmental Studies PhD program at Adelaide University. I'm an Adelaide University graduate (in planning), so they welcome me and agree to let me spend my first year in the field. The federal government PhD scholarship is another matter, as I lack a necessary qualification: an honors degree. That competition won't be decided for another six months. Nevertheless, I begin work on my plan to study what the Australian planning profession should do about climate change.

My first research proposal reveals both my scattered emotional state and my growing sense of desperation. I cannot write an "academic" proposal to save my life. I just want to learn from a forest:

How to learn about ecology? As I approach my fiftieth year, one thing is clear: I cannot learn it from books. Experiential learning has persisted as the trademark of my work and practice. I propose to live in a tropical forest for fourteen months, starting in late 1991. I will keep a structured daily journal and read about ecology (and related subjects such as the new physics, paradigm shift, and chaos theory). I will continue to write poetry. I will avoid paid work as much as possible. Most importantly, I will walk daily in the forest in daylight, moonlight, rain, and dry weather. I will learn to see what I now cannot...

YEGGE SEASON 1991
MEETING THE MENTOR
May to mid-June 21°-33°C

Yegge, from May to mid-June, is a relatively cool time with low humidity. There are clear blue skies, and the winds from the southeast bring cold air from the southern winter.

Early-morning mists hang low over plains and shallow wetlands. Billabongs are carpeted with water lilies.

Dry winds and flowering Darwin woollybutt trees tell local Aboriginal people it's time to start patch burning to "clean" the country.

2. The Call To Adventure

My Hippie Lover

For generations people have gone to the wilds to find and see their Perfection, their true nature, their inherent goodness, wholesomeness, and simplicity. We also go to the wilderness to see the Perfection of the extended body of creation of which we are a part.

Joan Halifax, 1993

$\mathcal{A}$t some time in her life, every woman needs a hippie lover. For a straight woman, ideally, he's a man who's not fretting about office politics, getting promoted, or how the stock market is performing. A man who's living in the moment, living for love. And for those of us who journey to find answers to big questions, a hippie lover can offer a kind of initiation through sexual awakening. That is what happened with Mica and me.

When I first meet Mica in 1976, his enthusiasm for everything—sex, drugs, and ecology—helps me find a softer self and be more open and flexible. I am 33, so it's about time. I start reading different sorts of books, taking more care of my appearance, and becoming interested in myself as a woman. I am wounded, and I need healing. Mica is shocked by my stories of the abuse I experienced at my mother's hands. My stories help him understand some of my skittishness and why my ex-husband (I call him *The Rational Man* or *TRM*) was little help in this regard.

Until I meet Mica, I am obsessed with my frigidity. And ashamed. I imagine thousands of imprisoned orgasms frenetically battling for a glimpse of daylight—festering inside me, screaming at each other, and growing increasingly desperate. A whole colony of wriggling, grey, drab under-nourished orgasms, like pale amoebas, with dark, angry, glittering eyes. Congregating somewhere "down there." Brawling among themselves to achieve a tiny squeak that might provide release.

I did not intentionally enlist in twelve years of passionless marriage with a husband who berated my obsession with "The Big O." I expected more. Much more. I was 20 when I married and was halfway through an undergraduate degree. I could read, and Vancouver did have public libraries in those days. So, before I married, I read what I could find about sex. Havelock Ellis was my favorite. He wrote *The Erotic Rights of Women* in 1918!

We marry in 1963.

"For God's sake, Wendy, orgasms are just not all they are cracked up to be," *TRM* moans not long after our honeymoon's painful, blood-letting disaster. (I was shocked at the bloody mess my deflowering produced on my wedding night. Not to mention the pain. *TRM* left a big tip for the motel maid.)

4.2. THE CALL TO ADVENTURE

To be fair, *TRM did* try. A bit. Sometimes painful friction would produce a miserable squeak from me and a sigh of relief from him.

Later, politics enter our bedroom: "It's ideologically unsound to be obsessed with the 'Big O', Wendy. What kind of feminist are you, anyway? Truly, Wendy, you are *not* missing **anything** special. Believe me. Please stop obsessing. It's so boring. And it's just not correct."

These words *TRM* mumbles sometime before exploding inside me, his cries reverberating off the walls of the tiny bedroom. He mumbles something similar again in the few seconds between his release and plunging into eight hours of deep sleep.

Throughout this reliably punctual episode, I monitor his pulse rate, my eye on the digital clock on the bedside table. He starts his ascent at about 60 beats and reaches his destination in about three minutes. His pulse decreases slightly at first and then rockets.

I roll over.

More than a decade later, *TRM* shares the problem of my frigidity with his colleagues (including the department secretary). Rhonda tells me about it right away.

"I am so appalled, Wendy," she groans.

"Don't worry, Rhonda," I smile. "First of all, it's not true. And second, it's not your fault. Men will be men."

I might sound upbeat to Rhonda, but inside I am paralyzed with shame and rage.

I am a virgin when I marry *TRM*. Well, technically, anyway. It's what nice girls did then. I did experiment in my late teens with a lovely college boy. I was eager and curious. And I trusted him. He gave me an orgasm, asking nothing in return. (I could not thank him enough!) So, I know perfectly well what an orgasm feels like. But, of course, I can't tell my husband. My virginity is my dowry. And I am, after all, "intact." (I know that because I was "examined" by his doctor father.)

After ten years of passionless marriage, I join a women's sexual therapy group. It's the seventies in Adelaide, a hotbed of liberal politics. As the sexual revolution hits Adelaide broadside, old taboos break down, and women begin to learn to experience their sexuality as a form of self-expression and a source of pleasure. In a federally funded program held at the Centre for Personal Encounter (COPE), I join half a dozen women learning how to masturbate, guided by a doctor and a psychologist. It is so easy. I score highest on the perineometer. The other participants have supportive partners to help. My husband refuses to meet with the psychologist.

As our sexual relationship develops, Mica sometimes expresses astonishment about *TRM*'s insensitivity and incompetence. "Where did that dude learn about women, anyway?" is his favorite question. It becomes a rhetorical question—a joke between us.

Of course, there's more to this marital story. By this time, *TRM* has been with his lover for seven years. (We've been married for twelve.) He ends our marriage by leaving a brief note on our kitchen table.

So, I lose my husband. *And* I gain my identity and a lifelong commitment to empowering sexuality in everyone.

4.2. THE CALL TO ADVENTURE

The Hite Report, published in 1976, causes a revolution among Australian feminists. I am hugely relieved to read Hite's "bombshell" finding that women can't reliably orgasm from penetrative sex. I feel a tremendous burden lift from me when I read that sentence. And Hite dedicates ten pages to women faking orgasms. She calls Freud the "founding father of the vaginal orgasm" and treats him with disdain.

Making love with Mica changes me completely. Before I meet him, I am an anxious, driven, outcome-oriented multi-tasker. By the time I've learned what Mica has to teach, I am well on the way to sexual enlightenment. I am free, curious, and hopeful. And I am healing.

Adelaide, December 1990

In our early days together, Mica, the naturalist, is the teacher, and I am the student. And not just in the ecology realm. It includes our loving. He teaches me about time, transitions, and the spaces between things and activities. We'll return to my inner-city terrace house from a political meeting or a walk in the Adelaide Parklands. And while I busy myself, putting on the kettle and feeding the cat, Mica stands in the hallway, rolling a smoke, just staring at me.

Then he grabs me and spins me around to face him.

Then he growls at me.

"Stop that, Wendy. Just stop and come here for a minute. Think of what you're doing and where you are. Allow yourself to be at home, to settle back into your own space. Slow down, girl. What's the rush? Just slow down!"

He teaches me to listen to my body's messages. And he teaches me lots about loving. Sometimes, his suggestions shock me, but I try anyway.

Under Mica's patient tutelage, I feel myself becoming a woman, at last, putting into practice the lessons I learned in my COPE therapy group. My image of myself as crippled and not whole begins to dissolve. But it is a slow process. Childhood abuse has messed with my mind—and my body. Some parts of me are still numb. I have chronic pelvic pain and don't feel whole. *And* I am desperate to learn how to be fully expressive. There are some things that therapy cannot shift. But a sensitive, competent lover can surely help.

Mica is visiting me for a month in Adelaide. We are teaching together. Social ecology to undergraduate architecture students. He's great in the classroom. His naturalist's erudition

4.2. THE CALL TO ADVENTURE

impresses the young men in my class (they are all men, of course). And we are living in the seventies in the progressive paradise of South Australia. Life in its capital, Adelaide, is in a state of perpetual undress. Our charismatic, controversial, and colorful State Premier, Don Dunstan, wears short pink shorts in Parliament. This sexually liberated bisexual man gives South Australians permission to be themselves. The twelve "Dunstan Years" witness the most significant social and political reforms in South Australian history. I am all for it!

Mica and I smoke dope, march in rallies against all forms of tyranny, and make love all weekend. We discover Tantra as we explore the territory of our bodies, minds, and psyches. I open to his enthusiasm like a flower. For the first time (except for that moment in Darwin), I make love on the floor. This is Adelaide in the late seventies.

In the warm glow of our closeness, we christen my Adelaide terrace house, my haven, *Independence*.

From the later vantage point of 1991, our early romance feels like a long time ago. Nevertheless, Mica still has qualities I never experience with another lover. He's nothing to look at: tall and scrawny. Don't think I idealize him. Because he's allergic to washing, I accompany him into my shower and scrub him vigorously before I let him touch me. Once he's scrubbed, Mica's enthusiasm and curiosity more than compensate.

Since our earliest sexual exploits, our loving goes something like this. Timing is everything. Mica resolutely refuses to do anything intimate when other things are on my mind. So, first, we must prepare ourselves for an extended period of uninterrupted pleasure with no responsibilities to follow. Mica introduces me to the delights of afternoon lovemaking, followed by a candlelit dinner, a bottle of wine, and more lovemaking.

When we first become lovers, Mica explains his theory that a woman has greater pleasure the second time she has sex during a day. The first is to open her to the experience and prepare her bodymind to enlist universal energies. The second (and third) time, she will be fully open and respond fully to a man and the wider cosmos.

"Life is a form of energy. To allow your sexual energy to flow, Wendy, really flow, you must set aside all previous judgments, expectations, and demands and surrender simply to 'being.' I mean it: surrender!"

His approach is a bit didactic. We start this conversation in a North Adelaide café, and I look around nervously to see if anybody's listening. They are not. Mica doesn't care, in any case.

"To begin with, you need to turn your attention to invite a flow of energy into your body and allow that energy to move as freely as you can. Then you can learn to stretch your capacity to contain higher levels of energetic charge without contracting."

The aim is to have uptight Wendy relaxed and surrendered.

Mica doesn't mince words: "Wendy, dearest Wendy, you have dense, tightly bound energy in your torso. What we are

4.2. THE CALL TO ADVENTURE

after here is you learning to walk the line between control and abandon. Got that?"

Soon we try out Mica's ideas in practice. After we prepare our loving space with candles, incense, and essential oils, we lie naked together. Mica doesn't have time for beds, so I make a soft, comfortable nest on the living room floor. I take the phone off the hook, lock the door, and draw the curtains. Then, generally in silence, he invokes some form of supernatural power. I can feel this extra energy as he begins to explore my body. He is the teacher instructing me to deepen my breathing and feel the energy moving within me. His breathing instructions feel upside-down to me, but I comply. I draw energy down the front of my body, soften it, expand my belly, and fill it with my breath. Then, I contract my pelvic floor and whoosh the energy upward along my spine and out the top of my head. At least I try.

I understand I'm training my nervous system to sustain high energy levels, magnifying the circulating energy, but I'm having trouble paying attention. The only other instruction is to keep my tongue on the roof of my mouth. I do what I can. Oh, and keep my eyes open.

Mica never begins in the same place and has a tantalizing capacity to keep me mystified about what is coming next. He does not seem aroused (I sneak a peek) and doesn't want to be at this stage. There's a single-minded focus to his attention, and I must be passive, concentrating on my belly and the whooshing. I learn to enjoy this passivity, although I find that other men of our generation appreciate a more active approach from a woman.

For me, what distinguishes Mica from other lovers is his insatiable curiosity. Not for me, those brief, boring, and unsatisfying clitoral climaxes, those timid squeaks.

"What we are after," Mica explains while I lie whooshing up and down, "is a mind-blowing, whole-body orgasm, accompanied by long, deep moans of surrender."

"Let's try to transform your whole body into an erogenous zone. I'm confident both of us can enjoy many erotic and sensual experiences. We must dispel the myth that intercourse is the only meaningful part of sex or that women want hard, aggressive, and speedy sexual intercourse."

(I keep my own counsel on that matter. Sometimes, some women do like it quick.)

Mica works over me during a successful sexual occasion with an archaeologist's deliberation, care, and curiosity. I sense the pent-up energy in our bodies in a warm cocoon that now surrounds us and fills the scented room. Sometimes, he uses verbal cues to keep me on track. He delights in finding new parts of my breasts, thighs, and belly to caress. Yes, my round belly—and the scars from many operations.

I often weep silently when he caresses my scars (still numb from the hysterectomy that ended my fertility). I am grateful, *so* grateful, that our loving is healing that deep wound. And it still hurts so much, even now. I'm terrified I will never be whole for other reasons, too. Maybe those childhood scars will never heal, and I'll be numb for the rest of my life. In the present Tantric moment, Mica pays precise attention to those scars, ensuring he traces every imperfection, caresses it,

4.2. THE CALL TO ADVENTURE

and gloriously celebrates it. I feel my body healing and those sorrowful memories fading, hopefully forever.

Because Mica knows I'm impatient by nature (a quality he deplores), he refuses to let me direct him. He has long since mastered his desire to ejaculate. Much of what I learned in my sex therapy group is irrelevant to Mica. We are on another plane. In those sessions, I learned to relax and not be anxious about performing. Mica celebrates that.

I struggle for years to shrug off *TRM's* "frigidity" label, so I am apprehensive that I will not come. But that is never an issue with Mica. He's preoccupied with my pleasure—and his desire that we both connect with this cosmic force he has invoked. And he is confident that he'll have *his* needs met. The force will not disappoint him.

With a sigh, I surrender my anxiety and impatience. Mica is stroking my body with scented oil (clary sage, sandalwood, and *ylang-ylang*). His fingers explore my ears, opening them. I sigh as he licks my eyelids and nibbles gently on my neck, coaxing my energy to flow. (Nibbling is new to me.) My hips begin to roll as he massages the entire bottom of my foot, licking between my toes and gently nibbling and biting my foot. New pulsations are growing inside me a few inches below my navel.

I am riding a wave of bliss.

While he's never guided me to touch him in any way, he firmly guides me into the zone where we will eventually unleash our passions. I breathe the scented air. I will my impatience to dissolve and open my whole being to a warm column of energy that enters me from above. My center breathes me.

Later, he gently turns me on my side. Still, I'm not allowed to anticipate his intent—or the intent of the sweet energy that now directs us. Another dimension absorbs us. The room vibrates, and the candles flicker. Galaxies of stars swim behind my eyelids in a vast, velvet sky. In our energy cocoon, we swirl among those stars.

I am lying on my front now. Mica places a cushion under me to elevate my ass as it receives energy streams from above. I can feel our breathing synchronizing as we circulate healing energy throughout our bodies. Now I am responding of my own accord, and I feel my nose twitching and my lips vibrating. I am getting close. A thin film of sweat covers my body. I feel my body relax, releasing tension. Now my pelvic floor is vibrating with every whooshing out-breath.

He's hot and intense now, and I am sure he's ready. But my gesture to guide him is gently brushed aside. Honey-sweet energy from above enters and fills me. I tremble with each new pulsation. The scent of woodsmoke in his hair and tobacco on his breath confirm Mica's presence, but for now, he seems lost to me—swept up in energy streams that swirl and vibrate throughout the room. I am opening in spacious surrender.

We are swimming in galactic space.

A sneeze returns Mica to the present, and he guides me to explore *his* body. He wants it now—gentle and firm—my mouth on his, my hand on his ass. I call to him and begin to pull him toward me—toward my throbbing body.

"Don't be so impatient, Wendy. Settle down, girl. What's your hurry? We are close, but you need a little more time."

Mica places a firm hand on my belly.

"Let's cultivate pleasure for a bit longer, okay? Let me open you up a little more."

I sigh. This is his way of teasing me, his revenge against my domineering nature. Finally, I stop trying to figure out if I am doing this right. *He* must prepare *me* so that *both* of us can align with the energies he has invoked.

His tongue is on my belly again, tracing my ancient scars, making its way closer. He kisses my scars. The feeling is returning after all these years. I'm holding onto him and waiting as his hand gently begins to open me up.

★★★

I don't want to give the impression that lovemaking with Mica *is* all about my being passive. It isn't. But I *am* wounded and I *do* need healing. As I grow in confidence in my relationship with Mica, especially during the month we live together in early 1977, I learn to take the initiative. That feels empowering. I also read everything I can about Tantric sex, and I love what I am learning.

Soon I also become comfortable being the initiator. We both love that. I become more confident as a lover when we mix things up a bit.

The more I embrace my sexual relationship with Mica, the more amazing I feel. Partly because when I am making love with him, I *am* powerful. I have what young Wendy begged for decades earlier: a genuinely liberated and liberating experience. Of course, I am not frigid. I just need tenderness, reassurance, and a bit of guidance. My knowledgeable lover quickly figures that out.

I pore over books to discover new ways of pleasuring him. He loves my touch, and pleasing him arouses me hugely. My natural impulse is to touch him, especially his thighs and legs, so I am happy to delight him further. I feel his sexual power building under my hands.

I look up to see his pale blue eyes glowing. "What would you like now, wild one?" I whisper.

"More," he groans. "More."

Mica is so enthusiastic that I keep experimenting. *We* keep experimenting.

Where Are Your Books on Ecology, Wendy?

… the male or female hero leaves his or her familiar dwelling, either intentionally or through a "call to adventure" from some outside force … [and] enters a realm of unknown and difficult challenges.

Christina Grof, 1993

*L*ast month Mica came to visit. For a few days, we do nothing but listen to Yothu Yindi's spellbinding new song, "Treaty," dancing in the living room and the courtyard, our arms above our heads, chanting: "Treaty now!"

"Treaty" is the first song by a predominantly Aboriginal band to reach the charts in Australia and the first song in any Aboriginal Australian language to gain extensive international recognition. Its message resonates with Mica's activist values. It highlights the lack of progress on the treaty between Aboriginal peoples and the Australian federal government.

Mica plays it over and over. As time passes and we grow closer, I learn why it's his anthem.

Shortly after Mica arrives, I have to leave for a few days' consulting work in Melbourne, but after a day, I phone to say I have pneumonia. I'm burned out. I've seen a doctor, bought the antibiotics, and must go straight to bed. Mica meets me at the door. He's cooked a lamb curry, tidied up, and even changed the sheets.

"Sitting outside won't hurt you," he suggests after dinner. "You'll stay warm if you lean back on me." His long fingers gesture to a cushion at his feet. I sit there.

"Can you hear that peaceful dove, Wendy? It's a tiny, delicate bird, and I love its lilting, musical call. It loves people, too. Too bad we can't catch sight of it here in your backyard."

I nod, not knowing what I hear or where it is. In my tiny inner-city courtyard in Adelaide, we crane our necks to glimpse the stars but never see them. There is always too much light. Light *pollution* Mica calls it. Wrapped in my quilt, I surrender my shoulders to Mica's massage. I cough and shiver in the soft autumn air.

Next door, Noni, my elderly neighbor, plays her new Vivaldi album, the bassoon concerti. She clatters away in her kitchen, humming happily. I lean back into Mica's lap and try to relax, drawing on my cigarette.

"I've been thinking about your ideas for your future," Mica continues, gently stroking the nape of my neck, "and I've had a look through your books."

4.2. THE CALL TO ADVENTURE

I turn toward him, wincing at the tightness of my shoulders.

Then Mica gets up and walks around to face me, staring down. He speaks slowly: "You're right about needing to expand your knowledge. Where are your books on ecology, Wendy?"

I lean back against the chair and sigh, but do not reply.

Mica asks again: "Where are your books on ecology, Wendy?"

It is a moment I will remember as long as my consciousness survives. I picture Mica's tattered bush library in the seventies in that sparse forest at Camp Concern and later at Deep Creek and his attempts to share his commitment and knowledge. He spent many early years in the library where his mother worked. He loves reading book catalogs.

"Where are your books on ecology, Wendy?"

"You know I don't have any, Mica." I turn to survey hundreds of books lining my living room walls. "That's why I'm so worried," I whisper. "I know I should know more about ecology. I'm so upset about where our planet's heading, and none of my colleagues seem to care. I'm having nightmares about the end of the world. Now my *work* seems to be going to hell in a handbasket. I'm losing *guaranteed* consulting jobs. The Universe must be telling me *something*, Mica. But what is it? What should I do?"

All is silent as Mica places his fingers lightly on the top of my head in that fatherly way he has. Then he walks to the other side of the courtyard, hands in his pockets, his back to me.

"This is a gravely serious matter, Wendy. Not to be ignored. You must heed these messages. Burnout is an affliction of the soul. It's a lot more than a psychological condition."

He turns to face me.

"I agree that you should come to live at Deep Creek. I believe you are ready to learn what I can teach you. You have important work to do that could help save the Earth, so I'll support your project. I don't have any money, but I have other things to give. I am willing to help you in any way I can. I'm at your service, Wendy.

"Just tell me what you want me to do."

Dr. Muldane's Prescription

August 1991

*I*t's because we're so close to the sun. Flying always makes me dream—and remember things so vividly I feel like I've traveled back in time. I think I'm here, eating airline food. But actually, I'm flying, traveling. Astral traveling.

On this cool August morning, heading back home after a rushed five-day visit with Mica in the Northern Territory, I realize how customary flying is for me. Ten exhausting years traversing this vast country, trying to convince reluctant clients to listen to their communities when they plan anything: libraries, new towns, transport systems. I've become an expert in community engagement. And I am fed up with it, fed up with the sound of my professional voice: strident, forced, worn, and impatient. I'm tired. Been tired for years. Tired of working long hours for low pay and less gratitude, tired of being alone, and tired of being responsible.

I'm planning to do the wisest or the stupidest thing of my life. I decide to spend a whole year living in solitude in the Australian bush on Mica's land, not far from Darwin. This will be no cozy home visit. I'll be there for a year. I'll have to build my own shelter. No amenities like electricity or indoor plumbing. Lots of the Elements: The Wet, The Dry. The Seasons. The Fires. The Storms.

I was raised in the suburbs, grew up in cities, and make my living as an urban planner. Very independent, I fancy myself. And about as thoroughly urban as you could get. Now I'm planning a big change. This year in the bush will be my experiment in *voluntary simplicity*. From my sanctuary in my Adelaide office, I read the future complacently: a year attending to my ecological literacy, with a hippie ecologist as my mentor and lover. Then I'll write a doctoral thesis about the whole thing. But by the time the wheels start to turn, the smooth, seamless landscape I'd painted in my imagination is beginning to develop some alarming features.

By August, I discover that my friend and mentor, Mica, the hippie naturalist, is an alcoholic. Deep down, I knew. For decades. He is very open about it. It goes with the territory (the Northern Territory). (I can spot alcoholics at 100 yards.) And it is easy to stay in denial. Mica has a lot to recommend him (including being the world's best lover).

But now it's too late to back out. I'm moving there in three months. I burned my boats, and I'd really lose face if I pull back. All arrangements are made, my business closed down, and the scholarship applied for. Of course, other people live at Deep Creek, but I don't know any of them. Everything is going to be very strange. Maybe that is just what I need: healing, some deep healing. I am an uptight, strung-out, exhausted professional woman of nearly 50.

4.2. THE CALL TO ADVENTURE

A year in the tropical bush with a hippie lover could loosen me up and be transformative.

And it could be a disaster.

The *I Ching* foreshadows Danger and advises caution. My friends have given up trying to talk me out of it.

So, I find a psychiatrist to help me through this challenging transition. I never go to psychiatrists, just as I rarely go to doctors. I don't believe in what they believe in. So, I turn to Dr. Muldane precisely because he does not have any "alternative" qualifications. He specializes in addictions, not goddesses. He is a straight (I mean "traditional") psychiatrist in an office with straight-backed chairs. He's not a healer and won't mess with my chakras. My inner child will not interest him. My connection to Spirit even less. No meditations, visualizations, birthing phantom mothers, or pounding cushions with baseball bats for Muldane. He graduated from the University of Adelaide, and his diploma with a gold seal in a black frame hangs on the wall behind his desk. It says he's a "Fellow." (I'm one, too, in a different professional body. That's about all we have in common.)

Muldane's office has wallpaper Muzak and is located in a very respectable part of Adelaide. Tree-lined, leafy, historic North Adelaide: the doctors' quarter.

I need that; I need someone sensible, someone reasonable to talk to.

"Being responsible," Dr. Muldane pronounces at our first meeting, "is classic codependency. You either abandon responsibility because of your dysfunctional childhood, or you decide to be good. To compensate for what you missed in your childhood."

He looks me straight in the eye the way he's been trained, I guess. I sit up straight and try to look impressed by the gravity of his message.

I figure I'm in the "good" category. Dr. Muldane enumerates the co-dependent's other reprehensible characteristics. His eyes brighten. I've seen that look in eyes before when they are confident that they are onto something.

"You're a classic example of a child of a dysfunctional family, Wendy. You have a real co-dependent personality. Tell me how it was with your father? With him being an alcoholic? Were you angry with him? His name was Gordon, wasn't it?"

Classic? Me? I lean back in my leather chair, my arms resting in my lap. My mind drifts away, split from my body. From an exhausted place inside me, a disembodied voice confesses with a modicum of bitterness:

I've always been responsible. I can't be angry. Can't feel it, can't express it, not even against Gordon, though he almost ruined my life with his drinking and irresponsibility. Or my mother, who acted like she wanted to destroy me: a spider trapping me in her web. Or my ex-husband—the philandering professor—and his adoring student lover (now his wife). My childlessness, my disappointments, my lost opportunities. So much anger. Buried anger. Can't touch the anger.

4.2. THE CALL TO ADVENTURE

I feel like lead. Trapped. Numb with anger. My body will never leave this armchair. And inside, I have a little conversation I don't share. I know there's an angry goddess inside me, tricking me, driving me crazy with her rage. An illogical, intuitive goddess, furious, waving her many glittering arms, rattling her garland of human skulls, gesturing frantically to catch my attention. In healing workshops, I hear the teachers and healers whispering over their herbal tea in the corner. "Anger. Swallowed anger. Don't expect too much from Wendy this weekend. She's a hard one. Contracted. Armored. She has a long way to go. Much to learn. She's not ready yet."

I remember my last appointment with Muldane before that brief August visit to the bush. The Darwin trip is part business, part pleasure—for a masochist. Muldane and I have been working together for a few months, and I feel it's time to explain my larger problem. I'm sitting on a straight chair, and he's swiveling in an expensive leather chair behind his desk. I note the brown suede elbow patches on his grey tweed jacket. For a moment, I remember what it was like talking about my feelings with my ex-husband, the professor.

"And so, just to summarize, now you want to live in an isolated place with an alcoholic man, Wendy," Dr. Muldane pronounces, mimicking my pained expression and leaning forward to make intimate eye contact.

"That could be a self-destructive act for an adult child of an alcoholic, Wendy, and quite dangerous for both of you."

I don't care if it's dangerous for Mica. I feel Muldane is a bit off the mark to mention that.

Dr. Muldane's Prescription

"It's too late. I'm going anyway."

I look over his shoulder through an open decorative leadlight window to a bed of neatly pruned pink roses.

"Do you have any practical advice?"

"You must decide what's reasonable."

What's reasonable. The words reverberate in my head.

What's reasonable. Images of Mica's bizarre behavior lurch into my consciousness. *My* infuriating behavior. Not reasonable. Certainly not Mica, my lover. Not me. Not reasonable. Not a reasonable situation. I am unreasonable. My unreasonable behavior is next in line for inspection. I can be a bullying, old harridan.

What I need is a breakthrough. Like right now!

I push Muldane further. At his hourly rate (not covered by my medical insurance), I figure I might as well go for it. And he comes through.

"Well," he mutters, inspecting his manicured fingernails. (I swear they have polish on them. I imagine immaculate toenails...)

"This is a very complex situation, Wendy. It could be the wisest or the stupidest thing you'll ever do. Depends on a lot of factors, and some may be beyond your control. One thing I can say with confidence, however. It'd be wise to stay out of his bed. Sexual intimacy could complicate the codependency issues between the two of you. And make it hard for you to cope. You will be very vulnerable there. Alone, with no support systems, you know."

His words land like a stone in my belly.

I *know* he's right. Poor chap, he's got so little genuine insight. Yet he nailed this one.

I swallow my fear and go anyway like I did on my first visit to Mica in 1976.

The one takeaway from Muldane I *do* implement is the "no-sex" rule. That turns out to be incredibly difficult. While I rationalize to myself that the price of an ecological education should not be coming across sexually, the truth is that it *was* part of my deal with Mica. Later, Mica calls me a "Trojan Horse." He feels shafted, "horsed," shocked that I did not hold up my part of the bargain. He let me build a house on his land and live there for a year. I was his student. But not his lover. The unfairness of it angered him deeply.

Later still, I am able to see it from his perspective. And to understand and respect his disappointment and anger.

But right now, I am desperate to escape. So, I exploit his hospitality and generosity. I am insensitive to his feelings and his needs. I charge ahead, looking out for Number One.

Much later, I forgive both of us.

Mica forgives me, too. Eventually. But that takes more than a lifetime.

An Unknowable Place

I'm making plans to live for a year in a strange place called Humpty Doo, a raggedy outback town of 3,000 people about 35 miles southeast of Darwin. I've heard a dozen stories explaining how it got its name. In 1908, a Northern Territory report referred to a station as "Humpiti Doo," the name meaning *upside-down or mixed-up*. It's also thought to mean back-to-front or just plain chaotic. Or maybe its origin lies in the disused Australian slang term *umpty-doo*, meaning intoxicated or topsy turvy.

In 1911, the *Sydney Bulletin* said *umpty-doo* was one of several slang terms that meant drunk. Like *skew wiff, tiddly* and *full*.

Some people think the name came from "Umdidu," the name of a local buffalo shooting station. And that came from an Aboriginal word meaning *resting place*. Gradually, the name was corrupted to *Umpity Doo*, then *Humpty Doo*.

In Australian vernacular slang, "Humpty Dumpty" means "upside-down."

You just couldn't find a better name for this madcap place!

Everyone agrees that Humpty Doo means something "unknowable." It's a place of light and dark. Life there is always a bit of a mystery.

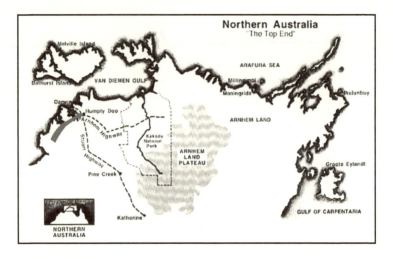

WURRGENG SEASON 1991
THE DREAMING
Mid-June to mid-August 17°-32°C

Wurrgeng is a cold season of low humidity. Creeks cease to flow, and floodplains quickly dry out. The magpie geese are fat and heavy. Burning continues, dampened by dew at night.

By day, birds of prey patrol firelines as insects and other small animals escape the flames. Flocks of black cockatoos forage in the burnt undergrowth for scorched speargrass seeds and hard charred nuts.

The trees flower. Bush bees make honey from the many flowering plants.

Dreaming My House at Two Couples Dancing

I'm lucky to have a planning consulting job that regularly brings me to the Northern Territory so I can visit Mica. Yesterday, we spent many mellow hours south of the creek, measuring a site for my house in a clearing on his land, scratching maps in the dry earth. I choose a sheltered spot near a small grove of trees. I call this place *Two Couples Dancing* because it has two pairs of *Pandanus spiralis* trees—screw palms about two meters tall. They stand like elegant female couples in formal attire, their long, dry skirts sweeping the ground. This place is close to Mica's, but it also feels safe and protected. My haven!

As the forest shadows lengthen, Mica brings out a folding chair from his house. He moves it around, then sits down on the earth and begins to direct me to identify features in the landscape. Mica sees invisible things: gateways, vistas, entrances, safe and sheltered spots, and taboo spots. He reads a lot into a landscape.

He reaches into a broken cooler and brings out a carton of iced coffee, which he pours, with a flourish, into two pickle jars.

"Look here, Wendy." He sets his drink down and stares at me intently. "You can see the cross-faults in the land exposed to view."

Then he jumps up, grabs my shoulders, and turns me around to face the northeast to observe the land's drainage patterns. When I don't seem to understand, he grabs a branch, clears away the leaf litter, and begins to draw lines in the bare earth.

They don't mean much to me, but I dream of our life together as a teacher and student. A life of field trips like this!

Since I first met Mica in 1976, I fantasized about living in a forest with him. Now, fifteen years on, my dream is becoming a reality.

Despite my trepidations, I am escaping from the prison of my urban life.

Later that day, alone at his shack, I sketch *my* dream of a house for my year's retreat.

My First Bushfire

The Deep Creek forest burned two days ago. I am awash with grief and pain. It's a shock and an education for me: way too much at once. The bushfire burned two-thirds of the property and transformed that barren and inhospitable forest into an absolute wasteland. How can I possibly live here?

I feel so undefended and unprotected.

My God. What am I doing?

That frightening day begins at breakfast with Mica and me shivering in the cool air in the garden of the café beside the Humpty Doo gas station. We sit with his friend, Kundu, at a scarred wooden table, drawing house sketches and location plans on paper napkins and lingering over our iced coffee and scrambled eggs. We've settled on *Two Couples Dancing* as a location for my house.

Mica and I spent most of the previous day measuring my house site. The house we imagine is about 10 feet by 10 feet square.

"This is great, guys," I enthuse. "It's a straightforward design, and I reckon it'll work. And I agree about the earth floor. You've convinced me about the risk of polluting the creek with a concrete floor."

The two men look relieved.

"The builders are already stockpiling recycled materials for your house," Mica chimes in. "It's gonna take them about a week to do the building, depending on the weather. November is unreliable, Wendy. It's the Build Up. It could be rainy. It could be dry. Certainly, it will be hot. But we are making progress. You'll be settled in that forest before you know it."

I smile back at him, buttering my toast. "I do feel better with a real site, Mica. I *am* a planner, after all."

As he returns with a second coffee, Kundu suddenly stops in the doorway. He frowns and signals to Mica to join him in the parking lot. Kundu has spotted a dark cloud on the horizon to the south. Mica stiffens at the sight of smoke, and I sense a sudden change in the two men. Then Mica comes running back to the table and grabs his pullover.

"That'll be paperbarks burning because of the dark smoke," he yells to Kundu, who is already making his way to the car, rolling a cigarette as he goes.

Soon we are thundering down the corrugated dirt road to Deep Creek in Mica's station wagon. On the way, the two men speculate.

4.2. THE CALL TO ADVENTURE

"Bloody hell, it's mid-August—almost the end of the Dry season—*Wurrgeng*. A late-season fire. Could be very destructive—very explosive—because of the dry grass and the strong winds," Mica yells.

Kundu nods.

Now we can see it.

I stare in horror at a fire burning to the east—separated from community land by a dirt road and a six-meter-wide firebreak. It is racing through dry grass and woodland, with flames six or nine meters high, roaring, and crackling. I gasp. We smell it as we approach the gate to the Deep Creek community.

"You be careful, Wendy," Kundu yells from the front of the car, turning to look at me and pounding his fist on the back of his seat to emphasize his point. "This is your first fire, right, girl? You stick to Mica like glue, and you'll be right."

We drop Kundu on the firebreak road to follow Mica's instructions yelled above the fire's roar: "Hey, Kundu, break a green branch that won't burn from one of those woollybutts and see if you can keep redirecting the fire with it. And try to deal with the floaters coming across the firebreak. Got that, Kundu?"

Later, Kundu says he tried, but the fire got in there, too. Working alone without water, he had Buckley's chance, that is, no chance. Boosted by a strong wind, the fire leaped 35 meters of road and a cleared firebreak in one go, sending Kundu scurrying for his life. Then it broke into the high school's conservation study area on the neighboring land to the north.

My First Bushfire

As the car nears Mica's 20-acre block, we see the fire has been and gone. My heart sinks. The cherished milkwood tree, Mica's driveway landmark, is scorched to its top leaves. On both sides of the driveway, blackened earth stretches as far as my stinging eyes can see. The ground is bare, and all the grasses and leaf litter are consumed. There is not a single patch of green.

In the middle distance, I spot dark smoke rising above a wall of shimmering orange.

The horizon, formerly hidden by trees, shrubs, and a rich woodland understory, expands for acres. It now reveals the scarred landform's features: hillocks, depressions, and stream banks. Scattered across this moonscape are burning and smoking stumps, charred skeletons of acacia, woollybutt, kapok bushes, ironwood, carallia, and billygoat plums, some without leaves or branches. Only the tallest trees retain a thin green canopy crowning their blackened branches.

4.2. THE CALL TO ADVENTURE

Black twisted stumps of leafless cycad ferns look like amputated limbs. Large birds I never saw before spiral overhead, wheeling and diving on insects and small animals scurrying to find refuge at the fire's margins. Mica says the birds are whistling kites.

The horrifying sounds startle me: giant trees crashing and thudding into the charred earth, throwing branches into the air as they fall. I shudder to imagine the fate of the denser creekside vegetation: the pale, fragile paperbarks and glistening, spiraling pandanus palms twisting from the banks. My mind registers only disbelief. I struggle to undo everything the fire has destroyed: the conservation research experiment, the community's 13-year project to exclude fire from their land, and years of backbreaking work.

Mica's land, his dreams. Up in smoke.

The battered old truck rattles onto the rough track leading to Mica's property. I lean out of the window taking in a vast expanse of flat, dead land. The fire destroyed the homes of countless creatures in minutes. Creatures I haven't even met and could never identify, their histories and ancient lineages obliterated. I gasp, numb with shock. I can't let it in. My mind races in a vain effort to make it un-happen. I am too raw for feelings.

When we reach his camp, Mica shouts with relief when he sees Rebecca and Tim, his son, in shock but unhurt. Mica slams on the brakes and jumps out. In a shaking voice, Tim explains that they saved two cars and the *donga*—the metal shed—with a wet sarong and the garden hose. Mica sinks into a chair on the porch and begins to roll a smoke.

My First Bushfire

"Jesus, Mica," mutters Tim, dabbing at his eyes. He looks like he wants to hug his father but pulls back, sensing his father's awkwardness.

Caught in mid-fuck, the young lovers did their best. "We saved the cars, but we had no warning, Mica, nothing at all. A wall of flame just passed through. That was it," Tim stammers.

They look startled, exhausted, and grimy, like the tiny creatures scurrying everywhere. Rebecca hangs back, busying herself inside the house.

"Well, at least you're not in any more danger," Mica reassures Tim. "It's bloody cold comfort, but it's true. There's fuckin' nothing left to burn here."

Now we hear another fire engine tearing up the road, siren blaring. We pick our way on foot through devastation to Mica's other house in a landscape of fallen trees, ash, and debris. The path, worn by Mica for a dozen years, wanders through the scorched landscape, pale and curiously unblemished. I find my breathing changing as an intense feeling of death chokes me.

"We'd better check the garden, Wendy." Mica's language sounds so quaint: "garden" to describe 320 acres of untamed forest. It is eerily silent, swept clean of birds and the usual small, scampering animals. A large pandanus has lost her skirt. Small fires smolder everywhere. Mica grabs an old tarp to put out flames in some fabric and an old book on top of the rubbish bin on the front porch. Burning pages flutter to the earth floor and disintegrate as black ash. I rush to extinguish them and stop. There is nothing left to burn.

Then, as I turn the corner to the back porch, I discover files in the wheelbarrow blazing like a barbecue.

"Mica!" I scream. "Quick! Your house is on fire."

He is yelling, and I am giving orders, and then we reverse roles.

"Give me a hand with the hose, Wendy," he cries. We are standing so close to each other and screaming—like an emergency crew.

"Fuck it! Hurry, Wendy!"

Together we untangle the garden hose, and I aim it at the latest blaze. Then Mica disappears, leaving me to douse the wheelbarrow fire. I aim the green snake of the hose to the side so I can read the pages. A blazing wheelbarrow full of research, dreams, and memories: Mica's patient printing—now silvered—on scores of black notebook pages. His journals and academic treatises are full of notes about climate change, desertification, insect populations, and sphagnum moss reappearing in the creek. I know these are the only copies, and I can't save them: the residue of years of documentation of the local ecology.

Toxic fumes are rising from radios and tape recorders burning in a rusted filing cabinet. As I am retching, Mica reappears.

"Quick, get a hose on that electrical stuff, Mica," I scream. "It's awfully toxic."

Mica obeys like a zombie. I grab the one undamaged length of hose from him and direct a stream at the wheelbarrow that has burst into flame again. Its melted tire reveals a rusted frame, scorched red handlebars dripping black rubber. It is like a series of still photographs.

One fire.

Another fire.

Move the hose.

We douse small, individual fires for hours on that porch.

"Okay. Enough of that, Wendy," Mica orders, regaining his authority. "We'd better check on the neighbors—Saturday morning. God knows where they all could be. Probably shopping."

We retrace our steps. Tim and Rebecca have driven off, a pale green patch marking where their car had been. We drive up the hilly track to the south.

Fire is everywhere we look. Above the din, men in orange clothing run behind trucks, dragging dusty black hoses, burning back, signaling, and hollering to each other. Their stumbling figures look insubstantial, silhouetted against a wall of smoke and orange flame.

4.2. THE CALL TO ADVENTURE

Mara, only sixteen, is fighting a small fire alone with a rake on a corner of her family's neighboring block, coughing, and mopping her eyes with a red cotton scarf.

"Hey, Mica," she yells. "Mom and dad are up the hill with the Fire Service. Could you get me a drink?"

We clank back to Mica's and return with a bottle of water. Mara grabs it, nods her thanks, gulps most of it, and stares past us, her face tight with grief and exhaustion. She picks at the cinders with her metal rake.

I feel sick. Later, the smell of my smoky clothes makes me throw up.

After Mica leaves to drive around the perimeter of the community property, I stay behind at his place, shuffling through ashes and charred branches as I make my way in from the road. Beside the path to Mica's place, a tree root bursts into flames, sparks spurting from deep in the ground. I run for the hose again.

Then from the smoky landscape, Helen appears, wearing a long black jersey dress.

"You're Wendy, is that right?" she calls hesitantly.

"Yes, I'm Wendy, Helen. Grab that hose, will you?" I call back. Together we drench the tree root. I drop the hose and turn to look at her, shaking.

"I've been inspecting the damage," she speaks slowly, turning to survey the blackened porch.

"Looks like you just managed to save the house."

"The house, yes," I reply as I root around for something to sit on. "But I couldn't save Mica's papers."

The sight of the burned books and papers is too much for Helen. She collapses into my arms, sobbing: "I thought this was a safe place."

I hold her and tell her, "Yes, Helen, a lot is lost. All the research."

Then I change the subject, blurting out, "I've had a gutful of men who can't cry."

Disengaging from our unexpected embrace, Helen stands while I sit in a burnt chair. I apologize for not offering her a seat. Other than the bed, there is not a stick of furniture left.

"I'm fine," Helen says quietly. "I was a physio for years, and we learn to stand for extended periods without getting tired."

"I'm coming to live here in a few months," I tell her. I explain my studies and how I'll live on Mica's land, but not with him.

"It'll be lovely to have you living here at Deep Creek, Wendy," Helen replies.

"I look forward to getting to know you, and I know Owen will feel the same way. We don't see a lot of Mica. Maybe having you here will change that."

4.2. THE CALL TO ADVENTURE

We chat for a while, and she offers me a drink from her water bottle. The water is cool, and the few drops I spill make bubbles like molten lead on the ashes on the porch floor. There is nothing more to say. After a brief hug, Helen disappears.

When Mica returns, we drive up the hill to visit Stan and Debbie's place, a modern architect-designed house with a yard cluttered with the paraphernalia of a young family. Debbie is standing on the lawn holding her daughter, Sophie, who is maybe two. A man from the Emergency Fire Service barks orders from his vehicle. Debbie's husband, Stan, is out on the Deep Creek community's fire truck.

I can sense Debbie's defensiveness as she leans beside the vehicle's window. As I come up and introduce myself, Debbie adjusts Sophie on her hip.

"Oh, I've been looking forward to meeting you, Wendy," she smiles, offering her hand. "I'm sorry it's under such awful circumstances."

"Hi, Mica," she calls out. "I'm so glad you're here. Can you help me, please? The boys were in the forest when the fire started. They've been gone over an hour. I can't leave Sophie, and I'm getting really worried."

"Sure, Debbie, I'll look for them," Mica quickly replies and strides off into the forest, coo-eeing loudly.

The man, still in his jeep, continues his rant. "This is very wrong of you, Debbie," he gestures through his vehicle window to dozens of small trees growing a few meters from the house.

My First Bushfire

"This is not the first time we've had this conversation, Debbie. You know perfectly well what the regulations are. The law requires you to clear a four-meter firebreak around your house. And you with a lovely new house, too. It might not matter much with a metal shack like Mica's, but this house is so beautiful. It's just plain irresponsible, Debbie—and I'll certainly be reporting this breach of the regulations."

He hurls this through the window, glowering. Then he starts the motor. Debbie and I back away.

"It's our community's policy not to clear the underbrush, and you know that," Debbie mutters, but it is too late. She buries her face in her child's body as the jeep smashes through 50 newly planted seedlings. He circles the house, engine revving as he takes another run at the hill. Then he roars off after yelling that he'll be back after the fire to burn the land he's just cleared.

"Here, let me do something," I offer, taking the sobbing child. Sophie stops crying to explain how she helped her dad plant all those seedlings. Then Debbie and I talk a bit about the fire.

We're sitting on the porch when Mica appears with Debbie's two boys, shaken but unhurt. They run to their mother.

"It was pretty close, Debbie," Mica explains, mopping his brow and reaching for his tobacco.

"They nearly got caught by a back-burning operation. I hate that fire-management stuff the Fire Service does."

4.2. THE CALL TO ADVENTURE

The boys can hardly wait to describe their adventure. "Mom, it was really scary. Really! We could hear the firefighters yelling directions, but we thought we'd got caught. We had to run from a really, really big wall of flames. We were just running and running! And that's when we found Mica."

"Or rather, I found you. You did okay, kids," he continues, lighting his smoke. "Well done. You knew what to do in an emergency. You're pretty experienced firefighters for nine and twelve. I wish I had known that much when I was your age."

After we say goodbye to Debbie and wish her good luck with the fire service, Mica drops me back at his place and drives off, searching for other neighbors. I walk down the hill to *Two Couples Dancing,* where we plan to build my house. Both pandanus couples have lost their gracious brown skirts of fronds to the fire. They look skinned and bare. The whole place feels desecrated. And it's hot there now with all the shade burned away. I sit in the ashes and stare at what remains of my house site. It's unrecognizable. I can't live here in a million years! I can't imagine that it will ever come back to life. I must find another place to build my house.

Mica briefly checks in on me and then takes off again. I accept that his frenetic activity is a way of keeping grief at bay, and I support it. What else can a heartbroken man do? So much is lost. When he returns from another round of helping neighbors and negotiating about backburning, I am shaking with tears, having retreated to the only surviving chair on his porch. He bends his six-foot frame over to hug me. But not for long.

"Stop being self-indulgent, Wendy," he chides me. "This is no time for chucking a sad."

I snap back: "This is my first bushfire, Mica, for God's sake."

Despite years of studying fire ecology, Mica has never confronted the topic of grief and bushfire.

He leaves me again to prepare for his birthday party, to be held at a neighbor's house: an informal event around the campfire, with guests expected later that evening. I'd completely forgotten. It's his birthday! Good God! I'm not in a party mood. I change into my long pants and heavy socks: my daily protection against the mosquitoes. Then I notice that none are about.

A smoky day slowly fades into a dusty night, and all around me, I hear burning trees collapse with deafening crashes. Behind Mica's house, the roots of a *Lophostemon* burst into flame. I rush back with the hose and then fuss around in the ruins of what's left of the garden, inspecting two cherished frangipani trees. Mica says their sap has boiled, and they will not survive. They are dying a slow, painful death in front of me, a reluctant witness.

Spot fires continue to burn everywhere. I labor into the evening, aimlessly cleaning up and damping down fires with nowhere to go. A terrible pain is growing under my ribs, and my throat aches from coughing. Feeling trapped, I wander into Mica's metal house and examine its charred walls, scorched ceiling, and flyscreen. My flashlight reveals the whole story. How we saved it, I'll never know. We had a minute to spare, or we would have lost everything. Blankets were already burning on the bed when we reached it.

I lie on the bed surrounded by death, breathing dry air saturated with smoke. Wakened by my coughing, I hear nearby trees crashing as they lose their ability to stand. Finally, I sleep. Later, fear jolts me awake again. I make my way down the moonlit path to wake Kundu, who helps me douse a couple of fires, carrying buckets in the misty air from the last length of hose. When I remark that it seems like a futile pursuit, he disagrees: "No. It's worth it. Really. We need to save as many logs as possible to provide refuges for small mammals and reptiles, Wendy."

The landscape glows with hundreds of small fires, like lanterns. Dawn is not far away.

Not a single animal visits that night. Those who survive are homeless and will have precious little food until the first rains. The fire has also destroyed countless homes and havens: litter that sheltered tiny ones, logs that were home to the larger creatures, material for nests, grass tussocks, and nesting hollows in logs and old trees. Missing their mutterings, mournful calls, thumpings, and rustlings, the night wears on, punctuated by falling trees and sporadic coughing. Even the mosquitoes have vanished.

There's one good thing about fires, the locals say. You can sleep without a mosquito net for a few days.

My First Bushfire

GUNUMELENG SEASON 1991
EMBARKING
Mid-October to late December 24°-37°C

In Gunumeleng, new rains bring more surface water and plant growth, and the waterbirds disperse. This season can last from a few weeks to several months.

The hot weather becomes increasingly humid and late fires still race through the dry brush. In this season, Aboriginal people traditionally moved camp from the floodplains to the stone country to shelter from the coming monsoon.

Thunderstorms build in the afternoons and showers bring green to the dry land.

The Geomancer's Report

I'm overwhelmed. Gasping. Breathless.

What *am* I doing?

I leave for Deep Creek in a week. *One week!*

I'm wandering around the chaos of my tiny terrace house. Can't decide about anything. I'm paralyzed by fear. The movers are coming in a few days.

What have I done?

Mica's friend, Paul, the bush builder, sent me a list of items to bring: a one-inch chisel, two other wood chisels, a brace and bit, a hand drill, some old sails, a half ax, and a shovel. Mica's list includes a mosquito net, a swag (bed roll and mattress), a backpack, a gas cooker, a gas fridge, gas bottles, and a flashlight with rechargeable batteries. Then there are books, clothes, and other household items for a year of camping. Mica has been living there since early 1981, so I guess he knows what I'll need to live there.

There's no mains electricity at Deep Creek, so the builders will use only the hand tools I bought. "Looks like an old-fashioned carpentry job," the man at the Adelaide hardware store remarks as he loads them into the trunk of my taxi. "You're certainly planning to do it the hard way."

I walk into my front courtyard in my slippers and dressing gown to see if the mail has arrived, and yes, it's there. What I have been waiting for. The geomancer's house location report. I grab my mug of coffee and take my treasure outside. I sit in the courtyard. The song of a peaceful dove nearby feels like good luck.

I open the envelope.

I groan.

Oh. My. God.

This will be very, *very* difficult. Well, I got what I asked for—for sure. A detailed analysis of house-siting options. And a clear direction forward. Juergen Schmidt, who's a geomancer and *feng shui* expert, makes his recommendations clear in his covering letter. He strongly recommends a site on the *north* side of the creek.

Not where Mica recommended.

I drop the letter onto the coffee table and wrap my arms around myself, rocking back and forth. I feel like moaning.

Boy, do I ever need comfort now.

4.2. THE CALL TO ADVENTURE

Comfort!

This situation is scaredy, for sure.

It's too late to mail the report to Mica. So, I'll just have to manage this sensitive issue when I arrive there in a few days.

And I know Mica will be furious. Juergen did his analysis using only Mica's mud map and a Lands Department map *without seeing the site*. He's never been there! Juergen calls his process "remote dowsing." All he uses is a pendulum and a map. He says it's a more accurate process than visiting an actual site because he can't influence the results. He only observes what the dowsing tells him.

Since *I* haven't seen the specific site Juergen recommends, it's impossible to imagine it. But I *know* that Mica will not be impressed.

He already thinks that geomancy is bunkum.

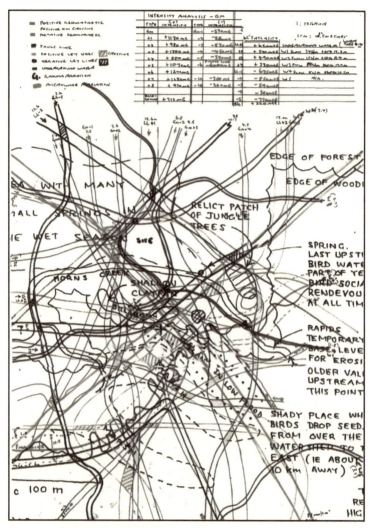

**Juergen Schmidt's Geomancy and *Feng Shui*
Analysis of the Deep Creek Site**

4.2. THE CALL TO ADVENTURE

I refill my mug with fresh tea and return to the courtyard, the geomancy map, and its accompanying report. Juergen worries that microwave energy from a television transmitter and a microwave tower crosses directly over Mica's proposed site. He says living in that exact location would be like living in Kings Cross in central Sydney. It will be *very* busy (energetically). I would be exposed to a lot of microwave scatter—up to fifteen times the recommended radiation.

If I follow *Juergen's* recommendation, I'll locate the house *north* of the creek in a spot that he says will be neutral to electromagnetic radiation. He calls his proposed site an *Old Qi* (energy) site, filled with ancestral wisdom. It has elevated levels of vitality and is energetically protected on all sides.

He says I will be in good physical and emotional shape living there. It's well suited to contemplation because major energy systems do not run through it, and the purity of the Qi energy softens its refined energies. His recommended house location has an accumulation of Gaian wisdom, which he calls "the essence of the whole planetary system."

I put down my mug and ponder. What on earth is "Gaian wisdom"? Will I be able to identify it when I see or experience it? Will it heal me?

I turn back to this document that will guide my life for the following year.

According to Juergen, Mica's proposed location is uncomfortably close to a fault line, which could discharge considerable magnetic turbulence. In his research on people living on fault lines, Juergen found cancer, leukemia,

The Geomancer's Report

multiple sclerosis, and what he calls "severe manic-depressive syndrome." Another reason for locating the house north of the creek is to avoid positive ions. In the north location, the wind would move positive ions southward away from the house. In contrast, Mica's proposed site south of the creek would have increased positive ion levels. That could bring respiratory disorders, particularly in wet weather.

(I already have dodgy lungs from a nasty lung disease 30 years ago. More lung problems I definitely do not need.)

I asked Juergen if he could find a good location for meditation, contemplation, and recharging my depleted system. And he found one! A large mass of ironstone just east of his proposed house site. I could recharge my batteries by sitting in the rock's eddy field. I was amused to hear him comment that the psychological attributes of people living at Deep Creek are likely to be torporific. He said they would be laid back, awfully slow, and lacking creativity. Local people might have difficulty making decisions. (I chuckle to myself about that.)

Juergen identified the presence of negative ley lines in several locations near Mica's proposed house location. He explained that where they cross, at inverted vortices, the high-frequency radiation inverts and moves downwards. I must avoid those places, as I'll suddenly feel uncomfortable and mentally and physically drained. When I asked how to identify them, he said they'd have a putrid smell. Standing barefoot there, I'd experience a sense of *cold*. Even in a warm climate, he said, I'd shiver because of the draining effect on my energy systems.

Juergen suggests I locate my front door away from the direction of the slope. It must be facing a flowing watercourse, so the *Qi* is retained, with the creek blocking discharge away from the house. The entrance should face the creek, be accessed from the creek direction, and align with the general energy direction (consistently north-south). He suggests I face my desk to the east.

There is no piped water to either of the proposed sites, so I will have to tap into the Deep Creek bore water supply by laying an underground pipe. However, Juergen reports that nearly all the water between the surface and the water table is pure, with less than 120 parts per million impurities. So maybe I can tap into a spring near my house.

I can swim safely in the creek. In fact, Juergen *recommends* sitting in the creek. As the water table is extremely high, most of the land around the house will become saturated in the Wet Season. That will be *Gudjewg*. I'd hardly call Juergen a humorous person. Still, he said that if I didn't want to paddle my house down the creek, I should see that the builders carefully concrete the house uprights into the ground to keep it from sinking.

I'm saving all this information to discuss with Mica in person right after I arrive. God help me!

Tonight, Mica rang to make sure everything was on track. He handed the phone to his mother, Molly. The line was crackling. Thunderstorms, Mica explained.

"Welcome now," she said. She has a deep, singsong voice. "Welcome, Wendy, to our block at Humpty Doo."

It was a lovely gesture.

Choosing Where to Build My House

You will experience the coming and passing of the seasons: the harmony and direction, the spontaneity and consistency, the continually rearranging balance. And you will feel them in ways that are at once universal and personal.

Diane Mariechild, 1981

$\mathcal{I}$ fly into Darwin on Sunday at noon. It is a terrible flight. I nearly lose my lunch on descent somewhere over Humpty Doo. Mica and I drive to Deep Creek and have only a few hours before Paul arrives to make the first (and final) decisions about where to build my house. I've talked to Paul on the phone a few times before I leave Adelaide. He's explained what he intends and what it will cost.

The ultimate house design will depend on the availability of materials. A shock to my system. For me, the planner, this is an entirely unfamiliar way of doing things.

Once we've settled in at his place, I tell Mica about Juergen's recommendations. I just blurt it out and hand him Juergen's report with the map attached.

Mica stares at me, holding the document like a rat he found in a basement.

Then he starts to rant, and I have no energy or skill to calm him down. I'm so overwrought myself.

Mica is furious about changing the house location. And how that's come about offends every fiber of his being.

As for me: I'm bedraggled after a long flight and several sleepless nights. I've just dismantled my whole life for a year or more. I have nothing left in my tank.

But Mica shows no compassion. I guess he sees this house-siting disagreement as a bad omen. While I slump in a chair near his house, he stomps around, waving Juergen's geomancy map and yelling, "Nobody can analyze a site without visiting it, damnit. Who does this fuckin' German geomancer dude think he is, anyway, Wendy? He must be a real fuckwit, this one. I bet he's also got an Irishman's gun that shoots around corners. For fuck's sake!"

We argue for hours, passing the map back and forth. Then, just when all seems lost, Mica suddenly capitulates. He's been fossicking around in his house, searching for some papers relevant to his case. He emerges, slams the metal door behind him, spins round to face me, and exclaims, "If you really want this 'feng-fuckin'-shui,' girl, you can have it. You are the one who is going to live there, after all."

4.2. THE CALL TO ADVENTURE

Later, when Paul arrives in his truck, the three of us walk across the indentation that marks the creekbed into a patch of remnant rainforest. Mica guides us on a tour of the small clearing north of the creek that Juergen chose for the house site.

A white cockatoo high in the branches of one pandanus tree welcomes us with a sharp, screeching call. (Or is it a warning?)

After we find a clear spot to stand, Paul doesn't mince words. He hates Mica's original location south of the creek.

"A fuckin' nightmare," he declares, stomping his foot in the damp black soil to emphasize his point.

Mica shakes his head, leans against a charred tree, brings out a tobacco pouch, and begins to roll a smoke.

Paul has been stomping around, and now he stops and turns to me. I hear despair growing in his voice.

"Wendy, I don't know you, but you don't look like a bush type to me. You look like you've spent all your life in the city. Do you know what you're getting into? If you build there, *south* of the creek, you'll be surrounded by mud (heaps of mud) when it rains. And that's any minute now. And the insects will drive you to distraction."

"Truly, Wendy," he implores, raising his voice, "you'll be much better in a drier place. Life here in the Top End is all about the seasons. Especially near an ephemeral watercourse.

Choosing Where to Build My House

I know you've never lived in such a place, but you will learn this, damnit. You will learn."

I nod. But I do not understand. Not yet.

All this is beyond terrifying. I am going to live here. Me! Alone! In this forest.

What am I doing?

We wander through the forest and stumble over vines and blackened stumps in deepening shadows and light rain. Mica comments, in passing, that he has given the name "White Gum Gate" to the entry to my temporary territory. Two soaring white gums make a ceremonial gate, and I pass through with a quivering heart. I beg this alien forest and its wild creatures to welcome this anxious stranger.

Paul stops, bends over and squints at Juergen's map. Soon he makes his preference clear.

"Wendy, I think the best spot for your house is here, where that German prick has put it. Right here. There's no comparison."

He aims a grimy finger at the map.

"I like this spot because it's higher, harder ground than the other side of the creek. It's greener, cooler, and shadier here. It will drain better and make your access a lot easier, though you will still have to cross the creek in the Wet."

4.2. THE CALL TO ADVENTURE

Paul does not embrace the *feng shui* idea. Far from it. We agree on where the house will be built and walk back to Mica's place. A few cold beers materialize from the cooler in the back of Paul's pickup. He tries to put Mica at ease, leaning forward as he pops open the can.

"I agree with Mica that this long-distance *feng shui* is a crock of shit, Wendy. But I *do* feel strongly that there's more shelter north of the creek 'cause that bit of remnant rainforest north of those two white gums escaped the worst of the fire. And deep down, I bet Mica agrees with me. But he's such a stubborn old bugger, he probably won't admit it."

Mica waves the idea away with his hand and busies himself searching for dry sticks for his fire.

"Whatever we do," Paul continues, settling back in the folding chair he's brought from his truck, "we must get our collective asses into gear. The rain's late. You know that, don't you, Mica? We could be flooded out any minute. So, we must start building tomorrow if you two lovebirds can get your collective shit together. I reckon we've got a week—two at the most—before the rain sets in. And then we're buggered."

And so, we agree on the house site with one dismissive gesture from Mica.

Paul and his mate Henry start work the next day north of the creek.

Later I think about how it must have looked to these two men: my hiring Juergen. Someone who did not live near Deep Creek, who could not visit the site, and worked only from maps. That was a dodgy thing to do. But I needed to assert some control and apply my housing knowledge to the house location and design. Employing a geomancer was my explicit statement that I valued the "invisible" energetic qualities of the land. But I had no direct experience. That decision certainly reflected my urban "disconnectedness."

And it was a radical act of trust in the invisible forces of Nature.

GUDJEWG SEASON 1991-1992
REFLECTION AND ACTION
December to March 24°-34°C

The change of Gudjewg (the monsoon season) provides great relief after months of the Build Up season.

Many animals mate during this season. Bush foods ripen, and the cheeky yam and the long yam are ready to be dug. Spear grass grows to over six feet tall, and the woodlands look silvery-green.

It is a time of water and nesting. A chorus of breeding frogs dominates the night air. Eggs and stranded animals are a good food source during this time.

Killing the White Gum

$\mathcal{W}$e're a week into house building, and my house is half-built. I am staying with Paul and Phyllis, his Aboriginal partner, on a large rural property about 25 miles away. They live in an open pole house with a high metal roof, a concrete floor, and no walls. Paul built it. It's like a huge open garage, not cozy or homey as I imagine my house will be. But it's a welcome refuge. Every night, Phyllis treats my sunburn with vinegar before I collapse on the couch. I can hardly drag myself to dinner. I sleep on their porch under a mosquito net. The rain often blows onto me, but I just sleep through it.

In the morning, Phyllis packs a gigantic lunch for me, Paul, and Henry, the other builder. She fills the cooler with fresh fruit and bottles of frozen water and juice. I'd never seen jackfruit before. We eat a gigantic breakfast of beef and beans and a blender drink of mango, pawpaw (papaya), watermelon, honey, and milk. Then we bomb off over dirt roads to start work by seven because it's so scorching by the middle of the day. I bounce around in the back of the open truck, wondering how I'll manage without *my* blender. (I'll have no electricity.)

This building process totally liberates my ideas about work. *Totally.* Initially, there are four of us: Paul, Henry, and Mica's young friend, Kundu. We're in a tiny clearing in a patch of remnant rainforest beside the creek. The sun filters through high branches of palms and gum trees, many with trunks charred by the fire that came through only three months ago.

The birds make a continuous, raucous song high in the tall trees above our heads.

And invisible critters scramble and slither at our feet. The three men work in sleeveless t-shirts, shorts, and flip-flops (sometimes even barefoot). No hard hats or boots on this building site. By noon on our first day, I check the temperature on my thermometer: 43 degrees C. (109.4 degrees F.).

We use Juergen's *feng shui* map and Paul's sketch to measure the site. (That's it for the house-siting process!)

With good humor, Paul finally accepts the "functional *feng shui* principles." "I reckon the *feng shui*'s going to dance around there," he pronounces, calling out in a loud voice as if to summon an ancient oracle: "Who are you, anyway, you Chinese prick?"

I hold the compass to make sure we orient the house true north, and Paul draws lines in the damp black earth with the toe of his boot. They become the outline of my house.

From the start, the house building is a race against time. Once it starts raining—*really* raining—we must wait for months to finish the house, and I'll have nowhere to live.

4.2. THE CALL TO ADVENTURE

On the morning of our first day of construction, I cleanse the site. A woman architect told me she prohibited arguments on building sites because the bad energy became encoded in the building. Before the men start work, I tape a photo of Sunny, my cat, to a tree with flaky bark that overlooks us. I stick the geomancer's circle to a tree.

I smudge all four of us and the building site with sweet sage burning in an abalone shell. That impresses Paul, who calls out to me: "Wendy, that's great what you are doing here. I *know* it will protect us here in this rough place. My Cypriot grandmother and aunts cleanse their houses using a special clay pot and dried olive leaves picked from a particular tree. I've always believed in that magic."

Henry, Paul, Kundu, and I stumble around in the damp earth, dragging away fallen branches, logs and small shrubs and pulling out seedlings. Then comes the worst part of my whole bush adventure. We have a painful conversation about killing one huge white gum tree. The men say it could drop its branches without warning. They call it a "widow-maker."

Without much conversation, Paul chainsaws down the towering White Gum.

I'm in agony. I feel incredibly sad to do this, as it is an ancient tree—maybe a hundred years old—and must be 17 or 18 meters high. But it is growing precisely where the house needs to go.

The White Gum

Before we kill it, I lean against this beautiful being and speak to it the best I can. I thank it for its help, apologize for the killing, and explain that I hope more trees will live because of the good work I intend to do. I can't pretend it responded and couldn't hear above the chainsaw. I am the transgressor; there is no escaping that.

At least nobody else is injured.

4.2. THE CALL TO ADVENTURE

Getting the tree to fall safely in the right place is a terrifying challenge for Paul. I'm shaking as the chainsaw bites into the tree's flesh, making a noise that sounds like murder.

Then Paul withdraws the chainsaw. The giant crashes down between the other trees and thuds into the soft earth precisely where he planned, tossing leaves and broken branches high into the air. Its long pale trunk stretches out before us, marking the northern boundary of what will become my front yard.

Killing the White Gum

"I believed in the strength of your magic, Wendy," Paul yells above the din, taking off his bandana to wipe his face. He lets out a long, deep sigh before searching around for his water bottle.

Later I hold the tape for Henry while we locate the spots for the house poles. Then, on our hands and knees in the soft black earth, using coffee cans for shovels so they won't get too deep, we dig nine holes about three feet deep for the upright poles.

After we dig the nine holes, we spend three days in a nearby research forest chainsawing plantation trees for the house uprights. They are northern cypress pine trees, tall and skinny—70 in all, about 15 to 20 feet tall. The three of us drive to the research forest in Paul's truck, and while I stand by nervously, Paul cuts down the trees with his chainsaw and then cuts off the branches. Strangely, I don't feel like apologizing to those trees. They feel like "resources," not living beings. I look around at the remaining trees in the research forest and remember how suburban developers always feature trees (and birds) in their marketing for housing projects. Yet on an actual building site, they never hesitate to chop down hundreds of trees for efficiency's sake.

Paul and Henry load the cypress pine logs onto the truck, and we haul them six miles to Deep Creek, making about 10 trips. The logs weigh the truck down, and it's harrowing, navigating the dry creek. We're terrified they'll get bogged. The men can't maneuver too close to the building site because the creek banks are getting so soft from the rain. The men sweat, puff, and groan as they carry or drag the logs across the creek the last few meters to the house site. These logs

4.2. THE CALL TO ADVENTURE

make up all the wood in the house. Except for the floor and the screen door, nothing will come from anywhere but that research forest.

When I take a break, I stand and stare at the line that apparently is the creek. I grew up in Western Canada, and I think I know about creeks and rivers. I know what a proper creek looks like. Wide banks, clear water, and large round speckled grey stones. So, I can't imagine there ever being a real creek in this dry creekbed. How could this mere indentation in the earth become a creek? Paul knows different: "I think we'd better whittle a pair of oars for you, Wendy, so you can paddle your house downstream in the Wet."

A Flexible House-building Process

After we've skinned 69 cypress pine logs, Paul and Henry maneuver nine of the biggest into the holes we've dug by hand.

We whoop with delight as the first pole goes up. Paul holds it as Henry tips the wheelbarrow, and the last of the wet concrete sloshes in.

"Henry, my boy, we've got an erection!" Paul calls out.

Henry chuckles and sets down the wheelbarrow. He wipes his brow.

I hold each pole until the concrete sets.

The poles are all slightly different heights, and they glisten blond and naked in the brilliant afternoon sunlight. Later, the men cut off the tops with a chainsaw. When all the poles are standing, I pull up a chair and sit where I figure my porch will be. I gaze out at the shimmering forest. The house will be at my back. The forest before me. It feels close—*scaredy* close.

The men are building my house to the call of white cockatoos screeching from the pandanus palms by the creek. And frogs singing in the creek.

My house with no walls.

They are tying my house together. They chisel wedges in the logs to fit each other exactly and tie them onto the purloins, using Cobb and Co. hitches with thick 14-gauge fencing wire. Like knotting it. It feels a bit like weaving.

4.2. THE CALL TO ADVENTURE

Then they use wide metal straps and bolt them together with six-inch bolts. Paul says it is a flexible, blow-through design. The hitches tie the house onto the ground, so it won't pull up in a cyclone. Here in the Top End, everyone is terrified of getting blown away.

From my folding chair, I stare up at my new friends. Paul found two more helpers, so now five sunburned, wiry figures are edged with golden light as they perch on the crossbeams of my house's skeleton. The forest's melodic cadence blends with the harsh sounds of their hammering.

Now the whole clearing is a building site. Skinned poles are stacked around, and nine poles are standing in pale wells of grey curing concrete. Some crossbeams are tied on. The bones of my house are materializing as it grows from the ground.

A pleasant childhood memory visits me. This scene is familiar to young Wendy, who watched the building of Norgate Park, house by house, over 40 years ago.

Mica's young friend, Kundu, makes countless trips to the local hardware store for more nails, bolts, and fencing wire.

"Sorry, Wendy, I know you're running out of money, but we still need more bits and pieces."

Kundu smiles apologetically through his matted head of dreadlocks. I fish out $25 for another 200 meters of tie wire, hand it to him, and slump back into my chair. I mop my forehead and slosh more lotion on my sunburn. God, I hope that the PhD scholarship comes through in February. I am almost out of money and credit.

A Flexible House-building Process

Most days, we start work at seven, with four of five people working on and off. Paul hoists the chainsaw, orders people around, and trims poles for braces. Henry measures crossbeams and cuts them to size. Kundu climbs onto the high crossbeams, hammer in hand, a mouthful of nails glinting in the sunlight.

And most days, at about 4 pm, it starts to rain, just as we are ready to finish for the day.

By Saturday, after six days' work in sweltering conditions, we have a house: a two-story pole house without a roof. When they nail on the glossy black marine plywood upper floor, the men invite me to climb their ladder so Paul can photograph me sitting on the floor. I am trembling with fear. The view is spectacular, but I can hardly raise my head to peer out. Do I have the skills and courage to live here alone?

Everyone thinks it is a great laugh: Wendy, the happy homeowner.

4.2. THE CALL TO ADVENTURE

Yesterday the roof went on—eleven days after starting work—to great cheers. Then, seconds later, the heavens opened again. The recycled iron roof is full of holes, but Paul says they'll caulk them later.

Earlier, after four days work, Paul calls a site meeting. Our ragtag bunch sits around on stumps and folding chairs, awaiting his decree. As I turn to survey our work site, I see that we've made only the tiniest clearing in the forest. Two giant gums and a wall of dark, thick, creekside vegetation dwarf the emerging house and the bunch of workers. And we are so insubstantial against the weather. Especially the rain.

We urgently need help. Like this very minute!

"This is not working, mates," Paul declares, mopping his forehead with a red handkerchief and drawing on a water bottle.

"It's too hot and not the right season for house building. Bloody hell! This is *Gunumeleng*, after all. Or close to. This

A Flexible House-building Process

fuckin' rain's gonna bring this whole project unstuck. It's dangerous and bloody hard using hand tools in these wet conditions. We need some electricity here. Like right now. To hell with the neighbors and their solar power. I can't go on like this. I honestly don't give a shit if they complain about the generator's noise. It's that, or I'm out of here. True. Sorry, Wendy, but you'll have to dig into your deep pockets again."

I raise my hand in a gesture of agreement and reach for my wallet. We're all relieved. Everybody nods. Nobody protests.

So Kundu and I drive 10 miles to Howard Springs and return with a small diesel generator and a can of fuel in the back of Paul's pickup truck. Paul quickly sets up his saw on a couple of sawhorses in the one dry spot under the house. It becomes a miniature assembly line. Then the drone of the saw drowns out the birdsong. But we don't mind. We have technology, and it's "all go" on our forest building site.

"Hey, Wendy, hand us some more nails, will ya?" they call, and I run to fetch a handful from under the house. I try to look busy, running around with tools and holding things while they saw or nail. I even try to start a fire to boil a billy for tea. But mostly, I stand in the rain, watching, as I did in Norgate Park. Watching men build another new house.

After a few days, we hire a bobcat to compact the site and move a ton of gravel (for the floor) from the other side of the creek near the White Gum Gate. It's a risky job. The daily afternoon rain makes the creek banks so soft and slippery. But I still can't imagine how this indentation in the earth could possibly become a flowing creek.

4.2. THE CALL TO ADVENTURE

Much later, my imagination returns to the creekbed. The creek is a powerful metaphor. When it rains, and the water runs again, it will flow over its old course. The creekbed will direct it. I ponder this tantalizing archetype. But my logical mind steadfastly refuses to accept that water will ever run along this shallow indentation in the hot, burnished, dry earth.

When it rains too hard for work, we drive to Darwin to buy hardware, repair our tools, and search for second-hand materials for a staircase and a screen door.

I am getting a new house. A container for my new growth. A refuge from the mysterious, unfamiliar forest. And a refuge *inside* that very forest.

It Can Be Fixed

*M*y staircase is my personal "rescue" project. We salvaged it from the Dinah Beach Boat Club for thirty-five dollars. Restoring it helps me feel more in control of my house. The builders abandoned it. They were racing against the monsoon rains and ran out of time, energy, and money. So, they never finished the staircase. Now it's a real eyesore. And I must use it every day and look at it from my desk and my chair on the porch.

A few days before my 49th birthday, I organize a women's working bee to fix it. The idea comes from my new friend, Linda Wirf. She squats on the muddy earth and examines it. It hangs crookedly from the upper floor, sitting in two buckets of concrete with metal star pickets (an Australian invention: pointed metal fence posts with three strips of metal). Not a pretty sight.

Linda draws a small, calloused hand along the flaking white and green paint, peeling it off with her short nails.

We stand together on the earth floor of the porch, inspecting our new project. She turns to me, smiling: "It's good timber, Wendy. It might even be jarrah. We could bring it back to life. It will look lovely with a little sanding and some linseed oil."

Her daughter, Laura, maybe 10, rubs the wood as if trying out her mother's words.

"It can be fixed," Linda continues, bending to inspect the foundation.

"You wait and see, Wendy. We'll come over next weekend and give you a hand. We'll buy a bag of cement, get some rocks from up the hill, and build a beautiful little rockery to finish the staircase. We'll use those concrete blocks to make steps at the bottom. And you can grow your herbs there. Basil would go well, and we'll plant lavender right by the steps, so you'll walk on it when you go upstairs to bed. (Don't tell Mica whatever you do. You know how he feels about exotic plants north of the creek.) You wait and see. It will be beautiful."

Her hands caress the staircase in anticipation of the job ahead.

Before Linda helps with the concreting, Owen comes over with a crowbar and straightens the stairs. Then Linda and I use concrete, bricks, and stones to create flat places for candles and plants. We plant lavender from her garden in the nooks and crannies.

We transform the staircase from rough to beautiful. We make a set of concrete steps at the bottom where I put plants (especially aloe vera) and a bucket for washing my feet before going upstairs.

Now, when I climb my stairs, the sweet scent of lavender follows me. My house feels more feminine. And I feel more balanced.

4.2. THE CALL TO ADVENTURE

My House, My Independence

December 1, 1991

My exhausted builders clean up, celebrate their triumph with a case of beer donated by Mica, and leave me to it. They're thrilled they outwitted the weather. They finish building before the arrival of *Gudjewg*, the Monsoon season.

The building process took about 40 person-days—with two builders and several helpers. Some days we worked for twelve hours in temperatures of 35 to 43 degrees C (95 to 109.4 F). And 90 percent humidity. It cost about $5,000.

Despite my fears, every time I think about my Humpty Doo house, I can only recall delight.

I love its simplicity, the beautiful staircase, a sense of openness, and flexibility. It's like I'm living on a small boat. I'm constantly adjusting my "sails": tarpaulins, shade-cloth, and bamboo blinds to keep out the rain.

My house sits in a tiny clearing in a forest landscape. It's soft and open. It fits in. We built it in a few weeks from 69 northern cypress pine trees. The tallest uprights extend the full height of the house.

I call my house "Wadi's Rest." While walking in the forest, I gasp when I glimpse its dramatic shape. It looks so modern. Imagine! A house with no walls that creaks and sighs as its timbers bend in the wind.

I have about 200 square feet of living space, an upstairs floor of marine plywood and a recycled galvanized iron roof. No walls upstairs. Only my large net tucked around the mattress. Sun on the long eastern roof creates a natural process of expansion and contraction. Rain plays it like a steel drum. It's not insulated, so I hear *pings, dings, clicks,* and *pops* as the weather changes. The tiniest tinkle of rain is a warning. The roof begins to tremble as if with excitement.

My downstairs space is screened. The floor is rammed earth. I didn't think I could live with an earth floor. (I'm fussy about cleanliness.) When the bobcat arrived, and Paul and Henry hauled a dozen wheelbarrow loads of earthy, brown gravel across the creekbed, I felt anxious. But it's cool and easy to clean. I love it. No worries, mate.

"This is the first house I've ever made for *myself*," I tell Sue, my neighbor. "This house is my haven for study, reflection, and hospitality."

From the porch, Sue surveys the house and smiles back.

4.2. THE CALL TO ADVENTURE

The screened downstairs houses my kitchen and working space with a small desk and a chair.

Twelve-volt wiring is so safe and forgiving. I've fallen in love with it. My electrical system is connected to a car battery sitting under a bucket. It's connected to one small solar panel on the fallen White Gum.

Downstairs, I learn to close the door quickly because the mosquitoes are so fierce. I look to my right into my efficient kitchen. It's working fine and is probably my favorite place.

From the covered porch, I can see the whole of the bottom floor. I love the wooden meat safe I found in an Adelaide antique store. Rural people covet this piece of furniture. It's excellent for protecting dry food like pasta and rice from animals. Sally, the bandicoot, tries to dig under the screen that protects my living quarters. (It's dug into the earth floor.) I regularly check that she doesn't dislodge the screen wall. I feed her leftover rice from my dinner. She's so tame that she almost eats from my hand.

I have three appliances. First, a two-burner, wrought-iron cooker. A friend loaned me a tiny refrigerator. My oven is a necessity for a person who loves baking. For these three, I need three gas bottles and one in reserve.

My stainless-steel sink sits on eight cinder blocks. It has one cold water tap, a pipe, and a hose that runs outside to a bucket. Later, I connect a tiny light above the bucket. After dark, glance out my kitchen window alerts me if the bucket is full and needs dumping up the hill. (Mica prohibits dumping dishwater near the creek.)

My House, My Independence

My kitchen is highly organized. Everything is in its place. Two chopping boards sit beside the refrigerator. A two-burner stove sits to the left. Herbs and spices are on a rack above it. A green compost bin and a red garbage bin. Everything with a tightly fitting lid to keep out the animals. Along the northern side, I installed a large sheet of galvanized iron to manage the heat from the stove. I hang cups and pots from hooks on the crossbeams. The scene is complete with glass jars, a filtered water dispenser, and a toilet paper roll.

I imagined this as my time for relaxed cooking, though I rarely cook anything fancy. I live on brown rice, vegetables, and canned fish. God! My diet's a lot like what we ate at Camp Concern in 1976!

My neighbors insist I wash dishes in hot water. I could get *giardia*, a dangerous tropical disease. Many local people have it.

The view north of my kitchen is incredible. From where I stand at my sink, I see maybe 15 feet of cleared land. Then the forest begins in concentric circles: small, spiky pandanus trees, taller pandanus trees, and more eucalypts.

During the day, it's tranquil in this part of the forest, as many animals are nocturnal. Not so at night. It's party time, with small critters crashing through the underbrush and bats and flying foxes jumping and flying between the taller branches.

My outside toilet is up the hill a few hundred feet (so I won't pollute the creek). It's not a building or an outhouse. Not here! Simply a small, bottomless oil drum over a three-foot hole. On the top is a standard toilet seat. A piece of shade

4.2. THE CALL TO ADVENTURE

cloth draped between four trees protects me from the sun. The toilet doesn't smell, and I'm surprised at how comfortable I am. I usually pee in the forest, well away from my house.

Everywhere I look are features to make life comfortable and convenient. Several small computer fans hung above my desk and bed are major modern conveniences. I remind myself that I'm a PhD student. I spend my time reading, writing, and trying to understand what is happening.

I have all the time in the world, and I spend it reading and writing. My laptop sits on an Indian tablecloth that covers my desk. My portable printer sits on a shelf behind me. Astonishingly, my desk chair works fine on the earth floor. From my desk, I take in the most beautiful view of the forest and one precious tree. I name her *Tristia*, and we regularly talk together.

Sometimes I use my portable printer on a table on the porch with my laptop on a nearby chair. It's funny. Here I am, in the darkness, with no telephone or proper electricity. I print reports, stuff them into envelopes, and post them to clients from the Humpty Doo Post Office the next day. That's all that remains of Wendy, the consultant!

To the left of my desk is a light that's not wired into my 12-volt system: a two-bulb battery-powered fluorescent camping light. For emergencies. I can turn it on if it's been raining and the solar lights aren't working well. Also, for emergencies is a kerosene lantern that hangs by my desk. And, of course, several flashlights and a stash of rechargeable batteries.

Beside my desk on a crossbeam (one of the few pieces of milled timber in the house) is a laminated collage of photos of my friends. Beside it hangs a quote from Emerson: "Nothing great is ever achieved without enthusiasm."

Also hanging there is Doug Swanson's sketch of his Adelaide house. I miss my dear, late friend, who helped me find the courage to visit Mica at Camp Concern.

The porch roof shelters the eastern side. The west is protected by tarpaulins and bamboo blinds. I am desperate to protect my earth floor, so I rarely open the western blinds.

I still have jobs to do. Weatherproof the house with tarps and bamboo blinds. Modify a few things to follow Juergen's *feng shui* guidelines (relocate the path from the creek to the front door, so it's not too direct). Move the porch entrance from the east to the south to keep those annoying *secret arrows* away. In *feng shui*, apparently, it's all about protection from arrows!

4.2. THE CALL TO ADVENTURE

I love to sit outside. My porch accommodates several folding chairs and a small, wheeled table. I work there during the day (when the mosquitoes are not so ferocious). I *can* sit outside after sunset in a long-sleeved shirt, long pants tucked into thick socks, and lace-up shoes. I must button my shirt and slather all exposed skin with mosquito repellent.

The porch never had a floor. Not even rammed earth. The builders ran out of time. So eventually, I redo it—with road gravel. It's a grueling job for an out-of-shape city gal. In the sweltering heat, I haul dozens of wheelbarrow loads from the drain up the hill at Robert's place. (Fortunately, the delivery stage is a downhill trip!) Then I mix in a bit of cement. The only way to compact my new porch floor is to put on my running shoes—and the radio—and dance. I dance my porch floor into shape to the sound of, amazingly, "November Rain" by Guns N' Roses! The song is a bit slow, but I'm tired, so it works fine!

My House, My Independence

From the top of the stairs, I survey my private realm. I listen to music and cyclone reports on ABC radio. It's only me here for a year. No lovers. (I listen to Dr. Muldane and never invite Mica into my bed. This adventure needs to be done alone.) The occasional guest sleeps on a mattress beside my bed. I hang clothes under the steep iron roof and pray they won't suffer damage from weather or animals. I store books and precious items in plastic boxes but worry they don't have tight-fitting lids.

On the western side, two bamboo blinds allow light and air through and keep the rain out. My bed with a futon mattress dominates the small space. It's so humid here so I'm meticulous about airing my bedding. I sleep under a gigantic mosquito net tied above the bed. It's named for the Aboriginal settlement of Maningrida. These nets are the gold standard.

Imagine my delight as I climb into bed and carefully tuck the net around me. It hangs high above so I can easily sit and read by a 12-volt light behind me. And though I'm always hot and sweaty, the crisp blue polka-dotted cotton sheets feel cool to my touch. I feel civilized—almost urbane—surrounded by the roughness of tropical life.

My thoughtful builders installed many horizontal rails so I can hang clothes, my sarong, and a towel beside my bed. Because the ceiling is 12 feet high, the upstairs has lots of light and ventilation when I raise the blinds. Bright cotton rugs on the bedroom floor are soft underfoot.

My house. My *independence*. When I first move in, I christen it by lighting my red candle. Its flame reminds me to bathe myself in courage, the quality I need for this adventure. When I'm more settled, I cleanse my house by burning sweet sage in an abalone shell. I smudge myself, downstairs, upstairs, and my porch.

Fourteen years ago, Mica christened my Adelaide terrace house, *Independence*. But *this* house is my *true* Independence. I am living here independently, making this house my home.

I still have a lot of work to do.

And I am home.

The Green Wall

$\mathcal{I}$'m sitting outside tonight to see the stars (using a new high-strength insect repellent). After a cloudy, hot day, the sky is clear. I keep thinking about my 1986 book, *Housing as if People Mattered,* and how fussy I was about the details—all those references. Long hours in the late seventies, sitting with Clare at her dining table in Berkeley reading research reports for our book. When I compare that with the house-building process I have just experienced, it's ridiculous. Hilarious.

How can I describe the bush? I think it's too early. It's still too foreign. I am still living in the other world—the world I left behind—and the world in my head. Daily I tell myself I have the necessary courage for this project. I pray to whoever is listening, something that goes like this:

Dear God, Am I making the most terrible mistake? What if I don't have the skill or endurance for all of this? Please guide me in this frightening situation. Give me the courage to take this risk. Amen.

God replies with something that goes like this:

*Dear one, you are right where you are meant to be. You are
not given anything more than you can handle. Breathe. Find
happiness in simple things. Calm your troubled mind.*

When I look out at the surrounding bush, I see nothing
except shades of orange, green, and brown. Sort of a blurred
collage. I guess this is the *Green Wall* my academic mentor
spoke about. She said it would take me a while to develop
"ecological eyes."

I think I have some sort of archetypal fear. The *wall*
looks like a fence or a hedge that separates the domain of
wilderness from the domain of culture. The wild from the
tame. Or maybe I'm frightened by *green chaos*. Psychiatrists—
and torturers—say that the human mind needs refuge to
maintain sanity. Without it, we can disintegrate and go mad.
So, before I can differentiate among elements in the natural
world, I might need to learn more about chaos, the *Green
Wall* and its implied darkness. I'll need more courage for that,
for sure.

Inside the Inside

Going into the forest requires us to let go of our old ways and identities; we shed defenses, ingrained habits, and attitudes, which opens us up to new possibilities and depth. We find what really matters to us and can reach the core or center of meaning in ourselves, which is the center of the labyrinth, and then we have the task of integrating this into what we do with our lives when we emerge.

Jean Shinoda Bolen, 1994

$\mathcal{I}$'m a planning analyst. So, I select my point-and-shoot camera for its ultra-wide-angle lens. For 30 years, I photograph with a plan, cataloging my images: neighborhood site plans, housing floor plans, layouts, annotated park plans, housing density, spatial arrangements…

No time for close-ups in *my* busy life.

Now, as I slowly settle into the Deep Creek landscape, I sit on my porch, cradling my morning cup of tea. My bare feet rest on the cool earth floor. A wall of green surrounds the clearing. I am terrified of approaching it, much less walking into it. Or through it.

Every day, I say I will.

And every day, I don't.

True, I've escaped the city. But now I'm housebound, terrified. And I chose my timing poorly. It's the suicide season: the oppressively hot and humid Build Up.

I'm living in a patch of remnant rainforest in a bare, open eucalypt forest that was severely burned a year before. Urban to my painted toenails, I am trying to learn to live alone here.

And, though I'm terrified of it, could this alien forest possibly heal my tortured mind?

Weeks after I move in, disoriented by culture shock, I do one simple thing. I attach the macro lens to my camera.

And *everything* changes.

I lose interest in trying to understand, confront, or pass through the *Green Wall*. My attention is drawn elsewhere.

I yearn to go *inside*.

And when I find myself inside a pandanus palm, a cycad fern, the bark on a paperbark tree, I discover life *inside* the inside. I long to get close to the essence of the trees and the

4.2. THE CALL TO ADVENTURE

ferns. Now I can see the colors, the graphic patterns, and the vortex that draws me in even more.

Then, months after I move to Deep Creek, my ephemeral creek fills with water. I sit in it. My whole being sinks into my depths and deepens in the singing creek. *I'm* singing now. I hear more than birds now. This whole forest is a living soundscape.

As I tentatively enter the realm of small Nature, my heart opens, and my eyes soften. My photography deepens.

Now I regard the *Green Wall* as a prospect. Not a terror.

Refocusing returns my life to me.

A Message from a White Cockatoo

$\mathcal{H}$ere's a typed message Mica left on my desk recently. I reported to him that a white (sulfur-crested) cockatoo made a great fuss one morning while I sat quietly on my porch drinking my tea. It was such a surprise. I can't figure out what caused it.

It sat in the top of a huge pandanus palm (maybe fifteen feet tall) within about 10 feet of my house.

It called out in its shrill voice and tore off all the top fronds with its beak. They scattered in a giant circle on the ground below. And all the while, the bird kept screeching.

**"White Gum Glade Memo," Deep
Creek, 13 December**

Wendy:

From your narrative, I conclude that you were "approached" by a White Cockatoo yesterday. I think that the Pandanus Tree employed in that "display" should be called "The White Cockatoo Tree" for the present. I rate the approach as momentous. And the fact that it caused me to brief you on aspects of the protocol to be observed as fortunate.

I wish to hand over the primary responsibility for considerate behavior toward White Cockatoos at the White Gum Glade to you. I am asking you to accept responsibility to stop visitors from handling or displaying feathers (with particular priority given to white feathers). The whole local human community is at risk of punishment by the White Cockatoos if such a precautionary rule is not established and policed.

And, in any case, it would be rude (and an abuse of the Cockatoo's hospitality) to make the bird feel avoidable anxiety.

I interpreted the Crow mimicking the frog call this morning as an indication that this bird, too, is resident and holding an exclusive hunting territory. It has not shown itself to you or "approached" you. I expect that it will do so soon.

Mica

I beg Mica to explain more about what the cockatoo's warning means. And about the crow. I'm so curious. Is this cockatoo teaching me something? Helping me somehow? Is it telling me that my life is about to turn? Has it come to save me?

4.2. THE CALL TO ADVENTURE

But Mica becomes glum and won't say more. So, I drive to the Research Unit in Darwin to visit their library. I search and ask the librarians, but we can't decode the cockatoo's warning. However, in my research, I learn that the sulfur-crested cockatoo is a significant bird. Arnhem Land Aboriginal people (who live not far from here) associate it with death and mortuary ceremonies. It keeps a sentinel eye on wayward spirits lost en route to the island of the dead. Its imperative call alerts Aboriginal people to the location of spirits in limbo among the rocks and scrub. A bird or two high in the trees warns a feeding flock against predators.

Mica tells me later that Aboriginal people were often wary of displaying cockatoo feathers in case the birds would warn birds further afield. I'm grateful for this advice:

Somebody who offends the white cockatoos gets a sort of criminal conviction. The cockatoos gather and say: "Would everybody gather here, please? Item of business. Security issue. There's a human you need to identify here. He's a danger to us. I will identify the felon to you."

You can get yourself a criminal record with the white cockatoos. I found that if you offend the white cockatoos, not only will they be gathered to you so you can be identified, but they will also travel ahead of you into the bush, putting out alarm calls as they clear the bush ahead of you. If you are a hunter-gatherer and get in their bad books, the cockatoos can spoil your hunting expeditions and deprive you of food. They can kill you. Jackdaws do the same sorts of things in Europe.

A crow is the other bird in my life. One wakes me every morning at 7:30. I am curious about this crow. I sense it will play a significant role during my year at Deep Creek as a wake-up call. Crows are associated with life's mysteries and have powerful natural magic. Later I read that crows can show a compassionate response to humans and even provide guidance. Joan Halifax believes that it is not us who will save the creatures, but the creatures who will save us.

I call this crow *Hermes*, this persistent trickster bird who wakes me every morning. Maybe this crow is here to remind me of the consciousness of the life around me.

A Bush Shower

$\mathcal{M}$y shower is the greatest delight of my bush abode. It's connected to an upright pipe wired to a tree on the hill, well away from the creek, so I won't pollute it. The water comes from the Village bore water supply, pumped by a windmill. My neighbor, Helen, an artist (she paints on silk) and a healer, built the shower as a housewarming gift.

I have a separate tap at the bottom of the tree for buckets to wash my clothes. Cold water only, of course. It's the tropics, after all, so cold showers are the go.

Helen sets 80 salvaged, golden-colored firebricks in sand to make the floor. She edges it with logs charred by the bushfire, adding a beautiful, poignant touch. Cycad ferns surround it. A small one that looks like a potted plant grows at the edge of the brick floor.

"Oh, Wendy," Helen exclaims, putting down her trowel and mopping her brow with her sarong. "This will be one of your favorite spots. I can guarantee that. You can see right into the creek from here. If you've never showered by moonlight, you are in for a real treat."

I repeat her words to every city guest who visits me. Everyone makes the same report: Wendy's bush shower is an unexpected delight.

Amazingly, the afternoon shade falls precisely where Helen laid the bricks.

Later, I run 50 meters of wire from my house through the forest and attach a one-watt light bulb to the tree above the shower head. Then, like magic, I can flick on a tiny light to guide me on nights when the moon is hidden. (I love wiring.)

I christen my shower in the starlight. I sing "You Go to My Head" in my outdoor voice as I luxuriate in the sensuousness of the clear, cool water. The butterflies love it—they dance in the spray.

My shower is one of the most beautiful spots in the tiny territory I now call home. Its blackened logs remind me of the grief and horror of the Fire, and the glistening pale green cycads announce the hopefulness of rebirth. When I am walking through the forest and glimpse my shower, it triggers a sense of contentment and expectation inside me.

And I imagine the same slow-growing cycad that brushes my legs with soft fronds flourishing 25 years later, more than three feet tall.

4.2. THE CALL TO ADVENTURE

Christmas Present

I spent yesterday with Sue, my new neighbor. It was a painful day. My first rural Christmas brought up all sorts of childhood memories.

"Just keep driving, Sue," I yell over the engine's roar as we crash along the rough dirt track at Deep Creek. "Stopping to look at it won't be good for me, and it certainly won't improve our Christmas."

In reply, Sue guns her ancient blue Suzuki. We career along the narrow cut in the forest, splashing through shallow puddles and knocking over several tiny paperbark seedlings struggling to stay upright in the damp black soil. A few pandanus fronds, glossy with rain, are caught in my window so I see everything outside in pieces—nothing whole.

Yeah, I think wryly. That's about it, all right. All in pieces.

We rattle within a hundred meters of the tiny one-room metal building with a campfire's charred embers glistening from the morning's rain. A healthy-looking dog roots about in a blackened fry pan, ignoring us.

We glimpse a figure standing in the afternoon shadows on the porch. So thin, he is nearly transparent. A tall, stooped man with a long white beard turns to watch us drive past.

"But it's that book you gave Mica for Christmas," Sue yells back. "It had a bright red ribbon hanging from it like a bookmark. Like the ribbon you used to tie up my present. It's just sitting out there on that stump beside the track."

(I gave the book to Mica for Christmas, and he left it where I could see it.)

"Forget it," I shout. "It will ruin my Christmas. If Mica wants to leave a book outside in the Wet Season, that's his problem. It's important to him, or he wouldn't have walked all that way to put it there. You know he can hardly walk with that sore foot. Let's just forget it, Sue. You and I will enjoy this bloody Christmas dinner if it kills us."

"It's not my fucking book," Sue yells defensively, gunning the Suzuki again. "I don't give a shit if it gets wet. I thought you might." Her profile was tight with her unspoken thoughts.

"For Christ's sake, Sue, I'd rather enjoy my Christmas. Let's forget it."

My first Christmas in the tropics isn't getting off to a good start. We are on our way to Christmas dinner at Sue's friend's place 10 miles away. A family barbecue with lots of kids. I hear my thoughts as we clank across the dip and turn onto the

4.2. THE CALL TO ADVENTURE

dirt road. Sad, lonely thoughts. Good thing I didn't decide to stay behind. Being alone with these thoughts always spelled danger. Better someone else's chaotic Christmas than *my* painful memories that crowd into the dusty jeep like insistent, hungry puppies. They press around my scratched, mozzie-bitten legs, gnaw at my sandals, tug at my grey shorts, and nuzzle into the stained armholes of my t-shirt. Little buggers. Hard to keep them at bay. Especially on Christmas day.

I always have problems with Christmas. Because I come from a sad family, Christmas is always the hardest time. It's about disappointment. When you go through the year being an unhappy family, there is nothing much to measure it against. You know that things aren't so chaotic or miserable in other families. You get to know that with experience, painful experience. But at no other time are these feelings as explicit as they are at Christmas when it's so hard to keep up pretenses. People come around; they see your presents, and your secrets inevitably leak out.

First, they see you standing with your Dad in the parking lot by the North Vancouver Scout Hall in the freezing rain. You are arguing about which Christmas tree to buy. Arguing about the last few straggly trees rather than getting there in time to find a good, straight fir that would support the angel nicely at the top. Instead, you leave with a distorted, scrunched-up sort of tree. Something left over. Something no other family wanted.

Then there are arguments back at the house about how to put up the tree or whose fault it is that we are out of replacement lights. Why did all last year's tinsel get tangled up? And why there aren't any more hooks for the balls? Or who lost the tree stand? And always the warning: this will be a lean Christmas because of some disaster with the Business or the Bank Manager.

When I am old enough to travel on my own (maybe nine), I take two buses to West Vancouver across the new bridge over the Capilano River to visit the Park Royal Shopping Centre. I am seven and three-quarters when Park Royal opens in September 1950. Daddy tells me it's Canada's first regional-class shopping hub (whatever that means). It has something I have never seen before: automatic doors with an electric eye. (Daddy tries to explain how they work, but I know it's just magic.)

One day—a few days before Christmas—when I am wandering through Park Royal with my allowance in the pocket of my pale green wool coat that was stained red in spots by my library books getting wet when I was carrying them, I find the perfect job for when I grow up. It is in Woodward's Department Store. Sometimes I'll stay inside the store for hours until it gets dark outside. I perch on a stool they have and watch the two women at work. My little floral umbrella leans against the counter, making a puddle on the linoleum.

This is my favorite department because they wrap Christmas presents here—and only here. I mean *gift* wrap, and they really know how to do it. First, they have shiny white cardboard boxes for everything, all sizes and shapes, so that all presents are easy to wrap and come out looking very neat. And that makes the presents look larger, too, because they use scads and scads of tissue paper in boxes much larger than the gifts.

4.2. THE CALL TO ADVENTURE

And these are not just old boxes from the shoe department, vacuum cleaners, sweaters, or mix-masters. They are tailor-made boxes, glossy, clean, crisp, and white. They have numbers stamped on the bottom so that you know which one fits a tie or a glass bowl or a man's shirt or a cardigan folded properly over a piece of cardboard with no ugly crease down the front.

The boxes start flat with the numbers showing, and when they fold them, they neatly stack them on special shelves that fit them perfectly. When they aren't busy wrapping presents, the women fold the boxes and stack them like in cake stores.

Every Christmas (from about August, actually), they set up a prefabricated desk in Woodward's with perfectly fitting shelves just for boxes. They must keep them in pieces, all numbered, in the basement for the rest of the year and then fit them together like a Meccano set. That especially appeals to me—being so organized ahead of time and knowing precisely what sizes of boxes to order. And they never run out of boxes, either.

Nancy, who is about 50, says to the younger woman, "Hey, June, could you please go down to *Stores* and pick up a dozen D5s and a couple of D8s? That tie sale on the first floor will make us run out of D5s."

"Gotcha," June responds. "I'll take my coffee break at the same time, Nancy, if that's all right with you. Be back in a tick."

(I imagine June loves the notion of Stores as much as I do.) And she contentedly putters off to Stores, stuffing a yellow packet of Matinee cigarettes and her Ronson lighter into the front pocket of her sleeveless turquoise smock.

I imagine *Stores*. I dream about *Stores*. One Christmas, years later, when I am a teenager, I get a part-time job in Women's Sportswear at Woodward's downtown department store. They let me go down to *Stores* to collect more boxes. But they won't let staff enter the box room, and I can't see the shelves with the boxes from my side of the counter. It is a big disappointment, even at sixteen.

Back in the early fifties, I highly approve of how they wrap the presents at Woodward's, Park Royal. First, they have everything that matches perfectly: paper and ribbon and little cards with holes for the ribbon already neatly punched in them. The colors all tone in, and there is a selection of more "masculine" papers with ducks and hunting guns for fathers or grandfathers, who might be embarrassed by Santas and trees. (They also wrap birthday presents for those lucky enough to have a birthday while the stall is up.)

And they have a little machine for making bows. They use a special ribbon that doesn't split, and the machine wraps the ribbon around its spindles just enough times to make a perfect bow for the thickness of the ribbon and the size of the present. That fascinates me.

I approve of the thinner matching ribbon to tie the bow in the middle once the machine snips neat triangular cuts. That way, the bows always fluff up perfectly. They would never consider ready-made bows with adhesive. These are still the days of real craft.

4.2. THE CALL TO ADVENTURE

The best part is the cellophane. It transforms any gift, adding that essential touch of elegance. I like how they often include a sheet of perfect cellophane with absolutely no crinkles for about 10 cents more. It comes off a large roll with a cutter, so the parcel has no embarrassing creases. They cut the edges of the cellophane short, so there won't be any unsightly bulges when they fold them under the Christmas paper. And they always put pieces of the same length of Scotch tape perfectly straight on all the edges, so nobody is offended by a sloppy job.

And then, when the ribbon and the bow and the tag go on, the whole effect is beautiful. And the bow isn't always in the same place, as though no special thought went into this present. Sometimes it is set off-center, or they wrap two strands of ribbon around the present. Every present is individual. And every present is perfect. And every present is boxed so you can't tell from its shape what the present is. Nobody could ever be embarrassed by a present like that.

★★★

Well, here I am, 40 years later and twelve thousand miles away in a foreign tropical place, on a steamy Christmas day, rattling along a dirt road in the tropics, thinking about ribbons, perfection, and Christmas past. And wondering how to deal with Christmas present. And the Christmas present I've chosen for Mica. In the past weeks, I've learned how affected Mica is by his childhood, just as I am by mine. Mica says his late father was a policeman, and he loved him. He says nothing more. His mother still tenderly cares for her only child.

Christmas Present

As for me, I had no mothering. I am a motherless child. Mental illness robbed me of that parent, leaving me with feelings of anger and sadness. I yearn for what I never had: a loving, nurturing mother who respects me. Secretly, I envy Mica.

I am terrified of a bushfire here in the forest, and even a hint of it tests my courage. I almost die of fright when I drive back from the Humpty Doo store a few days earlier, only days before Christmas. As my old car bangs over the bridge into Deep Creek, I spot two fire engines ahead of me, lights flashing. My heart sinks. I gasp for breath. I can almost smell smoke now.

Not another bushfire! No! Not another one! Where could it be? I've only been gone an hour. Did one of my gas bottles explode? Did I leave something cooking on the stove? Did I leave a candle burning...?

I screech to a halt alongside the first truck and jump out, breathless, my heart pounding. I don't notice the balloons and streamers. The local fireman, seated high on the back of the truck, smiles down at me through a curly white beard. He doffs his red cap before raising a green can to his lips. His assistant, in uniform, speaks first, grinning.

"Mornin', ma'am. Merry Christmas from the Fire Brigade. Any children at your house?"

"I thought there was a bushfire," I splutter, realizing my mistake.

4.2. THE CALL TO ADVENTURE

Then we all laugh together. I accept a cold one from their cooler, and we chat for a while.

"No need to worry yet, love," the Santa fireman reassures me.

"It's way, *way* too wet for a fire right now. You'll know when it's the fire season, believe me. When we hit *Yegge* and *Wurrgeng*, you better believe it. But now, you'll be right for months. Truly. Relax. Merry Christmas."

I wave goodbye as they chug up the hill. I climb back into my car—remembering other Santas, other Christmases, other presents, my childhood Christmases, full of anger and pain—and yet so full of hope.

As a child, I have lots of principles about Christmas and expectations, and I must be careful not to get too disappointed and depressed—which happens when things do not go to plan. *My* plan. But here—Christmas at Deep Creek—I am making a special exception to my rule to avoid giving in to emotional issues during the festive season. I decide to speak to Mica and give him my present.

I've had this gift for some time—long before I left the city. I consider it the perfect present: Robert Bly's *Iron John: A Book about Men*. I like its emphasis on legend: the moist, the swampish, the wild, and the untamed. I bet Mica will agree with Bly about retrieving and eating the Shadow and the black earth of darkness. There might be something for Mica in Bly's argument about men having difficulty trusting other men.

Christmas Present

The book is about truths and masculinity that go beyond our popular culture's stereotypes. That certainly is Mica's province. Bly explains that bonding with the father is the key. How can men retrieve their wildness and become one with the *Wild Man* without a real relationship with their fathers? he asks. I especially like the book's earthiness and its confidence in men. Both evoke strong images of Mica. Valuing men— notably *Wild Men*—is a topic dear to his heart. Bly advises brushing these naïve and fragile creatures with the wingtips of our minds.

I also like what Bly says about Hermes. Hermes is magical, detail-loving, obscene, goofy, and not on a career track. My hero. Bly says that men do not learn authentically until Hermes is present. I have always romanticized Mica, which is easy to do, for he is such a colorful, magical character. He is a lot like Hermes: the trickster messenger in *my* life.

All this is Mica's philosophical domain. Sexuality and the men's movement fascinate him. *Iron John* is an evocative, archetypal character, and the stories in the book have a healing quality. And the book's emphasis on partnership with the feminine gives me hope. So, I figure I'll still give Mica his Christmas present.

Things start well. Mica stubbed his toe. It's ugly, with the nail infected, so he can't do more than hobble a few steps at a time. And he certainly can't drive. He is holed up on his porch, calculating rainfall for the bioregion with a blunt pencil on some smudged graph paper, his foot propped up on an oilcan.

4.2. THE CALL TO ADVENTURE

Sue and I invite him for Christmas brunch. On Christmas morning, I walk over to ask if I can get him anything from the local store. I leave Sue back at my place across the creek, cooking and listening to Christmas carols on the radio. She is keeping close to me in case anything flares up. I am carrying Mica's present.

Mica places his order. "Just bring me two dozen full-strength cold ones, four packets of Peter Jackson dark blues, three boxes of matches, and two cartons of iced coffee, Wendy. That oughta last me through Christmas and Boxing Day if no guests turn up."

I record his order and leave, reminding him that Christmas brunch would be ready at about eleven. I hand him the book.

★★★

Mica does not show up for brunch, so Sue and I have our pancake brunch alone, drinking champagne and sharing outrageous stories about our lives. Occasionally from across the creek, we hear a curse or the sound of something breaking. Later that day, Christmas dinner with Sue's friends is what I'd expected: a loud and cheerful barbecue. And I keep wondering about the book. When we return near midnight, Sue aims her headlights at the tree stump beside the track. The book is gone.

Books in the rain.

Suddenly, I remember my green coat stained all those years ago by wet library books I clutched to me like friends, like family, like love, like understanding. My Easter coat bought to celebrate a festival of sacrifice, forgiveness, and renewal. Stains carried like badges of shame until I outgrow the coat.

There's a connection there somewhere, I think. I wore the consequences of that folly for years. I suspect I'll wear this one for a long while, too.

BANGGERRENG SEASON 1992
TERROR, ALLIES, AND INSIGHTS
March to April 23°-34°C

Banggerreng, usually lasting through March and April, marks the transition from the Wet to the Dry season.

Local people call it the "Knock-'em-down" storm season when violent, windy storms flatten the speargrass. It has periods of strong winds, dark clouds, heavy storms, high temperatures, and high humidity. This harvest season is a time of plenty.

Fish are prolific in the billabongs and rivers. When the rain ceases, the spear grass seeds. Most plants are fruiting. Magpie geese eggs will soon be ready to harvest.

A Visit from a Kookaburra

The true language of these [unfamiliar, non-human] worlds opens from the heart of a story that is being shared between species. For us to be restored to the fabric of this Earth, we are bidden to enter this tale once again through its many modes of feeling, to listen through the ears of others to the mystery of creation, with its continually changing patterns, and to take part once again in the integral weave of the narrative.

Joan Halifax, 1993

March 7, 1992

I am trying to develop compassion for myself. To calm my mind, I listen to a taped Buddhist loving-kindness (*mettā*) meditation in the morning. I sit upstairs on my bed under my net. I try to embody an attitude of compassion and sympathy for all living beings. On alternate mornings, I send loving-kindness to all beings. I focus on having a non-violent, gentle attitude toward plants, especially the gigantic trees around me. I even send prayers to any trees that might remain in the temperate Canadian forest of my childhood.

The *mettā* practice is supposed to foster compassion and sympathy toward all creatures and open space inside me for the re-emergence of a larger world. It sounds like this:

May we learn just to be a moment at a time. No expectations, just an open heart, sharing as we can. May all beings be happy. May all beings be free from suffering. May we all come home to our completedness.

In a second meditation, I re-parent my infant self. I use a taped visualization. Part of it sounds like this:

Now imagine that the grown-up picked you up and held you. You hear her tenderly tell you the following affirmations: "Welcome to the world. I've been waiting for you. I'm so glad you're here. I prepared a special place for you to live. I will not leave you, no matter what. I'll give you all the time you need to get your needs met."

I'm really trying here, but I struggle to achieve mindfulness and attentiveness. And meanwhile, I wrestle with my thesis topic. I came here to learn what the forest had to teach. Well, I'm learning, that's for sure. *And* what I am learning hardly fits into an academic thesis. I'm reading and taking notes and thinking deeply about how planners could embrace sustainability. But I keep coming up against the same problem. Planners just don't *care* about "the environment." It's so "out there" for them. (For me.) I ask myself the same questions repeatedly: How can I understand the reasons behind planners' seeming indifference toward the environment? And then, how can I learn compassion for them?

Gary Snyder recounts a Tibetan saying: "The experience of emptiness engenders compassion." I'm finding that living in the forest engenders both an interior and exterior sense of emptiness. Not compassion. Not yet anyway. Maybe I'm not ready yet. Still, at times, a great peace rushes into my empty spaces. I am experiencing a completely different way of seeing. Maybe this is Annie Dillard's "other kind of seeing that involves a letting go." She explains, "When I see this way I sway transfixed and emptied." Or maybe it's about being empty. My Buddhist friends tell me that first you must empty yourself before you can embrace compassion and love for all beings. Hmmm.

One morning about three weeks ago, I was sitting downstairs at my desk, gazing out past the old, mossy *Tristania* tree to the wall of trees. Then, out of nowhere, a male kookaburra flew close to my house. He settled on a tree by the path about five meters from me. Just sat there and stared at me for the longest time.

Then he started to call out—laughing and screeching. So loud, so dramatic! It seemed like an announcement— like a bulletin. Or a set of instructions. I'd never had such an experience. The kookaburra's call was so dramatic that my body started to shudder, and I could not stay standing. Energy pulsed throughout me. The more he laughed, the more alive I felt!

What is happening? This is the most dramatic event since the white cockatoo's frenetic announcement back in December.

I'm curious, so I walk across my creek to ask Mica what the kookaburra's message means. He says the kookaburra is a highly influential bird. I should wait to see what happens around me. That's about all he can offer. But I remember him telling me something about kookaburras, so I locate my journals from 1976 and 1977 in a box upstairs. In 1976, I recorded Mica's exact words:

A Visit from a Kookaburra

The kookaburras are critical members of the community. Many birds take their cue from them, so the moment they accept you, everyone relaxes. When the kookaburras decide you are all right, you are all right. Everybody who lives in the bush knows this.

I am still pondering the meaning of kookaburra's visit when Joc arrives from Adelaide for a few days. He's the most experienced bushman I know. He explains that kookaburras are territorial, dominant, and announcing. All other birds and animals defer to them. Maybe it was just an invitation to friendship?

That doesn't quite do it for me, so, seeking more guidance, I hop into my car and drive to the Research Unit in Darwin to speak with Debbie Bird Rose, an anthropologist. While she's warm and supportive, Debbie hedges her bets. She says that while some people regard kookaburras as announcing a death, these things vary from place to place.

So, I return to Deep Creek, my curiosity piqued, determined to watch and listen.

And what happens next astonishes me. Within three days of the kookaburra's visit, everything changes. *Everything changes.*

It's like living in a different forest.

It's the most curious thing! First, the animals start coming in closer. Hermes, my "alarm clock" crow, now wakes me from the tree closest to my house (not farther away). Pairs of tiny yellow butterflies perform their airborne mating dance *under* the porch roof, not *outside* it. A bowerbird hopped up the

4.2. THE CALL TO ADVENTURE

steps to the top floor when I was meditating yesterday. Even the hesitant agile wallabies nudge closer to my house, though they never stay. I spot them by my shower and drinking from the dishwater bucket behind my house.

Everything is different.

I can't begin to describe how I feel. I've endured four solid months of struggle and isolation since I moved here. And now this. I feel forgiven, accepted, and tolerated by this forest community. Maybe even welcomed.

I believe the kookaburra *is* influential. Here's *my* theory.

When we cut down the White Gum in November, that violence terrified the forest creatures. What they witnessed made them deeply afraid of this violent human. So, they hid from me, or at least kept their distance. How could they ever trust me after that? Then, after months of my behaving myself and living quietly here, they consulted the kookaburra. *Are we safe?* Maybe the kookaburra sounded an "all-clear" message?

Or perhaps he is announcing the change in season—a shift to a less highly charged time. And all of us, me included, respond to these seasonal differences.

For some reason, the seasons are all confused this year in this bioregion. The Dry *Banggerreng* season has not arrived properly. The Wet season (*Gudjewg*) has been extended. Nevertheless, time is inexorably marching on for a person (me) with a plan for one year. And some dramatic seasonal changes are happening inside me.

A Visit from a Kookaburra

The kookaburra's reply to the nervous forest creatures' question ("Can we trust her?") applies directly to my current situation. I sense he's communicating several messages to me:

Can *I* trust?

Can I trust myself?

Can I trust what I am hearing and receiving from Nature that surrounds me here?

Can I trust this new form of learning?

This forest challenges me to engage in a radical education in listening and trusting. Now I notice and reflect on *all* my experiences.

I'm living in a totally different season.

I write about my curiosity about the kookaburra's visit to my American friend Evelyn, a Deep Ecologist. She says about the response of forest beings, "They *did* reconsider, Wendy. You emanated trust and safety, and you all co-adapted. Simple behavioral psychology." Evelyn reminds me that I must continue to be respectful. For Evelyn, that is a message from the kookaburra's proud energy.

I sense that my reaction to the kookaburra's visit is my real lesson. The forest animals are timid, and I don't have much contact with them. (Many are nocturnal, of course, which limits contact.) Those I do encounter look right through me with tiny black eyes. It's unnerving, even if it *is* grounding. I am being seen through. That happens daily. It forces me to be present.

4.2. THE CALL TO ADVENTURE

Since the kookaburra's visit, I'm encountering lessons about kookaburras everywhere I look. Yesterday, I read something that might explain the kookaburra episode. I'm on a heroine's journey. Right? Right. Identifiable stages punctuate a heroine's journey. Right? Right. One list looks like this: *Innocence, Call to Adventure, Initiation, Meeting with Allies, Breakthrough*, and *Celebration*.

The stages of a journey fascinate me. I have passed through the initiation stage and crossed into strange new worlds. But what about *allies*? Allies are supposed to appear when the heroine realizes she cannot complete her journey within a known framework. She senses grace in the presence of allies. So, I am curious: is the kookaburra an ally? Could he be offering strength, help, or advice?

And what does *grace* mean in this context, I wonder? I always understood grace as something God bestows, something unexpected and unimaginable. But now I wonder...

This is my first time living with animals. In my childhood forest in Canada, there were birds and squirrels. That was about it. Nothing like this tropical forest. Thinking about the kookaburra brings to mind a quotation from Gretel Ehrlich. She proposes that living with animals helps us redefine our ideas about intelligence: "Animals hold us to what is present: to who we are at this time, not to who we've been or how our bank accounts describe us."

Anyway, since the kookaburra's visit, everyone is acting differently. And I feel different.

About this time, I read a poem by Mary Oliver called "The Gift." She did a clever thing with a mockingbird. She

A Visit from a Kookaburra

played him some Mahler. Later she heard strains of Mahler in his song. So, I ask myself: what song could I play to the kookaburra? It must be "announcing" music. I select one piece as unpredictable as the kookaburra's announcement: Debussy's "Golliwog's Cakewalk." I've loved this music for decades and forgive Debussy for its unintentional racist origins. It's the right music for my experiment. Just crazy enough, with its ragged rhythm.

My curiosity and feelings about the local animals mirror my changing feelings about this forest. I'm more curious now, and I notice much more: like the long grass turning golden; wild bush grapes growing by my shower, purple and ready to eat; how the creek seems different farther downstream away from the springs that feed it here; several different types of mosquitoes (some are dangerous, I'm told); mud-daubing wasps building a nest on the crossbeams inches from the foot of my bed; and termites nibbling at the door frame (it's not termite-resistant wood). My senses are sharpening. My creek's many songs are invitations to a conversation. Often, I sense its moods, mirroring my own.

My creek's songs seep into my dreams, and I feel *my* songs growing inside me. I am composing a song about—and for—my creek. Funnily enough, it's called "My Creeksong." I made up a tune that I hum every day, and I've written a few lyrics. I never wrote a song before.

Here's the first verse:

Into a forest comes a Wadi
Who dreams and dreams and dreams and dreams
Into a forest comes a Wadi
Who dreams and dreams and dreams and dreams

4.2. THE CALL TO ADVENTURE

Dreams and dreams and dreams and dreams

Walking barefoot every day is my solitary "pilgrim" effort, my brave attempt to move from here to there—to move beyond the confines of my perceptions. There are snakes around, of course. I know I need help, and I need to learn to ask for help. Walking barefoot feels like I'm testing the Earth. I'm worried. If I give it all I have, can it hold my weight?

Increasingly, I sense the Earth as benign and accepting. I am noticing individual features of this landscape. (I feel it's trying to speak to me.) And I don't feel as frightened and self-protective as I did four months ago. Now, at last, I can sit quietly with my *scaredy* feelings. I've always had a desperate, needy, lonely, demanding nature. For as long as I can remember, I've never been satisfied, never felt nourished, always felt empty. This empty feeling is my lifelong companion. And filling that void has preoccupied me for decades.

I've confused and bewildered myself and others by being independent, strident, bossy, manipulative, aggressive, and assertive. I've paid for that toxic combination in shattered relationships, estrangements, and lost opportunities for intimacy. (Sigh.) I still grieve the loss of my first marriage. Two young people who were passionate about everything but our relationship. So much time wasted. And then there's my second husband. An adorable man and a wonderful friend, but we could not sustain a connection. It was my fault for being too "driven" and work-obsessed. Now he's happily remarried with a child on the way... and I'm alone. Again. And then my last lover (not counting Mica). He decided he wanted children just after we really bonded. So, he found a fertile woman, and now *he's* got a child on the way.

A Visit from a Kookaburra

And my relationship with Mica. Well, that's hardly simple. Hardly "satisfying." We've finally settled into a "teacher-and-student" relationship. But it's not exactly "intimate."

Despite all those disappointments, a few weeks ago, I notice that *my feeling of emptiness has gone.* The sad, yearning feeling—my companion, like my second self—has disappeared. My emptiness gone.

I emptied myself somehow. I sense only its echo, a pale shadow of my emptiness.

I had to negotiate with life here, and that helped me find my resilient core. When things are difficult, I feel real. I am here, my life is real, and I have lost something naïve, idealistic, and romantic. And that's okay. *My emptiness has gone.* I thought I glimpsed it recently, but it's disappeared. After four months, I have come to my senses. Now, as I walk through the forest in a state of not knowing, I feel much lighter.

Today, I visited my sacred pandanus tree for a few minutes. I feel drawn to it and feel special there. I can't explain why I feel that that place (and that tree) are so sacred. It's partly that the August 1991 fire that destroyed thousands of trees in its path did not touch that tree. The ring of unburnt grass that surrounds it has a magical, protective quality. But it's more than that. There's a feeling—like an aura—about that tree. It has special powers. But they are so strong. I'm terrified of engaging with them.

And I feel so unworthy. That tree (I imagine it's a "she") might see through me and find me wanting. Find me weak, shallow, insincere, inauthentic…. Find me lacking. Not whole…

4.2. THE CALL TO ADVENTURE

Cyclone Terrors

April 11, 1992

I'm living 12.6 degrees south of the equator in the Thunderstorm Bioregion. And we have thunderstorms right now. *Right here, right now,* we've had a serious cyclone warning for several days: *Severe Tropical Cyclone Neville.* I know I'm living in the heart of cyclone territory, so I'm fully prepared to abandon my house and drive to a safer place. The nearest cyclone shelter is Bartlett Springs School, 15 miles away. Or I could drive south towards Alice Springs.

Although I am from Down South, I know that cyclones are part of life in this country. Every Australian knows that! In 1974, a year before planning for the Deep Creek community began, Cyclone *Tracy* struck Darwin early on Christmas Day, causing one of Australia's worst natural disasters. I can't imagine what it was like to experience 255 mm (10 inches) of rain in 12 hours. Wind gusts reached 217 km/h (135 mph) before destroying the anemometer. *Tracy* went on a rampage, flattening more than 70 percent of Darwin's buildings, including 80 percent of its houses. It killed 71 people (including 22 lost at sea) and seriously injured another 145. The damage bill was 7.2 billion Australian dollars.

Three-quarters of Darwin's population of 100,000 left within a few weeks.

My neighbor, Helen, told me a tragic story. At that time, she was a physiotherapist at the Darwin Hospital. All staff ordered to stay home. But one nurse (a friend of hers) decided she needed to get to work to help in the emergency. She was beheaded by a sheet of flying roofing iron as she stood on her back porch, bracing against the winds before she prepared to race to her car.

So, as you can imagine, the words *Severe Tropical Cyclone* communicate a lot here. I was horrified when a neighbor told me that Deep Creek was the epicenter of *Tracy*. The epicenter! And *Neville* turns out to be the most intense cyclone since *Kathy* in 1984.

But *this* cyclone is not *here* precisely (it's out in the Arafura Sea, near Papua New Guinea). It's close but not dangerously close. The radio warnings say it's a compact cyclone that is intensifying rapidly despite being close to land. But it hasn't landed. Not yet.

The scaredy part is that cyclones often change course and speed unpredictably. (That's what happened with *Tracy*.) I keep my radio on 24/7 to track its progress.

Neville brought a major storm the day before yesterday. The lightning strikes came terrifyingly close, and my creek flooded dramatically, completely cutting off my road access.

4.2. THE CALL TO ADVENTURE

I had to wade across the creek to reach my car. When it's running, my creek flows amazingly fast. And, because the track where my car is parked is only dirt, the overflowing creek could make it impassable. I might need to move the car to higher ground north of my house.

Now, the memory of the builders' mocking suggestion haunts me: "Let's whittle an oar for this girl to go with her house." I pray they were exaggerating.

When it comes to rain, I'm a contradiction. I love the rain and want my creek to run with me sitting in it—surrounded by luminescent weeds, fish, and the water goanna lizards. *And* I'm desperate to be dry and safe, with safe access for my car.

This rain comes in the middle of *Yegge*, which is supposed to be a dry, cold-weather season. My house has no walls, so I can't hide from a cyclone. I have no telephone, so I spend several restless nights listening to cyclone warnings on the radio and reading the cyclone protection, flood warning, preparedness, and safety manuals from cover to cover. I follow the instructions. I pack my car with the recommended evacuation kit. I pack my books and valuables in plastic bags and waterproof bins with tight-fitting lids. I have a container for my computer, printer, and electrical equipment and another for bedding and clothes.

I had my car radio repaired, and a can of gasoline sits near the house. I figure my little car would almost make it to Alice Springs (about 800 miles south) on one tank. I have a map with all the back roads marked if traffic blocks the Stuart Highway in the southbound direction. Depending on the cyclone's direction, I can still head south and east on other roads.

The bottom line is this: If the cyclone comes close, I must get myself out safely without relying on anyone else. All the advice I read says the same thing: "Never become complacent."

Complacent? Me?

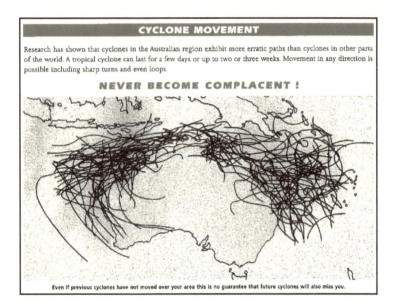

TROPICAL CYCLONE ADVICE NUMBER 8
ISSUED BY THE BUREAU OF METEOROLOGY,
DARWIN AT 11 P.M. CST TUESDAY
7 APRIL

Australian Bureau of Meteorology (1992). *Report on Severe Tropical Cyclone Neville.*

A CYCLONE WARNING IS NOW CURRENT FOR COASTAL AND ISLAND COMMUNITIES BETWEEN DARWIN AND GOULBURN ISLAND.

A CYCLONE WATCH EXTENDS SOUTH TO THE DALY RIVER MOUTH. THE WATCH BETWEEN GOULBURN ISLAND AND MILINGIMBI HAS BEEN CANCELLED.

AT 11 p.m. CST CATEGORY 1 CYCLONE NEVILLE WAS LOCATED ABOUT 40 KILOMETERS NORTH OF CAPE DON. THE CYCLONE HAS ACCELERATED IN THE PAST 6 HOURS AND IS NOW MOVING WEST SOUTHWEST AT 3 KILOMETERS PER HOUR.

GALES TO 80 KILOMETERS PER HOUR WITH GUSTS TO 110 KILOMETERS PER HOUR ARE BEING EXPERIENCED ON THE COBOURG PENINSULA AND EXTENDING OVER THE TIWI ISLANDS OVERNIGHT. GALES ARE EXPECTED TO DEVELOP FURTHER SOUTH TO AFFECT THE DARWIN AREA AROUND SUNRISE, ALTHOUGH THE CENTRE OF THE

CYCLONE AND STRONGER WINDS WILL PASS WELL TO THE NORTH OF DARWIN.

DETAILS OF CYCLONE NEVILLE AT 11 P.M. CST WERE:

LOCATION OF CENTRE: WITHIN 45 KILOMETERS OF 11.0 DEGREES SOUTH 131.7 DEGREES EAST

RECENT MOVEMENT: WEST SOUTHWEST AT 8 KILOMETERS PER HOUR

CURRENT INTENSITY: CATEGORY 1

CENTRAL PRESSURE: 985 HECTOPASCALS AND SLOWLY INTENSIFYING

WIND GUSTS NEAR CENTRE: 110 KILOMETERS PER HOUR

REPEATING—A CYCLONE WARNING IS NOW CURRENT FOR COASTAL AND INLAND COMMUNITIES BETWEEN DARWIN AND GOULBURN ISLAND.

A CYCLONE WATCH EXTENDS SOUTHWARDS TO THE DALY RIVER MOUTH.

THE NEXT ADVICE WILL BE ISSUED AT 2 AM CST WEDNESDAY MORNING.

4.2. THE CALL TO ADVENTURE

In the end, *Neville* slowly weakened, and winds eased below hurricane force. Its damage was mostly to remote coastal communities hundreds of miles from here. But it did cause widespread tree damage along the coast.

The stark reality of the cyclone activated new processes within me. I feel myself opening to a deeper connection with the beauty of this place. I'd already surrendered my simplistic view of *benign* Nature. Not *this* Nature. Terror is an essential part of my process now. It challenges my fragile sense of self and newfound courage, and I feel myself getting stronger as I wrestle with it.

My current fear could be like the terror this tiny forest community experienced after I killed the White Gum. I feel so guilty about that now. I'm also confronting my deep-seated fear of the wild. I'm slowly learning to trust and not to live in terror that I might die because of Nature's great power.

So, a lot is going on for me as this volatile (or temperamental), fickle (or unpredictable), erratic (or mischievous) cyclone circles the Top End of the Northern Territory. Mostly, it's about trust, of course. Again. This time, it's about trusting Nature. (Is there anything in a human life that's *not* about trust?)

3. CROSSING THE THRESHOLD FROM THE ORDINARY WORLD

YEGGE SEASON 1992
ASTONISHMENT AND DELIGHT
May to mid-June 21°-33°C

Yegge, the cold-weather harvest time, has clear blue skies and only occasional showers. Winds from the southeast bring cold, dry air from the southern winter.

Water lilies bloom in white, blue, purple, and pink colors.

Yegge is a good hunting season; bush foods are still abundant, and animals are in good condition. The native flora are yellowing, and their seeds blow across the land. Fishing continues to be good in rivers and waterholes.

The Only Being that Does Not Know Its Place

At the Threshold, the gate to the unconscious, the unknown, once closed, is now open. As it opens, there appears a landscape inhabited by ancestral patterns. And in this interstice between self and other, the gods appear as forms of energy emanating from external and internal landscapes. When we are in this liminal state, we find the place where the worlds connect and flow together, where form and space, figure and ground are one.

Joan Halifax, 1993

Lately, I've been asking, "What am I doing here?"

The best times in the forest are the cool mornings. I sit on the porch in my folding chair with a cup of tea, yogurt, and muesli. I listen to classical music on ABC FM radio. Some mornings I find myself weeping. I always sit facing east, as Juergen advised, to let the inspiration of the morning sun seep into me.

My days feature small chores: morning rituals of greeting the day, meditation, shower, and breakfast and then fixing ropes and mending tarps, watching for signs of a bushfire, reading, writing, driving to the shop or the post office, and cooking. On hot days, I spend a few hours in the local library, where they gave me a desk in a small, air-conditioned office. At night, I stay indoors downstairs to escape the mozzies. I usually read by a kerosene lamp or the tiny light I've strung over my desk. When it's cool, I read tucked up in bed.

Last night, I went to bed early. At 3 am, an unfamiliar sound startled me awake. What was it? The sound swept past my house like wind, from the White Gum Gate at the southwest to the deeper forest to the north. Was I dreaming? Then the sound came again, faintly, from a distance, from the northeast where I sometimes hear wild dogs howling.

It was a horse neighing.

A horse! In the middle of the Australian bush! Such a "domestic" animal in such a wild place.

In this context, it felt as incongruous as a wild boar wandering into the courtyard of my Adelaide townhouse.

A rich community life—wallabies, possums, bandicoots, quolls, fruit bats, even horses—dances below my upstairs nest. They go about their nocturnal business indifferent to the bewildered student in her eyrie.

Five minutes ago, I set down my notebook and stared into the darkness: *I am the only being in this forest that does not know its place.*

4.3 CROSSING THE THRESHOLD

Creeksong

Past, present, and future... flow together like the upstream and downstream of a river, only more organically.... to be alive in the present is to carry the past on into the future... we are constituted in memory and hope, and... where there is no vision, the people perish.

Holmes Rolston, III, 1981

*I*n five months of living here, I've learned only a few things. The forest tries to teach me more, but I am an uncooperative student.

But *creek learning* is something else. My creek teaches me about creative processes: a wild woman's pure flow. Here everyone talks incessantly about the risks of fire and fear of fire. I have an insight: if fire is the *process* of my transformation, surrender to my creek is its *substance*.

After I settle into living in this remnant rainforest, this ephemeral creek nourishes my healing, inspiration, strength, and courage. I discover that my childhood name, *Wadi*, that I chose because I could not pronounce my name, *Wendy*, has a precise meaning in Arabic. It's a dry gully or streambed that fills with water only when it rains. A *wadi* is a consistent, loving, and life-giving spirit. A distant storm can carry its lifeblood deep into the barren desert. Entire communities structure themselves around this path of hidden waters.

I am *Wadi* immersed in a *wadi*. Daily I experience its rejuvenating qualities. So, when the cyclonic rains from *Neville* came again last week, unbidden and unexpected, and its sourcewaters returned my creek to life, I was overjoyed. I feel blessed and forgiven. I am getting a second chance to participate in its life and transformation. I risked everything coming here, being here, and persisting here. And now, this unexpected gift is rewarding me by teaching me the rules of the world I now inhabit.

Here's an extract from my journal:

My creek! It's a miracle.

One day, it's a dry creek, sandy and dead. All the water deserted it. Suddenly, it's a wellspring again. Alive, pure, flowing.

Naked, I slip gently into its coolness from the muddy bank. Tiny fish nibble my hip. Laughing, I spill my morning cup of tea into the rushing stream. A water goanna lizard lumbers by on the bank, ignoring me. The birds are rapturous, celebrating.

4.3 CROSSING THE THRESHOLD

Right here, right now, life is joyous intensity.

To live beside a creek is to experience a microcosm of everything, seen and unseen. It's habitat and drinking place. Wallabies drink at sunset. Their paw prints decorate the soft banks. Frogs launch cadence competitions. Waterweeds astonish me with new iridescence. Where did they come from? Where do they go in Yegge in the Dry Season?

Creek is celebration, exuberance, joy.

Neck-deep in clear water, I dream for hours, *creeksong echoing the songs of my soul. A canopy of carallia, melaleuca, lophostemon, and pandanus trees protects me. Shards of sunlight glance off sharp fronds.*

A fire-blackened pandanus spirals from the sandy bank, bending down to creek, bending to observe me. To embrace me. I hold onto its roots when creek runs fast.

Upstream, a small spring contributes to the creek, its sourcewaters east of my footbridge. It meets muddy water rushing down the firebreak. But by the time it's here, creek is clear again, singing past me. And I, speechless with delight. Need nothing more. Have water, birdsong, and peace. And all around me—and within me—new life bursting forth.

Creek is landmark, boundary, protection, sacred. Creek is our nurturing Mother, our life source. Creek is shelter, food…

It's surrender. When fire rages, I immerse in creek, dig into creekbed, tunnel into creekbank. Deepening, I become creek. I am coterminous with creektime. Creekcells dance in mine, reciprocating.

Creek is our lineage, flowing into future.

Creek is hope.

Many women write about flowing water. Of creeks, Gretel Ehrlich confides: "Running water is so seasonal, it's thought of as a mark on the calendar… rather than a geographical site." In her 1978 book, *Woman and Nature*, Susan Griffin says this:

> *We say look how the water flows from this place and returns as rainfall, everything returns, we say, and one thing follows another, there are limits, we say, on what can be done and everything moves. We are all part of this motion, we say, and the way of the river is sacred, and this grove of trees is sacred, and we ourselves, we tell you, are sacred.*

My tiny creek—barely a mark on my first map of this place—is everything to me now. Its songs saved my life.

It reminds me of my calling. It implores me to sing. To sing *my* brave songs.

4.3 CROSSING THE THRESHOLD

WURRGENG SEASON 1992
BREAKTHROUGH AND PURPOSE
Mid-June to mid-August 17°-32°C

Wurrgeng is a low-humidity, cold-weather time, from June to July. Bush bees make honey from many flowering plants. After creeks cease to flow, floodplains quickly dry out.

Magpie geese and many other waterbirds crowd the shrinking billabongs. The making of bushfires continues for both "burning off" and hunting and will continue to the first rains.

Birds of prey, such as black kites, patrol firelines, as insects and small animals escape the flames.

Retreating from My Retreat

… an ecology of mind and spirit in relation to the earth, an ecology that sees initiation as a way of reconciling self and others, an ecology that confirms the yield of darkness, the fruit of suffering, an ecology of compassion.

Joan Halifax, 1993

June 8, 1992

I'm on retreat!

What a concept!

I'm utterly alone in an isolated part of the tropical bush. And now I need more isolation and solitude.

Yes! I do!

I could hardly wait. I've lived here half of my allotted time. Traveled too much. *Waaay* too many visitors.

It's time to pull back and take stock. I promise myself I'll do all the things I haven't done. Promise! Meditate, walk in my forest, visit my favorite pandanus tree, chant, and read poetry and spiritual books.

My plan is to deepen my experience.

Now, I have a serious, grown-up conversation with myself: "Remember, Wadi, that you are a PhD student, and the Australian Government is paying to keep you here. As a student."

So, I read six books in twelve days, including two beautiful novels. One is Mary Durack's, *Keep Him My Country* (a gift from Mica), and a powerful memoir, *Poppy*, by Drusilla Modjeska, about a woman trying to find out who her mother was. I cried all through it.

I am doing so well. I pat myself on the back. *Good job, Wadi. Excellent retreat skills, girl.* I read scholarly books and articles, clean up around my house, and bake muffins and banana bread. (Australians do both poorly—they skimp on the oil.)

I cook vegetarian soups and stews. I keep reminding myself that not much separates me from the forest, so I'm reluctant to push my luck. Can't get too close yet. Can't say why. Afraid I'll lose myself forever.

Every morning, I sit on a mat on my earth floor and dispatch deep prayers from my essence, first to God and then to the Earth Mother, to guide me.

I pride myself on tolerating silence.

4.3 CROSSING THE THRESHOLD

Things go well at first. The weather is fine. I greet each day as a new beginning. As we agreed, Mica occasionally leaves fresh fruit and vegetables in my car. For the first eight days, I am settled, peaceful, and well prepared. All my gas cylinders are filled, and there is lots of food in my fridge and the cupboard. Increasingly, I feel I belong here and am part of my forest.

A blue-winged kookaburra flies in close and sits on a nearby branch. A statuesque white ibis wanders over, digging for food near the creek.

I can see why relatives of this bird were sacred to the Egyptians. It has an unnerving presence, almost a foreboding quality. These visits make me reflect on the longstanding kinship between humans and other animals. How can I nurture that kinship in alienated urban humans?

I keep saying I'll go for a walk soon, but I don't walk or wander. For reasons I still can't explain, I can't move beyond the frontiers of my fear. I'm grounded. I accept that. I stick to my house and its immediate spaces.

Only once do I visit my sacred pandanus tree: the only unburnt tree in that part of my forest. And even then, I scurry away after a few minutes. It's so powerful there. Something is happening in that place I don't understand. Alone in the forest, I'm terrified of too much experimentation. My life is one big experiment right now. How much more can I take, I wonder?

I know I do not belong here. Not yet. (Maybe never?)

I read and listen to taped music, not the radio, because I am not interested in current affairs. My current affair is *right here, right now.* I need to find ways to be peaceful and learn to live with that.

Retreating from My Retreat

If I hadn't visitors coming next week, I'd change my plans and risk a three-week retreat. Or even longer. I'm so good at this. I'm an adept, though I did have one minor accident, nearly choking on a bay leaf. (That would have been embarrassing: *Died eating!*)

But on the ninth day, things go horribly wrong. Or right, depending on how you look at it.

I awaken with a jolt. **Panic.** My body is shaking, and I'm cold to my bones though it's already hot outside. I'm desperate to run. Right now! Run away!

Run away. *Anywhere.*

I untangle myself from my bed and sleeping net and carefully climb down the ladder to the ground. Find a sarong to wrap around me. Try to be normal. Although I am gasping and shaking, I try not to notice my panic. Instead, I focus on extending simple domestic tasks.

And I'm desperate to run.

I wash the dishes slowly, clean the fridge and all my cupboards, and sweep inside and around the house. Even dust. What a ridiculous concept in a bush shack with a dirt floor!

I change my bed and hang my quilt to air on the clothesline. I shower and slowly, luxuriously wash my hair.

Even though this activity looks normal, deep inside, I'm desperate. Desperate to run away.

But where can I run?

4.3 CROSSING THE THRESHOLD

Not to the local stores, the library, or the post office. That would not be an *escape*. No point in driving to Darwin (35 miles away). I haven't spoken to anyone for nine days, so talking to my Darwin friends would be agony.

And I have nothing to say. I might even have lost my ability to speak.

I could drive to Jabiru, but that would take all day—there and back. And where would I be? In a depressing uranium mining town (the enemy camp), fires burning all along the highway.

I could visit my neighbors, but most are away during the day. I heard Mica drive away earlier in the morning.

I have nowhere to go. I must stay put.

All morning, I battle my frantic urge to run away. By noon, I am breathless and paralyzed. I'm desperate to run and convinced I must stay. I wander across the creek to my car several times, but I can't imagine where to go in it.

I am terrified of venturing outside the Deep Creek boundaries. I even consider tying myself to a house pole to keep from running. I remember that Odysseus tied himself to his ship's mast to resist the Sirens.

This I know: *I must go through the door to myself and find out who I am.* (Whatever that means.)

I have no idea how to do it.

I stomp around until late afternoon, when I settle on a plan. I decide to double down. "Amp it up." I'll exaggerate. Make things big. Make a big statement that I'm staying put and not running.

I'll pull out all the metaphysical stops. (*Again*: whatever that means. Nothing means anything right now.)

I must be meant to learn something here. This desperate urge to run must be a sign. I think nothing is happening. But I'm sure that something *is* happening.

I desperately want to make it happen. Whatever it is.

By sunset, I've settled on a plan. It took all day. I am, after all, a planner.

I'll turn my Spartan downstairs into a New Age spiritual center. I've got what it takes—here inside my tiny shack.

I get to work. Just doing something—anything—helps settle my trembling heart. A bit, at least.

I place a woven mat and cushions on my carefully swept earth floor. I light at least a dozen candles and arrange them in a large circle on the floor. I imagine the circle stands for wholeness, a sacred place, protection, a womb, completion. I place crystals and sacred objects inside the circle.

I rummage through my plastic boxes upstairs and find my shamanic drumming and chanting tapes. I get a drumming one going on the tape player.

4.3 CROSSING THE THRESHOLD

Then I find my sweet sage and cedar and burn them in an abalone shell. I use it to smudge myself, all around my house, making sure to do the screen doors and the windows, as they are spiritual entrances.

My container is cleansed. I can safely sit inside now.

Then I pray. I call upon every imaginable power. I invoke "staying-put" help. I kneel and pray for the courage to allow myself to be changed by this experience. "Spirit, let your love come through."

From my place within the circle, I send a fervent appeal to all surrounding animals and plants, to all beings, everywhere. I chant every chant I know: Celtic, Hindu, Buddhist. *Om mani padme hum* is the last I remember. I turn up the drumming music. Chant louder. The tiny space hums and smoke wafts through the windows into the moonlight. I breathe in the sacred smoke and beg for support from any witnessing beings. *Please help this anguished human have pity on her own heart.*

Darkness falls, but it's strangely silent outside. Usually, the raucous conversations of night birds and other nocturnal critters punctuate the night. Not tonight. Nothing but stillness.

I sit and wait. What else can I do?

I don't know anything more.

I don't know anything.

After about an hour, my desire to flee evaporates.

I'm here. Now.

In its place is a new sensation, like a strong vibration. My chest is widening, and I feel an unfamiliar pain there. Then, my heart bursts, and the sweetest pain begins to throb there. Such a potent and tender feeling. I can't stop my heart from opening. And from my vibrating heart, streams of energy circulate throughout my body.

I've been close to this place before. But never this intense. Not like this.

My fear evaporates. *All* my fear.

I am little more than a vibrating heart when I blow out the candles and climb upstairs.

I sleep soundly for twelve hours.

I wake at eight from a place between the realms. Between one world and the next. Somewhere comforting and inclusive. Beyond my identity.

Strange forces are coursing through my mind and body.

A voice inside whispers: *Softly and subtly, you will understand how to be with yourself. When you come into the light, you will feel delicate and deeply understanding.*

And again: *When you come into the light, you will feel delicate and deeply understanding.*

I try to get out of bed, but I can't. My right arm won't work. It's crippled. I struggle to sit up. My arm has only one comfortable position—raised and pushing away, pushing *against*. If I try any other position, a sharp pain strikes me. My whole right arm aches like I've been exercising for days. I can't even pull my nightgown over my head.

I eventually escape from my mosquito net, stumble downstairs, and make a cup of tea. I can handle the pain if I hold my arm tightly high against my left shoulder. I find a triangular bandage in my first-aid kit and tie my right arm over my left shoulder in a sling.

I am bitterly disappointed. I prayed for healing and received only pain. I dreamed of emerging from this sacred time in a state of embrace with Nature. Instead, I can only hug my crippled arm. I need help now. I've failed "retreat." The prospect of re-entering the world terrifies me. I would stay here forever, but I'm disabled now and cannot care for myself.

I scribble a note with my arm held tightly against my chest. Then I tiptoe quickly through the forest to Helen's house and leave it on her doorstep, careful not to be noticed. Helen was a physiotherapist before she became an artist. She will understand. She knows I am trying to heal my brokenness by living in the forest.

When I return to my place, I pull a chair outside, sit down, and take in the landscape. Did the forest always shimmer like this?

I breathe in its fragrance, always with the hint of fire… and I remember…. This experience is oddly familiar. I do know something about this. My failure to push people away is a core issue. My clairvoyant healer friend, John Henderson, remarked in 1980 that every question I asked in a clairvoyant

Retreating from My Retreat

session was for *other* people. He found that disturbing. Why didn't I focus on *myself*? And why didn't I push away people I did not want to be close to?

I've always struggled with self-care. I'm bad at making myself the priority in my life. In 1982, at the Esalen Institute, with American psychic healer Elizabeth Stratton, I struggle to blow out my anger and mobilize my energy. The following year at Esalen, another healer, Daniel Long, comments that I must "make friends with my body."

Blessedly, Helen materializes silently from my forest just before dinner. By then, I'm shivering and can hardly speak. She mirrors that by whispering.

She's brought a flask of soup, puts on the kettle, and carefully checks for nerve and muscle problems. Each time she touches me, I wince as new grief arises.

"There is nothing 'wrong,' nothing physical, Wendy," she whispers as she helps me into my cardigan. "I am pretty sure your pain is psychogenic in origin."

Then she says, "Maybe later, when the pain subsides a bit, you might try gently opening your arm like a wing. There could be grief then, too."

Helen tenderly touches the sore places and recalls that the same shoulder has been bothering me for weeks. She opens a tin of tuna and a jar of honey, refills the kettle, administers painkillers, and offers a gentle, warm hug. Then she slips quietly back into the shadows.

4.3 CROSSING THE THRESHOLD

After dinner, I wander across the creek. Mica has returned, and Neil is visiting. Neil is a gentle, bearded man of about 30, Mica's longtime friend. We've connected over Darwin's housing issues, and I feel comfortable with him. And Mica knows all about spiritual adventures. So, I will be in safe company.

As I emerge from the forest, Mica calls out: "G'day, mate! Howzit goin'? You back in the land of the living again, girl?" He jumps up, finds a folding chair, and offers a cold beer from his cooler. For once, I accept. I don't much like beer, but this one tastes good. (Maybe it's sensory deprivation? I've had no contact with anybody or anything for 10 days.)

The two men are in a mellow mood, and they welcome me. They must see in my eyes that I need comfort and support. There's the slightest chill in the dry air. *Yegge* season. Mica's campfire flickers, illuminating their faces. A coffee pot rests in its embers. Mica has been strumming his guitar.

Mica is curious about how I "amped up the process" to combat my desperate urge to run. He agrees I had nowhere to go and a trip to Darwin or Jabiru was a ridiculous idea. He leans back and smokes for a while as he digests my description of the candles, chanting, incense, and finally, my bursting heart.

"What do you think your running away was all about, Wendy? Maybe your sore arm is a signal you've had enough of pushing the world away for now," he inquires, leaning so close I see the sun damage on his weathered, tanned face. His piercing blue eyes bore into me.

"Don't know. Just had to run. Desperate to escape from where I was."

Retreating from My Retreat

"Is it possible you were running away from *who* you are?" Mica whispers, turning away and reaching down to pull another can from the cooler.

I lean back and ponder. My whole intent for my retreat was to get closer to myself, deepen my experience of the bush, and feel calm and settled in my new identity as a person living alone there. I wanted to feel comfortable in my own skin.

"And so, you ran away from yourself?"

"But I *didn't* run away, Mica."

I jump up and stomp around.

"I didn't (*stomp*) run (*stomp*) away at all (*stomp*), Mica! I stayed put! *Totally!*"

(*Stomp.*)

"Well," mumbles Mica, looking down and fidgeting with the beer can pull. "I'm not exactly sure that's what really happened, Wendy."

I stare at him.

"But I stayed put. *I did!*"

Mica lets out a deep sigh that's more like a groan of exasperation. He puts down his drink and gives me his fierce, straight-on, Ancient Mariner look.

"I think you ran away, Wendy. Simple as that, girl. Ran away at the exact moment you were about to face yourself.

4.3 CROSSING THE THRESHOLD

You created so much commotion you couldn't hear your own voice. Now all you're left with is an arm that wants to push people and things away."

I stare back in horror. Then I lower my head and focus on the ground. Finally, I return to my chair. Neil hands me another beer. I let out the breath I've been holding in and settle back in the chair. I feel so sad. Like a failure. Such a familiar feeling.

Neil fusses about the campfire, clearly unnerved by our conversation. I blow out my exasperation and exclaim: "Oh, my God, Mica! Oh, no! I had my chance and blew it. I was *so* close. I didn't know what I was close to. And you're right about my arm. Pushing away."

Mica reaches out and gently pats my hand. It's been months since we were lovers, and it touches me. Then he grasps my hand and holds it tightly. He holds me with his eyes and speaks slowly, deliberately.

"Girl, you were working with potent energies when you chose solitude in that forest. That patch of remnant rainforest is filled with magic, partly because it survived that devastating fire last year. Not to mention surviving other fires that ravaged this country for decades before this community was set up.

"I've lived alone in the bush for over 15 years. So, I know the powers you can invoke when you're alone and begging for healing. And you *were* begging for healing, Wendy. *Begging.* And your begging *did* get a response. But to respond to *yourself,* you had to face your fear."

By now, the forest around us has hushed, and the crackling fire is its only sound. I'm staring at Mica. He's grasped his opportunity to reframe my experience. For my benefit. And I can only agree. I do not move my hand.

"You were seeking *union*, Wendy. (Or maybe *reunion*. You *were* whole when you were born, after all.) So, you begged for union. And the moment union was offered, its power was too strong for you. When you couldn't physically run, you found another way to escape.

"Now, we can only guess what might have happened if you'd stayed put. If you made yourself sit there and feel your fear. Feel how strongly you wanted to run away. And how deeply you wanted to stay with yourself.

"I agree with Helen. I think your arm will settle down in a short while.

"Wendy, all is not lost here. Consider the benefits you gained. Your center held. Nothing has been lost. Yes, you were on the edge of a breakthrough. Probably not like falling into the abyss. More like union with the Divine.

"Now, you'll need to wait and see, Wendy. You've been here only six months. And you've been traveling and had lots of visitors and distractions. I bet you'll experience a deepening of your connection with this land in the next few months.

"As for that *real* deepening you're yearning for, girl: we'll just have to wait and see. Let Nature take her course."

I slump back into my chair. This is vintage Mica. What I love about him. And what I fear. Mica is doing his Hermes job tonight. I hate it. *And* I accept that, in showing me the larceny of his friendly love for my foolishness and frailty, he's helping me see the message in my madness.

★★★

That was Friday. It is now Monday, and I've regained some use of my arm. But I have not re-entered the wider world.

And I've had a big think about my retreat. Despite my confidence, it was probably a dangerous idea. Such a journey needs a guide. Mythic stories always caution that an elder should always be standing by. Even Ariadne gave Theseus a ball of string to find his way back when he journeyed to the Underworld.

I decide to be more careful in the future.

And this bizarre experience has yielded one healing result. My right forearm was numb for years. Now I can feel it again. It feels alive, though sore.

But I can't *embrace*. Not at all! I often embraced or was embraced when I didn't want to. Maybe I've healed that tendency at last?

As to my running away, Mica has a point.

Now I must wait and see.

What It Means to Kill a Tree

$\mathcal{I}$killed a giant tree when I first arrived.

I didn't saw it down myself. I paid someone to do that. To kill it.

Now I live with the consequences of that violence. And now, I am learning from this forest. Everything I encounter is about trees. My forest provides instruction and wisdom and teaches me about the extraordinary place trees hold in our collective unconscious. Trees keep us alive and help us maintain our mindfulness. Trees are vital symbols in dreams, with meanings that range from evolution and psychic growth to psychological maturation, sacrifice, and death. The Old English root word for tree and truth is the same: *treow*. I am not here by accident.

The myths of many people warn against ignoring the sacred quality of a tree because trees form a bridge, connecting Earth wisdom and heavenly wisdom. They make the invisible visible, embody sacred qualities, and are sacred through their power as food, shelter, fuel, and medicine. The *World Tree* plays an essential role in shamanic initiation as the opening or channel to other realms. It's a "cosmic axle" that keeps the universe balanced while simultaneously being its center. And the *Sacred Tree*, a symbol of the confluence of the human collective, draws society together by directing its energy toward its powerful center.

Many cultures believe that certain trees' souls or spirits can protect people from evil influences and entities that cause disease, accidents, and death. I read in a paper by anthropologist Deborah Bird Rose that in her studies of the Yarralin people of North Australia, *all* the Dreaming plants people showed her were trees. Some plants acquire their Dreaming status by growing where a Dreaming was active in the past.

So why shouldn't trees be claiming me? I'm living in a tiny clearing in a forest in a house built of 69 living trees. The trees growing near me have releafed, so I can't see a single light from a neighboring house at night. I'm sitting in a forest, listening to the breeze in the treetops and flying foxes and possums rustling through the leaves. And I'm dreaming of trees.

I feel closest to a Tristania tree (whose botanical name is *Lophostemon lactifluus*). It's a close relative of the eucalypts and is also called Swamp Box, Water Gum, Myrtlewood, and Milky Box. One with a sorrowful feeling grows to the east of my porch. It's a spreading tree with three trunks, flaky bark, and large oval-shaped leaves. It blesses me with a cool, dense shade and showers my porch with small, tight cream flowers in *Yegge*, the Dry Season. I sense it's trying to communicate with me.

4.3 CROSSING THE THRESHOLD

Sometimes, I sit facing my house with my back against the old Tristania tree. And I dream there, nestling in before dusk when few insects are about. I lean back, and the tree takes over. I think about how we killed the great White Gum last November. At the time, I tried to be practical about it. The builders insisted it had to go. There was no other place to build the house. And I couldn't have branches falling on my head, could I? But my excuses evaporate when I read that the White Tree symbolizes growth and transcendence, with roots in the ground and branches spreading towards the heavens. Further, our psyche is balanced and whole if the White Tree lives.

Alone in the lamplight, I stare in horror at these words. I killed the White Tree in my pursuit of enlightenment. Did I sacrifice my Self in the process?

What It Means to Kill a Tree

The poet Antler claims, "To learn to die, cut down a tree." I did that. I killed a huge tree.

I notice I've stopped using the word *planet*. It's the *Earth*. Nothing less. The living Earth. Earth with a capital "E" and Nature with a capital "N." But language is only one part of my challenge. Atonement is a much greater challenge. How am I to atone, to reweave the tattered web connecting heaven and Earth?

4.3 CROSSING THE THRESHOLD

Dinner with Jessica

$\mathcal{T}$oday I spend the day preparing for my first dinner party in the bush. It's to be my thank-you to my neighbors, Helen, an artist, and her husband Owen, an engineer. Together, they helped build my house and shower, install all my plumbing, and construct a metal footbridge over the creek. Clare's daughter Lucy (visiting from Berkeley) is also my guest. She's visiting Kakadu, and I will collect her at 8 pm from the Humpty Doo Bush Shop.

I decide to prepare a special Chinese meal. It's an ambitious project in a tiny kitchen with two gas burners and no proper light, but I'm determined to make it memorable. Urban Wendy plans a rural banquet, I think, smiling for once at the jumble of misfit pieces that is my makeup.

It is getting on for 4 pm when I depart to do the last of my shopping. I'll just have time to finish cooking, tidy up, and be ready to receive my guests at seven with a glass of chilled wine.

I bang down the dirt track in my ancient Holden Gemini, laughing at the transformation brought by a year of forest living. I glance down at my filthy, torn, bitten feet, stained t-shirt, and ragged shorts.

As I turn onto the Arnhem Highway, I notice a familiar white pickup in my rearview mirror. I saw it when I crossed the bridge in Deep Creek. As the vehicle speeds past me, I can't see who is in it.

That gets me thinking about weirdness. In the eleven months I've lived here, I've learned to live with the locals: a rough bunch of derelicts, druggies, deviants, activists, and weirdos whose moods and passions are dramatically stirred by seasonal changes. In *Gurrung,* the steamy, hot Build Up "suicide season," people really do go mad. The scenes in the local pub sometimes frighten me. I meet men running from their wives, the tax office, the law, their pasts, and from themselves. One young friend exclaims, "It's a different world.

Nobody would believe Humpty Doo in the Build Up season: bent, deranged, marvelously insane, seedy beyond imagining." A local story captures it perfectly. Two old men had been arguing for years. During *Gurrung,* one finally shot and killed the other, who lived behind the Bush Shop. The police who attended after the murder returned the following day in the paddy wagon and stripped all the mangoes off the murdered man's tree.

My first stop is the pub, just past the Bush Shop, where I park beside several rusted pickup trucks. An angry-looking bulldog is tied up on the back of one, snarling at the "No Dogs

4.3 CROSSING THE THRESHOLD

Allowed" sign. Established in 1971, the pub has a colorful history highlighted by the apparently true story of Norman, the beer-drinking bull, who holds the record for drinking two liters of beer in 44 seconds.

I buy an acceptable bottle of Riesling at the liquor store. Then stop for a drink. The pub is getting busy, with small groups of men from the Ranger uranium mine arriving for the weekend. The outside patio, enclosed by a low wall, is popular in hot weather. It's roughly made with rust-colored concrete brick walls, a concrete floor, and a dozen picnic tables bolted to rusted metal frames. The horse races are running on a wall-mounted television, competing with cicadas' buzzing and the whir of 10 ceiling fans.

Leaning back with his knees up on one bench is a man about my age, wearing grey shorts and a crumpled blue checked shirt. I can see a network of purple veins in his feet. Through heavy glasses, he reads a racing form. A bottle of Crown Lager sits on the table in front of him; he slowly raises another to his lips as though his arm hurt. A dozen pins commemorating Australian tourist destinations decorate the brim of his battered brown felt hat. He reveals a slight limp as he shuffles inside to the bar to borrow a pencil.

I wonder about his life—what circumstances led him here? When—if ever—did he visit all those places? Does he work in the uranium mine? Does he have a decent job and steady pay? Does he have a beloved waiting at home for him? Is that angry dog his only confidante? Is he happy? Does he care about what is happening in the world? Do environmental issues interest him? Worry him? And further, what would it be like to be with a man like that?

Dinner with Jessica

My final question jolts me back to reality. What *am* I thinking? Too long alone in the forest. Months without sex. Horny as hell. I am getting desperate. I yearn for a lover, a man who will love me back.

And I have a dinner to prepare. Back to business.

I finish my Diet Coke, grab the wine, nod to the man, jump into my car, and putter a hundred meters down the highway to the shopping center. Life there is bizarre as always. An altercation about a paycheck slows things down for a while. I buy a few items and dump my shopping into the trunk. I need to make tracks so the ice cream won't melt. Not trusting my tiny gas fridge, I've bought extra ice.

I notice a note under my windscreen wiper. I gingerly step out and remove it. A shaky hand has written, "If you are interested in a massage and some excitement with silk scarves, look behind you." It is signed Jessica. Of course, I turn around.

The same white pickup I'd noticed is parked nose-in behind my car. The driver is leaning out of the window, gesturing. I walk over and peer in. Mirrored sunglasses hide the driver's face, and a floral headband holds a mass of curly, greasy, shoulder-length brown hair back from a pockmarked face. A huge, elaborate silver cross dangles from one ear. Then the person speaks, revealing a toothless grin. He removes his glasses. I recognize his eyes, his tattooed arms. It's Jesse, Sandy's lover, without his teeth, puffing on a big fat number and grinning fiendishly.

4.3 CROSSING THE THRESHOLD

"Wendy, at last, I've found you," he laughs, offering it. He speaks with a toothless lisp. "I've been driving all over Humpty Doo looking for you. I've come to visit you at last," he smirks. "Just couldn't remember how to find your house. Must have been outa it the last time I was at Mica's."

My mind races. Jesse is Sandy's new lover, and she is besotted with him. Sandy is in Indonesia for two weeks, and Jesse is minding her house and her truck. She would not approve of this expedition. But I must consider matters of common courtesy. Jesse has driven 35 miles and will expect a hospitable response.

"I've a bottle of wine ready for us," Jesse leers. He draws a bottle of Lambrusco from between his thighs and raises it for me to see. "And some silk scarves," he continues, his mouth in a wicked smile.

I recall with horror an offhand comment I made to Sandy about being tied up by a former lover whose tastes occasionally ran to bondage. Had I mentioned silk scarves? I shudder, more worried about etiquette than other forms of harm. He might be bent and crazy, but I doubt Jesse is violent. The massage, the bottle of cheap, warm Italian wine, and the silk scarves do not appeal. He is Sandy's lover, and I am a hostess bent on my task. An elegant dinner: authentic Chinese cuisine cooked up in a forest shack by candlelight. I have a critical path to follow.

I turn my head away from Jesse's mocking face and focus on my arrangements and the groceries melting in my car.

Dinner with Jessica

"I've got two of my neighbors and a friend from California coming for dinner in less than an hour, Jesse," I try. "I really don't have time. Maybe another time?"

"What do you mean, there's no time?" Jesse replies. "That's heaps of time, Wendy. Just you and me and mother's little helper." He gestures to a small Ziplock bag on the seat beside him.

"You can't stay for dinner," I implore, leaning against the side of the next car for strength. "Honestly, Jesse, there's not enough food."

That was a big mistake. Jesse pulls himself back from the window. He looks crestfallen, replacing his sunglasses as if to shut out my rejection. I am another insensitive urban impostor, failing the rural hospitality test.

"Wait, Jesse," I stammer, turning back to the truck. "I didn't mean it that way. Follow me. I'll cook, and you can have a drink and talk to me from my porch. But you'll need to leave before they arrive, okay?" He nods, grinning. He doesn't look like he means it. Lechery, my mind registers. Oh, dear. And Sandy, my friend and confidante. And me nearly 50. I thought menopause ended this. A hot flash is creeping up my neck; my breasts are dripping sweat. My mind is jelly, oozing.

Carefully, step by step, I offer directions to my house. "And Jesse, be careful," I caution as I turn toward my car. "You're pretty ripped, you know." Jesse leans back in the driver's seat and howls with laughter. As I walk back across the parking lot, I feel his eyes all over me.

4.3 CROSSING THE THRESHOLD

I anxiously back my car out of the parking space. As I putter toward the exit, I am thinking about the ice cream in the trunk. Then a huge campervan approaches, traveling on the wrong side. It's newly painted and has a homemade quality, although the standard of finish is exceptionally high. The new paint is glossy for Humpty Doo. I stop and wait for the driver to change lanes to pass, but he doesn't. Nervously, I inch past on his left, gesturing that he is on the wrong side. He stares through me the way men around here generally look at women over 30.

I am officially invisible. Tits and ass are *all* they care about, I think, recalling grotesque scenes at the local pub. I wonder what happened to Jesse's body clock. And where will I find the time to be hospitable, keep him at bay, and organize my elegant dinner party?

The sounds of breaking glass and metal striking metal stop me before I can look back to check that Jesse is following. What I see in my rearview mirror is not a pretty sight. Jesse has revved up and backed out at full speed, straight into the white campervan with its shiny new paint job. Its front fender and door are mangled. Pieces of wire, plastic, and glass dangle from the wreckage. But that is nothing compared to the back of Sandy's precious new pickup. Its fender is unrecognizable. The tailgate and lights are badly smashed, bits of orange and red plastic are scattered beside the back tires.

I park quickly and run back to the scene.

Is anyone injured?

After a struggle with his damaged door, the van's driver leaps out, a small, disheveled man in thongs and shorts. From the other side lunges the passenger, who is easily seven feet tall. He is barefoot, wearing paint-splattered shorts and sporting a huge belly. A screaming eagle decorates his left shoulder. The four fingers on his right hand spell out *L-O-V-E* just above the knuckles. Must be an old tattoo. He is purple with rage and very drunk. He's rebuilt the van, all right, from the ground up. Took over two years. Just finished it that afternoon. And then they had been celebrating. He is telling the world about it as he hurls himself toward the truck.

The van's driver is right on the heels of the tall, ugly one, and they both start yelling. Sandy could hear them in Bali. They are screaming about why the fuck hadn't he looked behind him. What the fuck were fuckin' rear fuckin' view mirrors for, anyway? For fuck's sake. The fuckin' years and money that's been wasted on the fuckin' repair job, the stupidity of fuckin' people who don't look where the fuck they are fuckin' going.

"You'll have to pay, you fuckin' little prick," they scream, one after the other, curse building on curse.

Humpty Doo stands still. At six o'clock on Friday evening, everyone is there, leaning against their pickups, sucking on their cans and bottles, and calling their dogs to their sides. People in the laundromat turn in plastic chairs to watch through the window. All the kids in the diner come rushing out. The driver, a smaller bald man of about 40, holds onto the giant's shirt, who continues his yelling as he pounds on the side of Sandy's truck. The small man looks like he's trying to keep him from picking up Sandy's truck and throwing it across the parking lot.

4.3 CROSSING THE THRESHOLD

Meanwhile, Jesse sits quietly in the crumpled truck, staring straight ahead, feigning deafness. Everything seems to be happening in slow motion. As the two men move from Sandy's truck's back end to the door, the tall one bends to look inside. That catapults his ranting into overdrive.

"Look at the crazy prick, Henry," he screams. "He's got fuckin' earrings through his goddamned, fuckin' nipples. Henry, can you see?"

I turn away, unable to control my laughter.

Henry is too short to see this amazing sight, so the giant lifts him. Clearly horrified, he hangs from his friend's arm, his mouth opening and closing like a fish.

"Who are you anyway, you crazy prick?" the big fellow screams at Jesse. He drops the little man and grabs the door as though to yank it off its hinges.

At that point, Jesse must have decided it was safer to exit under his own steam than be thrown across the parking lot by the giant. With what can only be described as an elegant flourish, he opens the door and steps down onto the pavement, facing them. A gasp is heard among the assembled onlookers.

Bare-breasted, except for the gold rings through his nipples, Jesse is wearing a black lace skirt tied at the waist with a long purple silk scarf. From below the skirt's fringe, his hairy legs protrude. A flower closely resembling the lips of a vagina is tattooed on his left ankle. His shoulders are heavily tattooed. The effect reminds me of my father's photo taken at a war-time Christmas party. The barefoot airmen were in drag, with hairy chests, leis, and grass skirts, singing and playing banjos on a tiny stage.

The effect is dazzling.

The sight of Jesse's skirt is too much for the burly passenger. He wheels around in a paroxysm of rage, screaming and panting, his face the color of beetroot, his chest heaving above his enormous belly. "He's wearing a fucking skirt, Henry," he screams, his eyes bulging. He lunges at Jesse, now leaning nonchalantly against the open door.

"Who the fuck are you, you stupid poofter?" the passenger howls. "Henry, the fucker's wearing a skirt! No wonder he can't bloody drive! You arsehole! What are you, crazy or something, you fuckin' poofter?" he screams again.

At that point, I step between them. I am calm; I explain my role as a witness whose evidence can benefit everyone. I offer pen and paper to Jesse. I give the driver my name and address and help them exchange details. Modeling sweet reasonableness, I remind the driver that he *was* driving on the wrong side and that he nearly hit me.

"We were celebrating the rebuilding of the van," he moans, much of the steam gone out of him. He stares forlornly at the damage. We move to settle the matter, and the two men sadly return to their ruined vehicle. The giant still snarls, but he's given up on fighting.

After they drive off and the crowd disperses, Jesse climbs back into the truck.

4.3 CROSSING THE THRESHOLD

"Thanks, Wendy," he says through the open window. "I'm feeling a little under the weather. Maybe I'll just go back to Sandy's after all." He unscrews the top on the Lambrusco. "I'll take a rain check if you don't mind too much, Wendy. You don't mind, do you, Wendy?"

"Of course, it's fine, Jesse." I smile graciously, my hostess smile.

Jesse backs out of the parking lot. As I watch him hurtle down the highway, I beg St. Christopher to protect all other drivers.

Meanwhile, I am bent on getting this bloody dinner together, but as I drive, everything looks different. I laugh all the way home. Nearly miss the Deep Creek turn-off. Then I finish off a couple of cold cans someone left in my fridge. I am laughing so hard, I sit down on the kitchen's earth floor, and can't get up. I don't think I emptied the car. Can't remember. Everything is chaos.

I leave my preparations to collect Lucy, but she is hours late. Twice I drive to the Bush Shop to look for her. That really blows a hole in my critical path. Relishing my story, Owen and Helen finish off the crudités and get heavily into the champagne while I am away. They sit on the porch and howl with laughter.

"That's a Humpty Doo story if ever I heard one, Wendy," Owen grins. "Everything's always a bit upside-down around here."

Thanks to Jessica, I don't remember my elegant dinner, and I've no idea what happened to the ice cream.

Dinner with Jessica

Living with Small Native Animals

Animals hold us to what is present: to who we are at this time, not to who we've been or how our bank accounts describe us. What is obvious to an animal is not the embellishment that fattens our emotional resumes but what's bedrock and current in us: aggression, fear, insecurity, happiness, or equanimity. Because they have the ability to read our involuntary tics and scents, we're transparent to them and thus exposed—we're finally ourselves.

Gretel Ehrlich, 1985

*W*hat will become of me? Will I ever be able to live (a) with anyone else, or (b) in a city again?

I've been taking long soaks in Mica's outdoor bathtub (it's sitting in an open patch of grass south of the *White Gum Gate*). And getting a few massages to nurture myself. The weather is terrific, Mica is peaceful, and today he came over and we talked for hours about termites and trees.

The butterflies are mating on the wing.

I finally worked out how to control Matilda, my resident marsupial mouse. Now I'm sleeping again. Matilda was waking me 10 times a night when she rolled over (I imagined) on (or in) a plastic bag under my bed. She persistently eluded the mousetrap. So now a bandicoot or possum is running around with a mousetrap on his or her tail or paw. I emptied the plastic bags and packed the contents into three large plastic boxes with tight-fitting lids. Now it's quiet under my bed.

Occasionally, I cause a mouse to drown, though I try not to kill anything here—except mosquitoes. This morning, cleaning up outside, I pull the pale corpse of a tiny, grey mouse from the bucket that collects my dishwashing water outside my kitchen window. Yesterday, just in time, I rescued one splashing around. I place a stick inside the bucket so the mice can haul themselves out, using it as a ladder.

The Business of Sustainability

If we weren't living in a state of denial all the time, the whole idea of sustainability would clearly be our first priority.

Starhawk, 1989

I'm going to the Solar Energy Conference in Darwin. I want to be presentable, so I shower, scrub my feet, find a bra and a modest dress that I hang under my outdoor shower to get the wrinkles out. I scrub my waterproof Teva sandals.

It's an easy drive, and I navigate the University's circuitous roads okay. I have many good Darwin maps, and I've visited more campuses than most people have had hot dinners. I find the building and park my beloved Gemimah. I mop my brow (Gemimah has no air-conditioning) and wriggle out of my stained shorts and into my dress (a skill women learn early in life). I have a neat handbag. I glance in the rearview mirror. Hair a bit raggedy but acceptable.

Before I know it, I'm sitting in the back row of a small lecture theater in Building E4.

Now to find out about solar energy and sustainability. And what I can do about it. I'm already doing lots, of course. I live in an eco-village, totally off the grid. I'm deeply proud of my one solar panel connected to a car battery. It runs a highly sustainable 12-volt electrical system. I have several small fans and tiny lights, and my basic system can power my laptop and a portable printer.

And I'm entirely off-the-grid for water, too. My water comes from a community bore powered by a windmill.

Now, what else can I learn to save the Earth?

At the front of the lecture hall stands a nervous-looking youngish man, fiddling with an overhead projector. He's clearly from "Down South" and is wearing a horrible beige thing that's probably his idea of a safari suit. He keeps putting his transparencies on backward as he tests them. But soon, he works it out. That must be Dr. David Miles.

I lean forward in anticipation. Miles is presenting on "Ecologically Sustainable Development." Now I'll find an answer to my question: where has the sustainability conversation been going while I've communed with Nature? I was so concerned when I left the city that people were ducking the deeper aspects of sustainability. Now, this young academic is going to update me.

Or so I think.

4.3 CROSSING THE THRESHOLD

Miles presents his paper on ESD (as they call it now). He can hardly control his enthusiasm and his hands are shaking as he replaces his overhead transparencies. He's what I'd call "aroused." He explains that the whole concept of sustainability is of immense importance to Australia because it involves the biggest piles of money in the country. Jobs and more jobs. He is wringing his hands with glee about the sustainability business—and its apparently endless economic development opportunities.

But not a word about how we should care for Nature or feel responsible for Her.

Not one word.

I gasp. How will I, as a planner, ever reconcile these incompatible worldviews?

After being bombarded for 15 minutes, I plunge into despair. I'm shaking in the back row, unable to speak, almost in tears. My dear friend, Vanda, flew to Rio at her own expense to attend the Earth Summit. The rallying call of Rio was "humanity stands at a defining moment." For the last few years, we've certainly sensed something changing. I thought that maybe Rio might solve all our environmental problems.

Listening to Dr. Miles, I'm not convinced.

The biggest piles of money in the country.

I stop taking notes, zip my notebook into my backpack, and rest my head on my arms on the desk. When I raise my head, I'm confronted by my scratched hands and blackened, broken nails. Yes, I've been doing the real work: digging in the Earth, delving deeply into the ethics of human responsibilities and relationships with (and for) the natural world. Immersed, embedded, my every fiber connected to the creek environment I now inhabit, I'm becoming one with that place.

So, making a "business" out of Nature, turning it into an enterprise or a profit-making entity! The whole idea fills me with horror. I cannot imagine it. And I don't want to face it.

I want no part of it. Ever! They're leaving the ethics out. That's what I'm trying to put in.

Then the tears come. My mother would say that people from the better families never cry in public. So, I lay my head on my arms again and breathe deep sighs of despair.

Later that week, I make another trip to Darwin, this time to my watering hole, the Research Unit. I speak with the librarians, return and collect some books, use the photocopier, do my laundry, and sit in the shady garden under the frangipani tree with a cup of tea to cool myself down. Then I meet with the distinguished Australian statesman and economist, Dr. Nugget Coombs. What a contrast! This gentle, diminutive man, an Australian legend by all accounts, including officially (he's called a *National Treasure*), ushers me into his comfortable office and offers a glass of water. Nugget used to be Governor of the Reserve Bank of Australia. He's 85.

"Please tell me about your research, Wendy. David has been regaling me about your PhD project. It sounds fascinating."

4.3 CROSSING THE THRESHOLD

David, the Director of the Research Unit, is a close friend. Years before, he was my boss in an academic job. I imagine he's told Nugget what I am attempting, living alone in the Deep Creek forest. Nugget relaxes back in his rocking chair and eyes me attentively.

We chat for an hour. Nugget tells me about his new book, *The Return of Scarcity*. He's working on a most urgent project: Aboriginal self-determination. He tells me he's still questioning the dominant assumptions of Australian society and trying to bring fresh insights to discussions of the underlying causes of contemporary problems. He is also a fearless campaigner for Aboriginal and environmental causes. (Years later, I read of his secret 25-year affair with the eminent poet and activist Judith Wright. She fought for the same causes as Nugget did.)

Nugget offers some encouraging suggestions about my research. Do the best I can with the resources I have. Do not aim low, but try to be practical. Because the situation is so urgent (socially, politically, economically, and more importantly, environmentally), all reasonable people must focus on issues of justice related to the environment. I assure him I am on his team.

Later, as I set out for Deep Creek, the sun is setting (blessedly behind me). Before long, I leave the city behind. As Gemimah rattles along the highway, I relax and reflect on how these two men frame our global emergency. Miles, the opportunistic, entrepreneurial young scientist, and Nugget, the elderly Renaissance statesman and activist. What a contrast! For one, sustainability represents a massive leap forward for business as usual, with billions of dollars at

The Business of Sustainability

stake. For the other, every moment counts, and every word and action is critical for the self-determination of Australia's Aboriginal people. We will have no sustainability without them. And they cannot flourish without sustainable solutions. A week apart, I meet representatives of two vastly different worldviews.

I don't know how Thoreau managed when he met Concord townspeople on the road during his daily walks in 1846. It often goes poorly for me when I leave my forest, especially when I encounter the *dark side of sustainability.* I should know better.

So, I'd better get back to work!

Postscript:
Months later, back in the city, my university office mate cautions me against dualistic thinking. Maybe there is a more balanced way of looking at Dr. Miles's enthusiasm. Wise young Aidan says this: "Many scientists, in particular, disguise their genuine ethical care for nature within economic arguments. They judge this to be the more practical way to achieve the goals they are passionate about. This strategy is, of course, dodgy, but their care may be genuine."

I'm blessed to have such intelligent friends.

Family Secrets

Suicide season has arrived! I'm so vulnerable! The slightest thing upsets me. Maybe triggered by the drying up of my creek. I miss the simple joy of listening to the frogs.

I feel so directionless and anxious. So, I decide to have a one-day intensive healing session with Carol Bacci. I've been studying with Carol for several months, learning how to listen to dead people. I've had a lifelong interest in clairvoyance and now I've met my teacher and we've become friends. She's a bit younger than I am, a warm, motherly woman, who was a nurse before she changed direction.

I arrive at Carol's Darwin house by mid-morning. I smile at her old-fashioned tastes in interior design: a knitted tea cozy, crocheted throws over the back of the couch, a glass water jug covered with an embroidered doily with a dozen dangling glass beads. (Things were a bit like that in Lindsay, Ontario.)

Carol greets me with a warm hug. "Good to see you, Wendy. I've a new plan for us today, so I'm glad you have lots of time."

Candles burn everywhere.

In Carol's warm embrace, I relax a little. First, I'll complete a questionnaire about my childhood. That will clear my mind and help me focus.

I take an hour to answer questions about patterns of anger in my family, how my mother managed her anger, how I held in and expressed *my* anger. I answer every question but struggle with the ones about my right to be angry. During my childhood, my parents strongly agreed on one thing: I had no rights. I let out a wail of despair at the question about permitting myself to express feelings in appropriate ways.

By far the most provocative questions are about my feelings about my mother: as a child aged 7 to 8; in middle childhood and my teens, aged 12 to 16; and finally, aged 20 to 30.

About life in my family when I was 7 to 8, I record *horror, shock, disgust, disappointment, anger,* and *sadness.* I scribble this anguished response:

> *My mother is always inside me trying to destroy my life. I feel embarrassed and anxious. Why is she always crying, so passive, and unable to do anything? Why isn't she interested in my school, my life, my friends? I hate it when she humiliates me in public. Furious that she's no good at "normal" mothering, I beg her to be different, pray she'll stop her endless complaining.*

4.3 CROSSING THE THRESHOLD

Remembering my life aged 12 to 16, I list these feelings:

Furious and impatient. Disgusted by her lack of trust in me. Horrified by her sexual flaunting. Disgusted by her lack of care for anyone, and her self-obsession. Terrified she'll ruin my life by not letting me be normal. Embarrassed by her class-consciousness and snobbery. Deeply disapproving that she has no life. Very fearful of her.

Remembering feelings at ages 20 to 30, I declare:

Horrified by her lack of control, her lies and manipulation. Feel sick when I receive her terrible letters about Daddy. Repulsed by her lying. Sad that she can't mother me. Horrified by her inappropriate behavior to everyone. Shocked by her continual lies and manipulation. Terrified I'll end up like her and ruin my life. Know she will never respect my boundaries.

Heavy stuff.

Five more pages to go!

The next section deals with *deservability.* I complain that when I was "insolent" (the word mother used), *cherished things were taken away from me, and they broke my heart.*

When I reach the final section, the paper is soaked with tears. Now I must record my greatest fear and see where it originated. (The questionnaire acknowledges this might be too much for me.)

First, a pitiful cry: *All I want is to be normal.*

My greatest fear: *I will not make a real difference in this world. I fail to use my powers of creativity, wisdom, or influence. I will be forced to live a lesser life.*

My second greatest fear: *I will end my life as I began it: in poverty and insecurity.*

I feel drained but strangely empowered. I've felt my younger self, deep in my body where all my sadness lives. I bury my head in my hands. It's agonizing to connect with so much pain.

Carol observes this painful process, offering tissues and filling my mug with more herbal tea. But nothing escapes her vigilance. She jumps on my terror that I will fail to make a difference in my world.

"Oh, dearest Wendy," she calls out. "Do not let this experience blind you to the reality that's right before your eyes. Firstly, your huge and passionate career and the activism that's always been part of it; secondly, the reasons you chose to do a PhD and live in the forest; and, thirdly, how desperate you are to reform your profession so you *will* make a difference in the world—today's healing is all about those three things that are true for you."

I'm listening now. All that is true. I am broken. *And* I am healing.

"We will listen to Spirit now. We earnestly seek guidance to heal the broken Spirit of young Wadi so adult Wendy can return to her life with a sense of empowerment, authenticity, and grace."

4.3 CROSSING THE THRESHOLD

A quiet lunch marks the transition between the "psychological" morning and the "spiritual" afternoon. Carol's bought my favorite salad from the Parap Markets: spicy green paw paw. I knew it as papaya down South. It's a Thai delicacy that Darwin people covet. We smack our lips and lick our fingers.

I am not broken. I am broken *open*. And in that state, I feel ready to receive gifts and insights from Carol's psychic readings. *And* I am beyond desolate.

From early childhood, I never felt right. Never knew how to walk properly, how to put one foot in front of another. I marveled that I even grew up. My mother tried to keep me "small." Last year I had a chiropractic x-ray of my spine because of this hump at the base of my neck. When I opened the envelope, I had to sit down in shock. There it was—an adult spine. Perfectly fine. Nothing to worry about. Despite my childhood's abuse and insults, I'd grown a normal adult spine. I was astonished.

One question plagues me, begging for an answer. *What is the matter with me?*

That question has tormented me for decades.

Carol smiles as she lights a second red candle on the coffee table. "For courage," she whispers. "Ahhh, Wendy, we've been working together for six months. And I wondered when you'd raise this question. When you phoned me yesterday, I knew it was urgent. So, I've had a lengthy conversation with Michael."

I know about Carol's unique relationship with Michael. I don't have a guide myself, but he's Carol's connection with the world of Spirit. She's been working with Michael for 20 years and relies on him. I've learned to accept and trust both of them.

"So, Wendy, normally, we don't discuss these matters while the other people involved are still living. It can cause all kinds of suffering in families. But Michael decided to make an exception."

I have no idea what she's talking about.

"You must understand, Wendy. Nobody will ever believe what we are about to tell you because it does not come from a 'valid source.' Just be warned about that. In my nurse's training, I learned all about the unreliability of 'recovered memories' of childhood trauma. So, when you tell this to other people, they will think you're crazy."

I sit back on the floral couch and cradle my mug of tea in my hands, feeling its warmth and comfort. (The mug has flowers on it, too.) This feels like the home I never had. And here, where I am safe, I will find the courage to listen to Michael. Later, I can work out whether I discuss it with anybody else.

"Okay, Carol. I understand I'd get into hot water telling a 'clairvoyant' story to straight people. But I'm at my wits' end here. I'm desperate! Officially desperate. Help me, Carol! What the fuck is going on?"

Carol leans back in her armchair and smiles at me with the sweetest eyes. She's in a trance now, but it's the most ordinary thing. She doesn't look different when she's communicating with Spirit or listening to Michael.

Afternoon sun slants into the cozy space. The room breathes.

"Well, Wendy, here it is, plain and simple. Your mother molested you. Everything flows from that. Your father is in Spirit, of course. So, Michael and I consulted him, and he's standing by to help us if needed. He's worried about you for years, but it was almost impossible for him to protect you.

"Your father discovered your mother interfering with you when you were two or three. Once, he found her bathing you in the bathtub, using the handle of her hairbrush to open up your vagina. Another time, also when you were tiny, he found her using kitchen tongs to keep your vagina open while she tried to stimulate your clitoris. She said she was preparing you to be an adult woman. By opening you up. At age two!

"Another time, he found her 'deworming' you, so she called it, with the handle of a plastic spoon. Sometimes, when he'd surprise her, you'd be screaming and fighting her off. Once, he found you laughing. That upset him even more."

Carol stops speaking and peers at me.

How am I managing?

I am not. But there's no point in stopping now. I lean against the back of the couch and Jocksie, Carol's tabby, climbs into my lap, purring. Ahhh, comfort…

"Sorry, but it gets worse, Wendy. Gordon tried to stop her, but he wasn't home enough of the time. First, he was away at the War. And then, he was traveling on business. Your mother was alone with you, and she kept denying what he'd seen with his own eyes. She told him he had a filthy mind that was in the gutter. It made him crazy. He tried to get you to tell him when she did it, but you were too small. He was terrified but couldn't figure out what to do. He decided she was a pedophile, but hardly knew what that word meant. He felt nobody would believe him, anyway.

"It's an awful story. When he told me, he was in heaven and he was weeping."

I steady myself, grip the arms of the couch, feel the crocheted *antimacassar* under my bare arms. The ceiling fan whirs. The lamp on the side table flickers.

I stare at the red candle. My body is wooden. Frozen.

"After your baby brother was stillborn and your mother was so depressed, things got a lot worse. In those days, nobody talked about things like that. Your father caught her again and tried to stop her. They had terrible arguments. She just couldn't control herself.

"Gordon was completely desperate. He was traveling on business for months on end. She'd turned away most of the neighbors, so they didn't have any close friends as a couple. He just couldn't figure out where to turn."

Carol reaches out to touch my hand. I grab hers and hold on tight.

4.3 CROSSING THE THRESHOLD

"So, your father blackmailed your mother. He told her if he caught her again, he'd tell her mother and brothers and sisters back East. He knew your grandmother liked him and banked on your mother knowing that. And one of your uncles was a lawyer she respected. Then he told you to tell him if it ever happened again."

"Why didn't Daddy just stay home and make her stop?"

Carol comes back to me, looks concerned, and scratches her head as if seeking guidance.

"Well, Gordon told me he had to keep traveling for his sanity, Wendy. He said he just couldn't live in that house for more than a few weeks at a time, even though he knew you were in danger. So, when you left to marry, he left for good. He said it broke his heart to stay, and it broke his heart to leave.

"He wanted you to know this, but was afraid to tell you. Afraid you might kill your mother. Or even kill yourself. So, he told me because he thought I might be able to help you because of my training.

"Gordon felt he did his best, but it wasn't good enough. It is heartbreaking, knowing he still has this in his heart, and he's been dead a dozen Earth years."

This explanation doesn't sit very well with me. My father abandoned me. I loved him. *And* I needed him to be a responsible adult. He ran away from our domestic chaos. So I had to function as a parent. I hated that role and rebelled against it. I told my parents they should go to parenting classes and work harder at being parents.

Family Secrets

Sadly, this last revelation only reinforces my earlier opinions.

Both Carol and I are crying now. As she reaches out to hug me, she sobs: "I'm so sorry, Wendy. Honestly, I am. This is so awful."

I am a piece of wood. Somebody else's voice speaks within me. "I guess that explains her hysteria at my first period, right? I was twelve. She went completely crazy and took to her bed, sobbing, 'It's too late,' for *days* on end."

"Yes, she couldn't have you anymore, Wendy. Your first period was a landmark. You were growing up, becoming a woman."

"So, that explains what happened many years later, too."

The horror of that bizarre incident flows back into me, cold, like ice water. About five years ago. I was visiting Mother in Vancouver. We were watching afternoon television, Oprah, maybe. Sitting together on the couch in her tiny, inner-city apartment. Then she abruptly put her hand into my groin. She did not rest it on my thigh in a friendly sort of way. She placed it firmly in my groin. And held it there.

I froze for several minutes until I finally collected my wits and went to the bathroom. When I sat back down, she did it again. Again, I froze. Numb. Motionless. Couldn't speak. Couldn't move her hand. I sat there until I came to my senses and stood up.

"When Mother finally left her apartment, I rang a friend who worked in the sexual health field. 'Write this down,'

I begged her. I was going crazy and wouldn't believe it an hour later. I was so horrified. My friend said the fact I froze indicated I'd been there before. More she could not say. I just felt sick.

"And then, a few years later, she tried to climb into bed with me when we were on holidays together. When I locked the door between our bedrooms, she threw her body against it repeatedly, screaming: 'Let me in! Let me in!'

"I feel horrified, appalled, disgusted, humiliated, raw, and burned. If my mother 'deflowered' me, how come I bled so much on my wedding night, Carol?"

"She must have used narrow objects that did not break your hymen. Maybe that was a mark of her peculiar skill: to make her violence invisible. I remember you told me she was fascinated by female genital mutilation. There she was—mutilating you—but the results of her mutilations were scars that would remain invisible."

★★★

Later, when I can listen, Carol explains about Borderline Personality Disorder. She and mother's psychiatrist agree about the diagnosis. Carol explains the "oral greediness" that characterizes BPD people, how they cannot soothe themselves because they were themselves victims of abuse. The "border," Carol explains, is between good and evil, between loving and rejecting, caring and harming—the fine line between sanity and insanity.

Carol explains that Borderline mothers can fall into despair or have explosive tirades, often without a visible trigger. At other times, they can be loving and supportive. Impulsivity and unpredictability are characteristics that are very hard for a child to manage, she says. While children experience a mother's sudden emotional shifts and obsessive or paranoid behavior, those outside the family may not notice that anything is wrong.

I begin to understand. Mother felt robbed as a child, so she felt entitled to take back what she needed—from her daughter and her husband. That explains her stealing. One terrible memory comes flooding back. Mother visited me at Yale shortly after my wedding and stole a precious photo of my grandmother from my wedding album. I secretly retrieved it from her suitcase, but the experience shocked me deeply.

Carol tells me, "You missed a developmental step during your adolescence and were not adequately prepared for separation and individuation. Your inability to relax and have fun and your chronic illnesses are typical of children of Borderline mothers. The one thing you yearned for—mother love—was the one thing you could not have. You wanted your mother to say, 'I believe in you,' but she could not give you this gift because she never received it herself."

★★★

Later, after lots of tears and hugs, we share a simple dinner. I wrap my shaking hands around the bowl and feel its reassuring warmth. I lift a spoonful of soup, and, as I examine the perfect cubes of carrot and potato, I realize something old and new. This is the next step on my path to freedom.

While Carol's revelations help me understand my brokenness, they are a sad tale to absorb, especially when I'm living alone in a remote place. I take to my bed for a week, lying in my upstairs eyrie, surrounded by pandanus trees, sensing the wisdom of one old lophostemon tree close to my porch. I weep for the childhood I never had. For the pain and suffering of all abused people. I pray for support as I move forward into middle age.

Other people may deny the source of my new insights, but I know Carol's telling the truth. I do have memories, particularly the bathtub ones.

I could turn my back on my wounding. But that's not me. So, I'll do my best to embrace it and move forward. I'm a wounded healer. And will share my gifts the best I can.

Sitting with Carol in 1992, I could not imagine that my mother would live another 21 years. Dying at 100. Unrepentant and raging to the end.

Or that in Vancouver, in late 2020, as I am recovering from a tragedy that nearly claimed my life, my mother would return to me.

Repentant.

Begging my forgiveness with all her heart.

And I will forgive both of us.

Soaring

*F*lying! I'm flying! I turn my head to my right and glimpse black wings and feathers. Me! Wearing black feathers! Soaring on an updraft, then gliding on the softness of the Dry Season air. The horizon knows no end.

Full moonlight reveals the contours of the tropical Deep Creek community. From my vantage point, I spot my creek, silvered by moonbeams. It's much more than an ephemeral watercourse. It's the center line of a vibrant zone separating two different plant communities.

I swoop to take a closer look at the north side. Life here is rich, wet, and dynamic: a swampish place where trees prefer to have wet feet. Carallia, pandanus palms, and paperbark trees bend down to converse with the creek.

I soar again for a view to the *south*. Silhouetted in the moonlight is a vast expanse of hot, dry, open, sclerophyll woodland scattered with skinny gum trees that somehow thrive in the infertile soil. Brilliant yellow flowers glow like ornaments on the high branches of the kapok trees. Not a single ancient cycad fern grows here, *south* of the creek where I park my car.

I descend again to inspect my side, *north* of the creek. There not a single kapok tree blossoms. I peer at the cycad ferns growing up the hill, where the paperbarks, lophostemon, and billygoat plums flourish. None of these trees grows south of the creek.

Ecotone! What an idea! An intermediate space where life has different plans. The essence of transition. Liminal. Marginal.

Physically and spiritually, I am living in a place between domesticity and wildness, between conformity and the original meaning of the word, *radical*: rooted in the natural world. Coasting, spinning, and diving, I am at my Edge. I *am* my Edge: a place of crossing over, vulnerable to change, in-between, separate, sometimes alienated. Different.

My life here is *so* different from my former life on the southern margin of this ancient continent. Traffic, sirens in the night, air pollution, hard-edged cities with hard-edged people. Now I embrace forms of thinking and being my old self could never imagine.

As I soar and change my perspective ever-so-slightly, I discover a new take on *New Wendy*. I observe this vulnerable, confused, middle-aged woman straddling the boundary between inner and outer landscapes. She's deepening her intimacy with a terrain where woman meets Nature, propelled into this tropical hothouse by dreams of healing, intimacy, and peace.

4.3 CROSSING THE THRESHOLD

Swooping again, I settle on a tall pandanus palm and take a closer look at my creek. Flowing gently between its narrow banks of soft, black volcanic earth, it's like a *mandorla*, that almond-shaped segment created when two circles overlap. It's my personal place of poetry and soul growth, where Heaven and Earth intersect and bind together that which was torn apart and is now made whole. Made *holy*. My holy creek.

My bird's-eye view reveals my creek as a source of nourishment for my body. And my soul's growth and awakening. In this magical in-between ecotone, I open myself to a visceral connection with the Earth. Like the connection with the mother I never had. The Mother I yearned for.

My raspy voice calls out: three raucous syllables, *caw, caw, cawww… Mummy, hear me!*

It's morning now. I land back into myself outside my house. Hermes, my reliable 7:30 crow, bounces on a branch where my wind chimes are hanging.

His call mingles with its boogie-woogie blues.

I chime in.

We sing the blues: me, the chimes, and Hermes.

But, curiously, this morning, *his* call sounds different.

Feeling Crazy, Unstuck

I expected challenges during my seasons here, but I didn't expect to deal with all my issues. *And* learn to live in these rough tropical conditions.

This country's dramatic seasonality really takes a toll on my energy.

When I first arrived during the Build Up (*Gunumeleng*) season, it was 38 to 42 degrees C (100.4° to 107.6° F) every day. It was humid. The monsoon rains had not yet arrived. I was crazy, overwhelmed. The oppressive heat and humidity, the mosquitoes, the heavy building work, the strange locals. I never felt so incompetent in all my life.

Adopting the role of the acceptable incompetent might be valuable for the ethnographer. But after months, I ask, How will I manage *with such a fragile sense of self*? Some days I feel so frightened and crazy that I catalog my few competencies. I found an article with a list of qualities I need to survive here: "strong ego boundaries, a firm sense of identity, consistent reality orientation, an openness to inner experience, motivation for growth and change, sufficient psychological resources, a precedent of intense emotional experiences and rapid personality changes, a positive view of traumatic experiences, and courage and fortitude."

I'd put my money on *courage* and *fortitude*.

A person with a weak ego would go crazy here.

My Nest

May 1992

I did everything backward. I built my house, moved in, and then tried to figure out how to live here.

Me! With no camping or bush living skills! In the early days, a branch breaking on the forest floor, footsteps in the crisp leaves, an animal scurrying away—all those things terrified me. I felt so exposed. No place to hide.

When I first arrived, my house was my refuge from the forest because everything was new and frightening. I felt alien, separate, hiding, struggling. I named my house *Independence*. I could find no meaning in the unfamiliar landscape. My hands shook as I untangled my sleeping net and tucked it under the mattress. I gasped at the sound of a snake slithering through dry leaves below. A highly venomous snake lives here: the common brown snake. "You'll be dead in a few minutes," the locals say.

At first, my anxiety verged on terror. I struggled to comprehend what I was doing here. And what my house represented.

Now, six months later, I've settled in and settled down. And the forest has settled down around me. We're friends now, greeting each other through a more transparent space. Time slows, and wind and weather swirl and gently pass through my house.

Brushing against the forest smoothed off my rough edges and my tough armor. My soft body is emerging as I shelter in my Nest.

I stopped calling my house *Independence.* Everything I learn here is about interdependence. I cannot have one without the other. So, this place is, now and forever, My Nest.

4.3 CROSSING THE THRESHOLD

My Nest occupies two places at once. Like me. Part of it—part of me—high in the glossy, spiky pandanus palm trees, is wide open. Upstairs, life sparkles: bright, airy, and connected to sky. Upstairs, on the eastern side, a steep iron roof protects my vulnerable waking state from harsh morning rays. I wake slowly, gently, as morning wanders in, glances about, lights on something, transforms it, softens, and gently balances life around me.

In my eyrie, I have perspective: Propped up, drinking my tea, I peer out on two sides, through the small clearing, into the close-up rainforest and then the open woodland beyond. My enlarged view imagines my courageous future. I will be a crusader protecting the living Earth. I will teach people how to care for Nature. I will make a difference in the second half of my life.

Upstairs, I read and sleep, learn and dream.

Downstairs, the trees are closer; it's cooler, and life feels *deeper* on the earth floor. I cook, read, write, and type at my desk. At night, I sing there, I chant, I drum.

I sit outside on the porch every day until dusk brings the ferocious mosquitoes.

As I embrace the honey-colored blue cypress poles my house is built with, I inhale their earthy fragrance (a bit like licorice, but fruity). My house is enclosing me, breathing with me.

Basking in the unfamiliar delights of solitude, I am discovering who I am, unearthing courage I didn't know I had. I am learning to listen to the rain clattering on the iron roof, splashing on the piece of iron that covers my fireplace, and pattering on the singing, rushing creek. I sit transfixed. All ears.

My Nest, my container of solitude, is like a Russian *nesting* doll. It represents Mother, fertility, and lineage. I imagine myself taking my new insights into the world like my children. I will encourage them forward, empowered by the forest's blessings of creativity.

At night, I sit in a lamplit circle, inside a circle of clearing, within a patch of glossy tropical rainforest, nestled in the wider open eucalypt woodland of the Deep Creek property. Above me is a latticework of woven pandanus fronds. Above that, a sparking night sky.

True, I am still a bewildered woman seeking solace and understanding. And I am resting now. In *Wadi's Rest.*

A gentle voice intones: *Be at ease in your Nest, Wadi. There will be time enough for action.*

4.3 CROSSING THE THRESHOLD

Finding My Purpose

You first must be on the path, before you can turn and walk into the wild.

Gary Snyder, 1990

*N*one of my neighbors held much hope for my success as a pioneer. My house would probably survive a storm, but most people thought I wouldn't. The builders and my neighbors bet on how long I'd last, Mica told me recently. The average was about six weeks.

But I just figure things out. Like a Romani person, I'm always tinkering. Fixing blinds and tarps, caulking holes in the roof, and draping speaker wire everywhere so I'll have another fan by my bedside or blowing on me when I work downstairs at my desk.

I'm much clearer now than I was six months ago. My future must be about working with others to help heal humanity's estrangement from the natural world. I'm no longer bogged down by massive, unanswered questions about my general purpose, goal, or direction. Each day, I read and spend time in solitude. And I allow my mind to wander and consider which path to follow.

What's more, I feel the healing growing inside me. And my creativity is bursting like the spring at the headwaters of my creek. I'm passionate about sharing what I'm learning.

The 7:30 Crow

The insistent cry of the 7:30 crow draws me back to the present. Hermes! That blasted crow! Hermes screeches from the tallest tree north of me before flying to perch on the bent paperbark branch where I tied my wind chimes.

He can't see me from there, and hearing no sounds of activity, he intensifies his morning announcement by jumping on the branch. He rings the chimes in a wild cacophony.

I climb the stairs and walk out onto my porch to confront this messenger. This curious bird. He's a mystery to me. What *is* his message? Is he bringing opportunity? Is he a manifestation of the god of *kairos*? This certainly is a potent time of transformation and new life for me.

I resolve to relish this moment.

It's Sunday morning. The chimes sound like church bells. Announcing… what?

"All right, Hermes," I call back, "I'm up already. Cut it out."

Hermes flies from the chime branch with a loud caw and observes me again from a higher branch.

I open the screen door, head to the kitchen, and put on the kettle.

Hermes returns at 5:30 pm. To announce the end of the working day.

GURRUNG SEASON 1992
OPENING

Mid-August to mid-October 23°-37°C

Gurrung is the hot Build Up season when the temperature and humidity increase. There is increasing cloud cover but little rain.

Days and nights are sweltering. The skies are blue, and creeks and billabongs are drying up. The scent of the blossoms of many plants, including red apples, milky plums and black plums, fills the still air.

In the swamps, Aboriginal people hunt flying foxes.

Remembering Last Year's Bushfire

As scary as it can be in the midst of the forest, as long and as alone as we may be there, it is a psychological landscape that is alive and full of potential. It is a far better place for the soul to be than in the wasteland.

Jean Shinoda Bolen, 1994

August 19, 1992

It's 7:30 pm, just dark. In the fading light, I rake leaves and then take a long, luxurious bush shower.

I turn on the radio and come inside to write. Fierce mozzies keep me from the double pleasure of writing and sitting under the stars.

We're entering a new season, and, for once, it's familiar because I visited here this time last year. We're entering *Late Gurrung*, the hot end of the dry spell. The weather changed dramatically in the previous two weeks. It's getting hotter (up to 35 degrees C or 95 F). It's stickier and warmer during the day and at night as well. It cooled down a bit last night. I packed away my quilt and warm socks—for good. Under the net, it's so stifling that afternoon naps are a thing of the past. Although the Build Up season is familiar, I dread its heat.

I've been home all day, pottering, raking leaves, sweeping the floor, washing undies, and cleaning my fridge. Can't leave home, feel frightened again, still can't wander anywhere. I'd like to go on bushwalks like ordinary people and draw and photograph plants, but I'm stuck here.

I'm a living contradiction. I walk daily, but never into *unfamiliar* territory. At night, I frequently take long barefoot walks south through the *White Gum Gate* and onto the dirt roads. It's a delight for an urban woman—walking alone at night. But I can't walk *into* the bush. An invisible wall—like an electrified fence—curtails me within the ambit of this house and my tiny yard. I allow myself an occasional short excursion to my sacred pandanus tree. But I am at my limit here, my growing edge, and this is as far as my courage permits me to wander.

It's so still here. I hear Robert (about 250 feet to the east) drop a wrench and curse as he tries to get his truck running.

Tiny amethyst flowers sparkle in a jar on my desk. Turkey bush. Such a delicious woodsy, lemony scent.

It's exactly a year since the Big Fire.

I am obsessed with Fire. Can't think of anything else. (Except for my lack of courage.) We're in *Gurrung*, the season of cloudless blue skies when everything is stagnating, dried

4.3 CROSSING THE THRESHOLD

up. The water in the creek is black and oily. Everyone I meet is muttering about fire.

Where will the animals go for shelter? For water?

My relationship with this land began a year ago. And it's deepened. After a nine-month gestation period, insights are flooding my mind. I can barely keep up with the speed of my evolving consciousness. Fortunately, the daily tasks of bush living anchor me.

It's hot. Now I need to wear shoes during the day, crunching through the leaves, telegraphing my movements to the whole forest. The only real shadows are here by the creek—in my cool haven.

This afternoon, during my fire watch, I drive around the community's boundaries, sniff for smoke, and report anything suspicious. The country is baking, parched. There's dust everywhere. The earth is hard like metal on the other side of the creek. The scraggly trees barely stand in the direct sun. Their leaves have fallen or are hanging pale and limp in the heat. I love the language Gretel Ehrlich uses to explain: "Leaves are verbs that conjugate the seasons."

I can't understand why some trees are losing their leaves. Trees are supposed to lose their leaves in autumn. But this *Gurrung* season is like spring, and it's so dry. So different from my early childhood recollections of Ontario—the sweet smell of burning leaves in autumn, especially in Orillia, my grandmother's hometown. I wonder what scents will linger in my memory after I leave this place.

Remembering Last Year's Bushfire

Living in this season at Deep Creek is my trial by fire.

But something as destructive as fire can contain the seeds of new life. Like me. I am a seed in a crucible that needs fire to germinate. The germ of myself is vulnerable, but its rigid, hard shell needs to be broken open. I cannot grow without this catalytic fire, this transformation. What Alan Watts calls my "skin-encapsulated ego" is breaking open in me. My skin is an organic limit. But my symbolic self has no limit. Nine months here opened a channel, and now I am being burst open by the heat of my experience.

Elemental fire features in the stories of all cultures. In this country, many stories by Aboriginal people describe an original owner who lit a fire that spread uncontrollably, causing a huge bushfire. From that time, knowledge of fire became universal. I sense a similarity with my neighbors. For them, bushfire is the ultimate darkness or evil that could destroy their community's dream. They call it "The Fire." They call it evil, though they know that fire has been part of the life of this land forever.

Daily, I confront the threat of fire as I enter a shadow realm. I accept that my shadow is elusive: the dark side of my life and my lack of mindfulness of Nature. Writing helps, so I write as much as possible between bouts of terror and paralysis.

Sometimes I try to draw my relationship with the creek and the "shadow realm," sometimes represented by Mica. But I rarely understand my drawings. And always, I draw that mysterious, sacred pandanus tree that stands north of my house.

4.3 CROSSING THE THRESHOLD

No Boundary

… I have no boundary, the light has extinguished my skin, I am perished in light, light filling you, shining through you, carrying you out, through the roofs of our mouths, the sky, the clouds, bursting, raining, raining free, falling piece by piece, dispersed over this earth, into the soil, deep, deeper into you, into the least hair on the deepest root in this earth, into the green heart flowing…

Susan Griffin, 1978

I was exhausted and terrified when I arrived at Deep Creek many months ago. I felt homeless, estranged, bewildered, and incompetent. Separate from everyone and everything. I could not imagine walking into the surrounding *Green Wall* of the forest.

Now I don't feel separate any longer. A permeable membrane separates me from the forest. At night, the softness of that boundary frightens me. It's so unfamiliar. This whole place and all aspects of this experience are so strange! I was an armored woman living a tense professional life. Often, I'd be the only woman working on planning project after project.

But the forest worked its magic on me, and I've gone all soft. I leak out.

I long to spend the night inside the unburnt circle of leaves surrounding my sacred pandanus tree. But I always turn away at the last moment. Then I'm so disappointed. I'm so eager to stay in that magical place. But I always run away. I feel unworthy.

Nowadays, I live in a state of perpetual fascination. I'm learning to see again—with new eyes. I'm learning that seeing requires attention, intense engrossment, a commitment of time, and the readiness to be surprised. Ken Wilber describes a similar experience: unity consciousness or no-boundary awareness, where the sense of self expands beyond the narrow confines of mind and body.

That prospect terrifies me.

These days, I prefer embodiment to transcendence. At night, I walk barefoot in the starlight, palms open, edging toward my sacred pandanus tree.

I'm feeling anchored and settled.

4.3 CROSSING THE THRESHOLD

GUNUMELENG AND LATE
GUNUMELENG SEASON 1992
LEARNING AND ACCEPTANCE
Mid-October to late December 24°-37°C

In Gunumeleng and late Gunumeleng season, water birds congregate in the large remaining water bodies.

Local people move from the floodplain to shelter from the forthcoming violent storms. The first monsoonal rains begin by about December, but the heat and humidity continue.

Spectacular electrical storms flash across the sky. Several fruits ripen.

Fire Ecology, according to Alan

I interview Alan on Sunday morning. He's in his mid-twenties, a welder who moved to the Deep Creek community from Darwin four years ago. At that time, he had absolutely no interest in ecological matters. He was just buying a cheap house.

He offers a cup of tea and cookies before we go outside to admire the view from his deck.

Alan's been a good neighbor to me. He helped rebuild the poorly designed porch roof and caulked dozens of holes. When I need an agile young man for a tricky job up a ladder, I call on Alan. And he always responds generously.

Of course, being so handy, Alan built his own house, mainly from recycled materials. He's a skilled tradesman. The ingenuity he put into his simple house shows that.

"C'mon, Wendy. I have something to show you," he suddenly announces, putting down his mug.

He hauls on his boots and leads me down the rough track that is our western firebreak. He wants to show me the difference between burnt and unburnt land.

From the boundary, we survey the neighbor's land. It's probably the same size as the Deep Creek property: 320 acres. The owner burns the whole property annually. That's what everyone does here in Humpty Doo. Actually, all over the Top End.

Except at Deep Creek.

"Oh, Wendy," Alan exclaims, gesturing to the west across the firebreak. Hear the passion growing in his voice.

"Let's not talk about *repair. Natural healing* is what we're trying to do. Before I moved here, I didn't have any concept of this. Now it's bloody clear to me, and I don't understand why those fuckers in the Fire Brigade can't see it. Just look at all the different plants growing on *our* land. Look at the understory.

"The other side of the firebreak looks like a bloody wasteland. I'm no fuckin' ecologist, Wendy, and I've never been to university, but I can see it with my own eyes. When I first came here, I thought Mica was a raving maniac. Now he's making a lot of sense, and I'm *totally* convinced. Keep out the bloody fire, I say!"

I stare at him in astonishment. Alan! Who would have thought!

4.3 CROSSING THE THRESHOLD

Then he grabs my hand and leads me as we navigate our way down the steep, rocky firebreak. From there, we have a closer view of the land on both sides: ours and our neighbor's.

Alan points out the small number of plant species on the neighboring land. Then he explains fire ecology principles exactly as Mica does. Ee survey hundreds of acres of burned land across the firebreak from Deep Creek. The difference is as clear as day. Even with *my* urban eyes, I can see it.

"You know, Wendy," Alan continues, kicking at the stony ground with a dusty boot, "the people who started things here were scorned and scoffed at. And they still are. I used to be embarrassed that I lived at Deep Creek. Now they can all get fucked. My attitude has changed completely over the last four years. Because I've grown with the land and because of my neighbors' attitudes."

This conversation really gets me thinking. These pioneers are fire ecology radicals. Since the community's establishment in 1978, the residents (only 25, including children, living on 10 25-acre properties in 1992) and their firmly held position put them at odds with the Fire Service and many ecologists.

Mica is the chief spokesman for this radical position. But *all* the founding members of Deep Creek are diehards.

I read that the calculated use of fire over many millennia altered the whole ecology of Australia, causing low forests to become grasslands. Aboriginal people used fire to drive animals from the long grass when they hunted. They called their fire regime "cleaning up country." They also lit fires to

Fire Ecology, according to Alan

encourage the growth of new shoots to feed kangaroos and other herbivorous animals.

My sojourn here has taught me the enormous difference between early and late-season fires. The destructiveness of fire increases as the season progresses. *Early* fires leave islands of green in a sea of ash and kill only the smallest seedlings and shrubs. They destroy some bird nests but kill few vertebrate animals. Because there is still some soil moisture, perennial grasses send out new shoots.

It's entirely different with *later* fires (from late August to October). Intense winds can fan them into explosive holocausts. Late-season fires consume everything in their path. Flames reach 20 feet and reduce shrubs and seedlings to ashes. They kill many animals and burn all grasses and leaf litter. After a late-season fire, most birds and other animals are homeless and have no food. And the forest will remain apparently lifeless until the first rains, when new grass shoots and some trees put out new leaves. But not everything returns. That's the point.

My Deep Creek neighbors (Mica, in particular) argue that deliberate burning diminishes *all* species (except some herbs). It removes forest litter that shelters and feeds small animals, as well as logs, nesting materials, and nesting sites. And it directly or indirectly removes life and food from the understory. Fire-damaged trees do not produce as much nectar or fruit and cannot support as much birdlife. Late-season fires cause significant loss of soil nutrients and increase the atmosphere's carbon dioxide load. More rainfall runs off burnt soil, silting creeks and causing water loss and erosion.

4.3 CROSSING THE THRESHOLD

Fire exclusion is bloody hard work. Deep Creek residents (mainly middle-class professionals with jobs in Darwin) follow a rigorous regimen of cutting and maintaining fire breaks, rostered daily fire watches, and careful monitoring of the local ecology.

I'm pretty juiced up when I return from Alan's. I find a beer someone left in my fridge, pull my only comfortable chair inside from the porch (the mozzies are so fierce tonight), and prop my feet on my desk chair. There! I am comfortably settled.

Then, I ruminate. Most days, I barely understand what's happening at Deep Creek. I can't say I'm "learning from the forest," but I'm pretty sure I've changed. Maybe I *have* learned *some* lessons. I sip my beer and reflect. In my small way, I'm part of a grand experiment here at Deep Creek.

At this moment, Aunt Hosannah arrives and settles in my throat. Her perfume fills my downstairs space. I hear her gentle, singsong Armenian voice: "Wendy, my dear niece, you *are* doing well. You *are* one of us. You *know* who you are. You know your blood. Your trials are making you strong, Wendy. And the lessons you learn on your journey will bring you joy."

I touch my throat, smile, and bless her. And she disappears.

Sleazed out of Deep Creek

December 17, 1992

I surrender.

They've sleazed me out of Deep Creek. Germ warfare got me.

It's 9:30 pm, and I'm sitting in the Pizza Hut in Darwin. Thirteen months to the day, and I am out. Out!

Out of Deep Creek.

I returned from four weeks in Canberra yesterday afternoon. Barbara gave me a ride from the airport. My car was here. My house is a filthy mess. I stand by my door and scream.

Tim (Mica's son, who was minding my house and will inherit it) is not here. I spend five exhausting hours in this steamy weather cleaning up his mess. It's been raining, and it's incredibly muddy. I ferry his belongings and smelly clothes across the footbridge to Mica's place in my wheelbarrow. It's a muddy, awkward job, and I'm not happy.

After a day of cleaning, I sleep poorly. Something is wrong. I'm sitting inside to escape the mosquitoes the rain brought. Then I hear Tim's motorbike and rush outside. I stand waiting for him.

"G'day, Wendy, Glad to see you're back home," Tim calls from across the creek.

"Where do you think I'd be, Tim?" I shoot back angrily. "I've been stuck here for a full day cleaning up your mess."

"Sorry for the state of your house," he stammers when he reaches my porch.

I nod and gesture to a chair.

"I'd better stand," he replies, looking down at his feet. "I'm pretty contagious, and I don't want to get this on your chair."

I sink into a chair and stare up at him.

"It's like this, and it's a mess. I'm sorry, Wendy."

He looks upset, but that is not unusual for Tim.

"I hope you haven't slept in your bed or touched my clothes," he mumbles.

It is a bit late for that warning.

4.3 CROSSING THE THRESHOLD

"Spit it out, Tim," I snap back. "What the fuck are you talking about? Of course, I've slept in the bed. Where did you expect me to sleep? In the creek?"

"Bloody hell, Wendy," he responds. "I'm sorry. It's scabies. Look at this."

Tim unbuttons his cuff and gingerly rolls up his sleeve. A rash of scabby, running red sores covers a wide area of his wrist and forearm.

"They're also on my legs and elbows, the little buggers." He looks embarrassed.

"Shit, I don't know anything about scabies, Tim. What does this mean?"

Tim explains what the rash is. I am furious and desperate.

"Jesus Christ, Tim. Why did you let me sleep in the bed and touch your clothes? Even a note would have done the job. It's not just scabies; it's that I've been here for more than a day cleaning up your bloody mess. I've slept in the bed and touched all your things, so I've got it, too, you bastard. Now, what am I going to do? I suppose you've used my car, too, and it's all over the seats?"

I'm trembling, and my voice is shaking. Tim stands awkwardly on the porch. Then he nods and hangs his head.

I can see he's genuinely sorry. And upset in a way I've never seen before.

"Look, Wendy, I know you think I'm an irresponsible asshole, and you'd be right about that lots of the time, but this time there really is a reason. It's Boris. He's gone, Wendy. Gone for good."

It's a tragic story. While I was away, Boris, who's hardly more than a puppy, broke into my neighbor Robert's turkey pen. Again. This time, Robert chased after him with a shotgun. The dog ran off into the forest, probably full of gunshot. Nobody has seen or heard him since. Tim searched but could not find him. I hear later that Tim's loud parties at my house were the last straw for Robert. He's deeply pessimistic about managing Tim when he moves into my place. He was also desperate to make a strong statement and take decisive action.

Even if he had found Boris, Tim has no means to help his dog. His car is unroadworthy and unregistered, so he cannot drive any distance. He can't afford a vet. Mica is in Darwin, so he can't help.

"You might as well sit down, Tim," I splutter, tears welling up. "Just sit on that plastic chair, okay? I want to say something. Last night before I knew what happened, I had a vision of Boris loping through the forest in slow motion, like he was floating. The forest was golden, and his coat was shimmering in the sunlight slanting on him. I woke up at 4:30 because it was such a clear vision. When I went back to sleep, I dreamed about him. I'm sure he's gone. I'm really sorry, Tim. He was a beautiful dog. The first dog I ever liked. I'm terribly sorry."

4.3 CROSSING THE THRESHOLD

Before he leaves, Tim explains about scabies: it's highly infectious, and the treatment is toxic. Of course, I can't use standard chemical treatments here because the house is so close to the creek. And I can't disinfect the dirt floor! Basically, I'm fucked! What an ignominious ending to my grand adventure! Creeping away in disgrace, infected, unclean… I feel so disappointed and humiliated.

There is nothing more to say. I have some quick thinking to do, and Tim is the last person to help me. So, I send him away. It's dark by this time, and I have a real problem: *where to sleep?*

What can I do? Can I stay? How could I possibly stay? Where would I sleep? Everything—me included—must be infected. I remove the cushion from my chair and sit down angrily. The metal frame hurts, but not as much as my pride. I've failed. Completely failed! I'm so ashamed. But I can't possibly stay!

I start to rip off my bedding. And I stop, turn to the forest, and ask again: "Can I possibly stay here? Is there any way out of this?"

The forest answers: "No. You face a brick wall. Your time here is up. Leave now, Wendy! Leave!"

I throw the clean bedding I've just removed from its waterproof box into the washing basket. It was sitting in neat piles on the infected bed. Then I gather what I can for a stay somewhere else, find my suitcase upstairs, and pack some essentials into it.

I drive into Darwin, praying they'll have a spare bed at the Research Unit. I don't have anywhere else to go. The manager is away at a Christmas party, so I leave a note on his door, telling him where I'm headed.

I can't believe what's just happened to me. This ignominious event is the end of my Deep Creek adventure. How embarrassing! But I can't go back and I must get rid of the scabies (once I find out how to do that).

I must move on now. Yes! I must move on.

Fortunately, I have a place to move to. Thanks to my portable federal government scholarship, Murdoch University in Perth accepted me as a PhD student. Just last week. The first term doesn't start for a couple of months, so finding a place to live there shouldn't be too hard.

Right now, I'm focused on finding a place to *sleep* tonight. I can't spend the night at Pizza Hut, much as I love pizza!

4.3 CROSSING THE THRESHOLD

Farewell to Deep Creek

I'm living at the Research Unit. Bless them!

I move all my gear and furniture there on Saturday. Linda and Wolfgang help with their flatbed truck. Before they arrive, I say goodbye to my house, drawing hearts in pink chalk on the house poles and inspecting everything closely.

I know my house is alive, like a bandicoot or a skink. I pat and hug the upright poles. I love my house. And I release it.

I will store everything in a carport at the Research Unit while I pack to move to Perth.

Of course, I spend my last moments in my creek. I undress and hang my clothes on the little carallia tree that just finished fruiting. I settle down on the sandy bottom, rearranging a few rocks that somehow crept into my haven. I lie back in the bubbling creek and take in a sky sparkling through a lattice of palm fronds.

I breathe in the creek's song. So sweet, so comforting. Now so familiar.

I sing a few bars of my *Creeksong*: "Into a forest comes a Wadi." The creek sings along, as always. It takes the lead, the melody. I'm happy with the harmony.

Tiny fish nibble my right hip. Shimmering waterweeds and soft sand nurture me.

I stroke a soft lemon-green frond of a pandanus. It's bending low. Offering a final embrace.

All is peaceful except for the frogs. They are just starting up.

And then I hear three crows. They shriek a coarse farewell. They swoop west/southwest and disappear from view.

(Funny. That's where I'm headed.)

4.3 CROSSING THE THRESHOLD

Listening to Tristia

I felt a positive yearning toward one bush this afternoon. There was a match found for me at last. I fell in love with a shrub oak. I love and could embrace the shrub oak with its scanty garment of leaves rising above the snow.

Henry Thoreau

$\mathcal{T}$ristia is the first one I meet at Deep Creek. She is by far the oldest of the community's inhabitants. She lived her whole life in the paperbark swamp north of the creek. She teaches me about the importance of being at home. "You can't learn to be at home on this whole Earth," she admonishes me, "until you know what it is to belong, to be at home in one place."

Tristia is committed to understanding relationships that happen in one place. She stayed put when other Deep Creek residents rambled in search of enlightenment. She has a solid quality, so just listening to her keeps me from falling apart during tough times. Tristia embodies a patient, worn sadness. At first, I sit on my front porch and listen to the sad cooing of the bar-shouldered dove. I never see that dove, but I hear its repetitive call from the southwest, two calls, a pause, and two more. Tristia senses my sadness, too.

I begin listening to Tristia about three months after I arrive. I worry that I don't feel connected to this experience; I feel stressed, overstretched, and worried. I suspect I've exhausted my inner resources. So, I listen carefully, allowing her to direct my learning. And I record this conversation in my journal.

The forest creatures are wondering who you are. You're a bit different from the others. They want to know what you are doing here.

Well, I'm trying to learn a new way of living. Can't quite explain it. I thought that living here close to them would help.

You need more peaceful and joyful times—feeling in touch. Like great sex.

You're trying to tell me that the forest has sex?

Sex? Are you kidding? It's one constant orgasm around here— everyone bursting out—one way or another. What did that English poet you like so much have to say? "Earth's crammed with heaven."

My favorite poet. How did you know? Elizabeth Barrett Browning. I want to be whole. I want to be healed. What do *you* think I can learn here?

Aha. So… not about "ecology," eh?

Well, I'm not going to be much good to "ecology" if I'm not healed, am I?

4.3 CROSSING THE THRESHOLD

Exactly. So, if you want us to teach you about healing, you must get dirtier. Sit in the mud for a while. And listen, just listen. More carefully, more often, regularly, every day. Write down what you hear.

Tristia also teaches me to listen to my body. I don't have one sick day over the next nine months.

Tristia is always available, the way older folk often are. But she doesn't say much directly. We sit quietly in the gathering darkness, and her wisdom seeps into me. I find her speaking when I least expect it. I'll be sitting on my porch before moonrise, craning my neck to take in the stars or glimpsing a wallaby near my shower. And suddenly, Tristia will ask embarrassing questions about what I am doing and why I am doing it.

Everyone at Deep Creek defers to Tristia because of her wisdom and great age. She's lived all her life in my forest, so she's in touch with its moods and quirks. At times, her communication is sparse. She is quiet in the Dry Season in *Wurrgeng* and *Gurrung*. Then, just after the rains begin and well into the Wet, she is fruitful with advice and instruction. I pull up my chair and stare at her, leathery, lined, and weathered, and wonder what she will not tell me. Tristia wears pale cream flowers from late *Gunumeleng* (the Dry Season) until about Christmas.

While other Deep Creek residents play at interpreting the forest, Tristia is more interested in how the parts fit together to create the overall picture. She loves the subject of caring. "You can't come to love the forest by studying its minutiae in isolation," I hear her explain. And then she says: "I've heard that before. I hate the idea that 'it's not real if you can't see it.'"

That's too scientific. It's too detached. Sometimes people try to dissect the Earth, leave it, and rise above it to connect with it. That'll never work. You'll learn much more if you listen. Just sit quietly and listen. There's much more to life than that dissected, separated way of looking at things. Grasping what's happening here takes close attention, with all your senses. You could start by feeling through the soles of your feet.

I'm already walking barefoot, so I try to feel through my feet. They are becoming rough and cracked. Through them, I learn to sense the softness, warmth, and harshness of the many seasons and changes in the Earth's energy. I am learning through the soles of my feet.

"That's soul-work," I hear Tristia say.

By April, when the leaves turn yellow and drop, it's too hot to walk barefoot by midday. But Tristia encourages me to keep sensing and feeling through my feet. It doesn't matter that I don't walk far. She hasn't, she reminds me, her journeying being mainly in inner space.

"Just keep listening and taking it all in. And don't overthink. Try to listen with your third ear," she suggests.

Sometimes we discuss ethics and the subject of forgiveness. I want to explain the clumsy things I did when I first arrived, but I feel ashamed and always manage to change the subject at the last minute. Sometimes ecology is our topic. Mica reckons that careful attention to ecological *literacy* is the way to save the Earth. For him, ecological illiteracy is the main political and practical obstacle to maintaining good land health, locally and globally. Ecologically literate people are easy to spot, says Mica. They demonstrate a good grounding in the fundamentals of ecology, a grasp of language and jargon, an awareness of scientific literature, and the ability to talk about it. He thinks I should learn to read the living landscape as an ecological document displaying its past and future.

Mica's ideas do not impress Tristia. For her, *context* is everything. Sensing the landscape over an extended period makes its secrets accessible. She teaches me to smell the limp dryness of May. To taste the mantle of bark the white gums dropped in October. To hear the trees screaming under the bulldozer on a neighboring block of land. For her, the task of understanding ecology is primarily sensual, not intellectual.

Tristia loves standing beside the paperbarks in the muddy black soil of the swamp. I emulate her in the Wet Season, particularly during *Gudjewg*, squishing black mud between my toes. She guides me to a tiny spring beside my porch, where I collect sweet water for my tea with a piece of hose and a bottle.

Besides my guilty conscience, I'm shy about talking directly with Tristia because of her age and mysterious quality. Also, I still have so much to learn about this community. I arrived thinking I knew how to communicate. Slowly, I begin to learn about my insect and animal neighbors and the birds that congregate by my creek. But Tristia represents a whole new challenge. Like a neophyte devotee, I regard her a little sideways. Sometimes she intimidates me. She thinks verbal communication is obscene.

Tristia explains the ethics behind her teachings and how she expects me to make my contribution to what she calls the *gift economy* by teaching others. Giving without expectation of return is what she means. I quickly catch on. I think I understand how the *gift economy* works because I've been trying to do that all my life. I promise to keep at it.

Tristia knows how to highlight the guilt I can't articulate. By teaching me about trees. She waits until I feel ready to learn, so 10 months pass before my urban eyes notice the differences among the trees. Ten months! I finally discover that I'm living in a paperbark swamp, a creek community, with pandanus, lophostemon, paperbark, and some gum trees I can't identify. Up the hill and to the east, I can still see lophostemon trees, but the paperbarks and pandanus do not live there. The billygoat plums, cycads, acacias, and woollybutts choose the drier spots.

Tristia explains that I live in a pharmacopeia, a craft store, and a vegetable garden all in one. To begin my education, we concentrate on pandanus trees. From my porch, we can see a great profusion of those dramatic, glossy screw palms near and on the creek bank. "You need to learn to understand what's close at hand, the local and the particular," Tristia instructs. "Then you can apply your observation skills elsewhere. Despite its unfriendly exterior, pandanus is decent food. You can eat the tiny ripe seeds from the orange nut and the raw cabbage at the base. And it's good medicine. Aboriginal people use it for treating diarrhea and stomach pains. Some even use the nuts for contraception."

The practical benefits of the pandanus appeal to Tristia's sense of the gift economy.

We speculate why some pandanus palms are straight and others bendy. "Some are growing in a whirling circle of Earth

4.3 CROSSING THE THRESHOLD

energy," Tristia says. Juergen Schmidt, the geomancer, said the same thing. I can sense that strange energy to the west of my house. I never go there.

Tristia also explains that the trees we used to build my house: northern cypress pines (*Callitris intratropica*) are also healers. Noticing resin seeping from the joints in my house structure, she remarks that colonial settlers used the tree's clear resin to coat pills and fill decaying teeth. Tristia also knows about the vital role trees play in humanity's survival. Since the dawn of history, people everywhere revere trees for their life-giving and life-affirming nature.

Sometimes we talk about my relationship with Mica. Tristia has lots to say on that subject. It goes something like this:

Well, Mica had to point you in the right direction, but it turned out that that direction was away from him. You both thought that it was with him, in tandem, but we knew better. He had to get you started on the path, like pushing a rider in a cycle race to give them a good start. But then you were in different lanes. And every time you changed lanes, you collided. We tried to show you so many times by making you sick or tired. But you were very persistent. And he was, too, in his way. Mica does love you, you know.

I say I know. I do know.

When she feels I'm learning to listen better, Tristia often speaks what is on my mind before I say it. The day before I discover my house is infested with scabies, Tristia has already made up her mind.

"Sorry, dear, you must go," is her cryptic instruction.

I'd be lying if I said that Tristia approved of everything I did. Growing to love her only increased my pain, and by far, the worst thing I did was sawing down the huge White Gum that stood to the east of my porch. Now I accept it was an appalling act of violence. I'm horrified that four adult humans agreed to kill that ancient tree that was 50 feet tall. I feel utterly inadequate, and I can do nothing about it now.

I often sit in Tristia's lap, my back against her warm body, facing my house, feeling her supporting me. I close my eyes and feel her energy flow through my hips, warm and strong.

The day I leave for good, I stop and walk slowly back to Tristia, who now seems preoccupied with other matters. Looking down at my scratched, scarred feet, I remark: I made my path by walking. Every day, I made new paths: through

4.3 CROSSING THE THRESHOLD

the cycad forest to my car, to my shower, to my toilet, to Mica's place, and, occasionally, on my courageous days, to visit the sacred pandanus tree. But there, I always edge away.

"I can't leave without talking to you." I face Tristia and stand my ground.

"I've been in such a rush lately. I was terrified about the scabies. Really, Tristia, I've been in an awful state. I didn't dare talk to you. But now, I must. I can't leave here without finishing this once and for all."

Tristia seems impatient, even weary, but I can tell she's listening. My abandoned house has no furniture, so I sit on the porch floor in the fading light while Tristia stands beside the paperbarks.

"Please forgive me for killing the White Gum," I beg. "I pray you might forgive me by now. You might have some compassion for my predicament when the house was being built. My being at the mercy of more knowledgeable local people, and all that."

It sounds so formal. Tristia gives no reply.

I struggle on: "I hoped you might have noticed my good intentions?"

Tristia is unmoved.

"It was murder," I hear her say flatly. "You killed my friend. There's no excuse. That debt is yours and yours alone. She was very dear to me. I was already middle-aged when

Alba arrived. I saw her grow from a tiny seedling. We survived that big cyclone nearly 20 years ago, and all we lost were a few leaves. For a hundred years, we stood together peacefully in this swamp beside the paperbarks. Until you came along. I had such wonderful conversations with Alba.

"You're becoming a good listener, Wendy, and I'm happy about that. And I know you will do good work back in the city. But you can never replace my beloved.

"And that's why the other beings and I decided it was time for you to go. We're all connected, you know. It was easy to get the scabies' cooperation. Everyone always defers to us trees. Even the kookaburras. The scabies agreed that you'd overstayed your welcome."

There is nothing more I can say. I kneel beside her as I'd done so many times. Lean my face to touch her. Feel the roughness of her bark, the strength of her presence, her grief. *My* grief.

After I leave Deep Creek and find a new direction in a new city, Tristia's final words continue to resonate in my heart: *We will protect you, Wendy. Just get on with it. We are waiting to see what you can do.*

4.3 CROSSING THE THRESHOLD

GUDJEWG SEASON 1992-1993
HEALING
December to March 24°-34°C

Gudjewg season is a time of water and nesting, violent thunderstorms, heavy monsoon rain, and flooding. It is the "true" Wet Season. Heat and humidity generate an explosion of plant and animal life.

Waterfalls thunder and creeks flow, breathing new life into the landscape. Magpie geese nest in the wetlands, and their eggs are ready for gathering.

The native grape is fruiting in open forests and woodlands. Widespread flooding may cause goannas, snakes, and rats to seek refuge in the trees.

4. THE RETURN

Consecration: The Kiss of Knowledge / My Creeksong

… the Return is to a place we never left, although we did not know that we were there all along …. [We return to] this life thread that sews together the fabric of our world. Here we can stitch together the robe of society with the stuff of creation and renew the life of our peoples and help them see that culture only blossoms in the field of nature.

Joan Halifax, 1993

Grace simply happens, and although we cannot work for it, we deserve it. If… we are each composed of a small Self and deeper Self, it is our birthright to become familiar with that deeper Self.

Christina Grof, 1993

To bring about a paradigm shift in the culture that will change assumptions and attitudes, a critical number of us have to tell stories of our personal revelations and transformations.

Jean Shinoda Bolen, 1994

4.4. THE RETURN

Consecration:
The Kiss of Knowledge

*… our Mother will speak to us, if we will listen. Her words
have earth clinging to their roots; her statements are grounded
in gigantic truth.*

Max Oelschlaeger, 1991

December 31, 1992

I finished packing and decide to stay in my room at the
Research Unit, even though it's New Year's Eve. A few things
are sitting on the bedside table for my carry-on luggage. Two
sacred objects I can't risk losing. A piece of aromatic northern
cypress pine (*Callitris intratropica*), that broke into two during
my year at Deep Creek. It's from a log that built my house.

And a basket woven from *Pandanus spiralis* fronds by an
Aboriginal woman in Maningrida. To remind me that my
human life is woven into a larger story.

Then I hear a voice.

Something important. You've forgotten something important.

What have I forgotten?

You must go back there before it's too late, a voice deep inside prompts me.

For what you've missed. Something important.

I step onto the balcony and turn to survey the carport below. Earlier today, a young mover packed and stowed the vestiges of my year's forest adventure: gas bottles, camping stoves, tents, nets, scorched and battered pots and pans, bookcases, a bed, gas lamps, tables, chairs, and hundreds of books and papers.

Now they are heading to urban life in Perth. I will follow on the morning plane.

I had a lucky break with scabies. I used all the patent remedies I could find, and they worked.

I wrap a sarong around me, kick off my sandals, and rummage in my suitcase for my flashlight.

The drive to Deep Creek, only 35 miles, is much easier than I expect. It's well past eleven when I arrive. Mica is in Darwin, so the place will be deserted. I drive down the gravel track and pull into my parking spot. Barefoot in the moonlight, I navigate the bridge. It's been raining, and the earth is soft underfoot. The frogs are singing.

My house is deserted, stripped of all my little touches that made it homey. It served me well and protected me so I could learn to relax and listen to the forest's voices. As I sheltered there, I discovered and nourished my courage. Now I feel refreshed and healed and have mostly recovered from the shock of my abrupt departure. My study of environmental ethics went well. I did not waste my time.

I open the door, search the downstairs, come back outside, and climb the stairs. Emptiness greets me. I notice the pink chalk heart on a doorpost: my childhood ritual, my marker of love.

Something important, something important, the voice repeats inside me.

Then, I remember. I pick my way through the underbrush north of my shower. I remember the first time I saw the stars whirling in June: the "starry vortex." I hid from the sky then and struggled to keep its vastness at bay.

Now, I stand before the single pandanus that survived unscathed the Big Fire of August 1991. The tree is a giant: easily nine feet tall. Its crisp, brown skirt brushes the earth. In the moonlight, a crown of spiky fronds casts sharp, black shadows on the forest floor. The flames stopped before this tree. They consumed several small saplings and severely damaged many larger neighboring trees, but, unaccountably, they did not touch this pandanus. A pale circle of dry leaves about six feet in diameter is witness to its mysterious protective powers.

I'm positive this beautiful tree is the local Earth Mother, Gaia's forest representative. I know *she* is sacred. This whole place is sacred. Yet, for more than a year, I could not muster the courage to reach out. Sometimes, terrified, I'd creep through the forest carrying offerings. Occasionally, desperate for solace, I'd burn candles and incense at her feet.

I *know* this tree has knowledge to impart to me, a terrified supplicant, but she never invited me to share in her goodness. Maybe she sensed my weakness and lack of courage.

Now, alone in my forest, I stand in her presence: a barefoot, humble human.

4.4. THE RETURN

In the starlight, the Mother beckons. I stand my ground. She beckons again. Now she is shimmering.

Something important.

I gasp.

I find myself asking, "Am I ready? Is this meant for *me*?"

An order is given for silence. The forest stills. All the creatures are listening, tiny ears and eyes alert. I cannot move.

Again, the Mother summons. I place a hesitant foot on the dry leaves and draw near. Extend a hand to touch her dry skirt, like a child reaching for an apron. Reaching for Mother—every mother I ever dreamed or yearned for. I bend forward, remembering I am, forever, a motherless child. I hang my head.

The forest encircles me. Cycad ferns, pandanus, carallia, melaleuca, and lophostemon trees breathe together, bend forward, witnessing.

I stand still in the forest of my life.

"Look upwards, my child," a voice instructs. "And hold yourself fast."

I raise my head and turn my eyes to a patch of sky. The air pulsates. I breathe through every pore, I sway. The sky begins to spin, sparkling far beyond the circle of witnesses. In this sacred, animated world, the trees breathe, the Mother breathes.

Then I hear her summons.

Planting my feet and drawing a deep breath, I find a strong voice that cries out to my forest, the sky, and the Mother.

"Yes! Yes! Yes!"

A sacred *Yes*, fashioned of swirling stars, binding me to them and the Earth.

The Mother commands my consciousness again. The words sound familiar: *listen, journey, wait, purify, dance.*

Then, from the heavens, it happens.

A bolt of energy spikes through me from the crown of my head to my toes. Strikes something ancient and new into being. Binds Earth and sky through me.

Taut as an arrow in a bow, I stand. Rapture inspires my breathing.

The air crackles like an electrical discharge. And in this divine activity, all duality dissolves.

I stand like a tree: feet in the Earth, arms in the sky.

Then I hear my words: "I am now consecrated." I announce it again. I feel like a cathedral.

The witnessing beings release the softest sigh I ever heard. When I can move, my shoulders relax, and I kneel.

4.4. THE RETURN

I take the fireflower from behind my ear and place it before the Mother. I bow my head and fold my hands before my heart.

Then: nothing more. Silent, witnessing trees breathe, night birds high above resume their chorus, sharply as before.

I steady myself as I rise. Before me, the forest shimmers—a dance of energy.

Everything I waited for, need to remember, is here. Now I understand. Radiant, twice-born, my inner and outer spaces reconciled, I *am* one with everything. The oneness of the sacred whole. I experience unity. I *am* unity.

In this sincere, intimate, and sublime moment, I know that only love matters. I will remember this moment of divine ordinariness forever. I listened to the forest. I revealed my true self to the forest, and it accepted me.

Finally, hear its message.

I have brighter sight and sharper hearing now. Before me, the Mother glows. Crystal filigrees edge every frond.

This must be grace.

I notice everything as if for the first time.

I sigh my last farewell, turn, and tiptoe past my house and across my creek. I remember all the occasions when I tiptoed to this place and felt so unworthy. I risked rejection and my true self. I needed to let go of my need to be perfect. To discover that I am worthy just as I am.

My footsteps on the dry leaves sound so much softer now.

As I pass through the threshold of the White Gum Gate, my breathing softens and my heart settles. I stand in the clearing south of the creek. The whole landscape looks different now. The divine worked through me the whole time I lived here, cleansing me, healing my estrangements, learning new things, finding clarity, and having the courage to let go.

Now the Earth is waiting to see what I can do.

Back in Darwin, I sit on the bed, breathing hard. Intense energy surges from my tailbone, draws fire from my genitals, and pulses toward my heart. I rock as I sense renewed energies nourishing my heart opening. The crown of my head vibrates.

The feeling is of honey flowing deep in the secret places bees guard. Fashioned from the wellspring of the creekbed, the glancing aspects of sunlight on pandanus fronds, tree shadow, and the wash of memory. Overseen by the Mother— the immanent divine, within and around me. Earth energies are surging into my heart.

The room vibrates. The night birds screech. Rich fragrance from the tropical garden swirls through the open window. I breathe it up from my roots. My shoulders broaden, and my chest expands. My arms open like wings. Can I contain more joy? And I hear these words again: *When you come into the light, you will feel delicate and deeply understanding.*

4.4. THE RETURN

I breathe the new word that describes my new direction. *Consecrate:* to dedicate, devote as sacred.

I cross the room, open the screen door, and step onto the veranda. All around the tropical city sleeps beneath a sky of soft, luminous pink. Dawn is moments away; its promise having swept away the stars. I breathe in—breathe with—the frangipani tree, the peaceful garden, my distant, sacred forest.

With my face to the dawn, I open my arms. I embrace the warm day, the New Year.

The new day breathes me. *Yes.*

I must return to a new life of service and share my gifts with others.

My Creeksong

Into a forest comes a Wadi
Who dreams and dreams and dreams and dreams
Into a forest comes a Wadi
Who dreams and dreams and dreams and dreams
Dreams and dreams and dreams and dreams

And when she hears the forest's silence
And when she sees the forest's hum
Very soon, she is enchanted
And then she knows why she has come

And now that eager, seeking Wadi
Finds she's sitting in a creek
Singing all the things she dreamed of
Every hope she'll ever seek
Every hope she'll ever seek

And then, one day, the Mother summons
She calls her back to tell her so
She wants this Wadi in Her service
Because she loves the Mother so

And now the Wadi's in Her service
Learning all she needs to do
To serve the ancient Mother Goddess
And sing Her love for me and you
Sing Her love for me and you

Into a forest comes a Wadi
Who dreams and dreams and dreams and dreams
Into a forest comes a Wadi
Who dreams and dreams and dreams and dreams

4.4. THE RETURN

5. AFTER THE RETURN

Three Afterwords

Afterword 1: Fine Woman, 50

After a lonely, celibate year in the bush, I need a lover. And I'm ready for a new partner. What's a girl to do? I advertise. The "Possibilities" column of the local *Fremantle Gazette* has a 25-word limit.

1	FINE WOMAN	13	FRIEND
2	50,	14	WHO
3	PASSIONATE	15	~~MEN WOMEN~~ LOVES
4	WISE	16	ADVENTURES
5	SPIRITUAL	17	OF
6	AND	18	THE
7	~~WILD~~ BOLD,	19	~~OF~~ SPIRIT,
8		20	ICECREAM,
9	SEEKS	21	PICNICS,
10	MAN	22	THIS
11	AS	23	PLANET
12	INTIMATE	24	AND
		25	MORE

sent in 3/2/93. Well, I wonder what this will bring?!

As I drop my letter into the mailbox on February 3, 1993, I ask, "Well, I wonder what *this* will bring?!"

The answer (delivered by fortune with splendid efficiency) is a spirited man with a wild mind and a vast appreciation of magic. Karl enters my life a few weeks after I return from Deep Creek to urban life.

In my forest, the Earth Mother, Gaia's forest representative, consecrated me in Her service. Imagine my delight when I read Karl's letter about the GAIA concept:

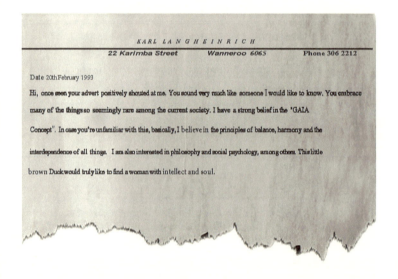

KARL LANGHEINRICH

22 Karimba Street   Wanneroo 6065   Phone 306 2212

Date 20thFebruary 1993

Hi, once seen your advert positively shouted at me. You sound very much like someone I would like to know. You embrace many of the things so seemingly rare among the current society. I have a strong belief in the "GAIA Concept". In case you're unfamiliar with this, basically, I believe in the principles of balance, harmony and the interdependence of all things. I am also interested in philosophy and social psychology, among others. This little brown Duck would truly like to find a woman with intellect and soul.

We fall in love. We study environmental philosophy together. As deep ecologists, we dedicate our lives to loving and protecting Nature. We marry. After we graduate, we work together, greening my planning consulting business. Our radical planning and community engagement work challenges accepted paradigms, wins many awards, and brings remarkable results to communities across Australia.

AFTERWORD 1

We steadfastly dream together, fiercely caring for each other and the living Earth. Together, we build an eco-house in an eco-village. We campaign to protect our neighborhood from coal seam gas mining. We dream and dream and dream. Karl is the love of my life.

Afterword 2:
Farewell to My Mentor

In October 2015, I accompany Mica to the Camp Concern site in Kakadu to celebrate 40 years since its establishment. We drive three hours along the Arnhem Highway through tinder-dry land scorched by burning. The annual rains are late. It's hot, humid, and dusty: the oppressive, humid *Gurrung* season.

Suddenly, we're here. Where my life as an environmental activist began 39 years ago.

Right here!

Waves of emotion assail me as we climb out of the truck and wander together through the bush. After a while, we work out where Mica's house was. And his fire. I smile at one rusted filing cabinet left behind in 1979.

We stumble over rusted roofing iron, find refuges, remember lookouts and vistas, inspect the vegetation at the edge of the billabong, observe flocks of white waterbirds, and listen to their raucous cries…

A termite mound occupies Mica's house site. We laugh together over that.

Gasping for breath, I sense my deep, rooted connection to this barren place. I honor its pivotal role in transforming my environmental consciousness.

Right here!

Sweet memories wash over me. This remote, inhospitable place—and this eccentric man—anchor me in the living Earth. I found my green heart at Camp Concern. It was the birthplace of my environmental activism.

Surrounded by friends, Mica muses about what he sees:

"Forty years ago in this place, we made the decision to stay until the government decided the Ranger uranium deposit would be mined in a national park. Thousands of people in the big cities down south were working on the same issue."

We're celebrating years of activism, but characteristically, Mica's naturalist focus is close-up, close-in:

I'm pretty happy with the vegetation in the water. It's heaps better than last time. This other closer vegetation wasn't here before, and the grass was confined to that other corner of the lagoon. That's because the buffalo have gone. And it's so amazing that all these paperbark trees have grown up on our old archery spot. See how big they've got in 36 years. Paperbarks like wet feet. And the pandanus suggests where there's water, so that could be the high water level where the pandanus are growing.

So, Wendy, do you like the smell of this little purple flower? So spicy and delicious.

Later, we farewell the others and trudge back down the track, dragging our folding chairs. Mica drives for a few minutes along the Arnhem Highway. At the mine gate, he parks and turns off the engine.

Mica is dying. We sit in silence. Then he speaks in a deep, gravelly voice.

"You know, Wadi," he begins, turning to me and grinning. "Remember how much you loved sitting in your little creek. Well, about 10 years ago, in the Wet Season, in *Gunumeleng*, we had a crocodile baby living there. It was about a meter long. It wouldn't have killed you, but it would have given you a fright!"

He reaches over and pats the top of my head with two fingers. We laugh, and it's a great release.

Before us lies the uranium mine. After a glance at the sign, Mica turns to face me. He speaks slowly, as though in a dream. Then, blue eyes twinkling, he steadily holds my gaze and announces:

Maybe what seemed like defeat in 1979 might have been a success, after all, Wendy. We may have actually won

Farewell to My Mentor

this one. Maybe it was not defeat, after all. Open-cut mining here at the Ranger mine ended in late 2012, and the uranium ore is still in the ground at Jabiluka.

I nod.

On the plane the next day, I ask myself: *Did the Earth Mother send Mica to me?* I smile at my response. Of course. She sent this goofy person to press-gang me into Her service.

And what did he teach me, this emissary traveling between realms?

Well, just about everything.

★ ★ ★

Before his death in December 2015, Mica worried about what I'd write in this book. Rightfully, he wanted to preserve his legacy. I do, too. I believe I've honored it. And recent events confirm that. He added these words in three telepathic messages in 2021 and 2022.

Dear Wendy,

I noticed how careful and respectful you have been in your book.... Thank you for taking me, my complicated life and my desperate yearnings, and treating them with respect.... You can relax now about me and the writing. There is nothing to be changed.

I want our loving to be in the book so people can understand what is possible between activists who have different perceptions....

AFTERWORD 2

So, what can I say about this work you've struggled with for 30 years?

First, you have my support and admiration… You are on the right track. Caring for Nature is something that humans must do. And the Earth will benefit from different ways of caring for Nature.

I say this to your readers*:*

The Earth is dying. The situation is much more catastrophic than we ever imagined. Sacred places are in peril. Whole countries and ecosystems are being destroyed. When you fear for your life because of climate change, you are not exaggerating!

Love the Earth as you love yourself, the future of your families, and all Earth communities. Protect the Earth with everything you have. Some people choose political work like the activism that guided my life. Some plant seeds. Some seeds are ideas.…

We stand together as Earth faces its greatest crisis. Any good deed on behalf of the living Earth is valuable. You have my blessings and support.

Mica

Afterword 3: Mothering

At a certain point, because we decide to forgive, Healing occurs in the present, not the past. We are not held back by the love we didn't receive in the past, but by the love we're not extending in the present. Either God has the power to renew our lives, or He doesn't. Could God be looking at any of us and saying, "I'd love to give you a joyful life, but your mother was so terrible, my hands are tied"?

Marianne Williamson, 1992

Hearing My Mother's Voice

North Vancouver, September 9, 2020

I'm 77 and grieving a sudden relationship breakup. I cry out to the Universe:

I am finished now. Just when I thought I was healed. Just when I thought I was strong. I thought I had courage. None! I am dying of grief. Oh, help me, please! I can't bear any more pain.

I am no stranger to loss. Quite the opposite. I befriended and sat with grief for several years. And not that long ago, either. Only three months ago, I finished writing a book on healing grief. I am a widow, the survivor of a car crash that killed my husband. Yet, even now, my feelings terrify me. I have nowhere to turn. I feel like a victim, stranded on grief's shore.

Then I hear a child's voice coming from my mouth: *Mummy, oh, Mummy, Mummy, where are you when I need you, Mummy?*

"Mummy?"

Who said that?

I am shocked. I spoke the word I banned for 65 or more years. There is something so primordial in my reaching out to the human who gave me life. My gut is crying for solace. I feel my life is in peril.

I hang my head and weep, horrified, humiliated, and ashamed.

I've been sitting for several hours on the edge of McGuire Trail, the Logging Road of my childhood. Only a few paces from my childhood home. Weeping and drawing with pastels in a small notebook. I gather myself together, pack up my folding chair and art materials, trudge past the diner on Marine Drive, some stores, and the motel to the bus stop. I catch the bus to my West End apartment. In all, it's a journey of nearly an hour. I am sobbing as I leave the bus. I can't see and must remove my glasses.

Back home, I put the kettle on, light my red candle, wrap a warm shawl around my shivering body, and settle into my armchair. I cover my heart with two hands.

I am breathing deeply. Self-soothing is almost impossible for abused children. I keep at it. I drop down into my physical body.

Suddenly, a woman's voice is calling out in my tiny apartment: *Wadi, Wadi, is that you?*

I gasp.

"What is this? *Who* is this? This is *not* happening!"

My mother's voice.

Mary's voice. Mary is listening. Mary hears my cries. Mary is reaching out.

I hear Mary's voice: *Wadi, Wadi, is that you? I am here, Wadi.*

Only days before, vivid sensations of childhood shaming surface when my lover suddenly rejects me. Now, my brokenness blesses me with new hearing. I cannot ignore this voice. I cannot deny it. Life is asking me to show up.

I struggle to my feet and pace around my living room.

Following my mother's death at 100, I shed not a single tear. That was seven years ago.

I devoted my life to a hundred hues of self-healing and psychotherapy. Counseling, analysis, somatic psychotherapy, bodywork, hands-on healing, reiki… But not *this* healing!

Now, as my broken heart cracks wider still, I begin to hear, understand, and, ultimately, accept my larger story. My cries as a child have reached my mother. Mysteriously, they must have activated Mother Love within her. Maybe the veil rent because I sat weeping for hours next to what was her home for forty years.

Maybe Mary waited until I was so broken before she reached out. Maybe she knew I'd finally hear her call?

I hum a much-loved song from my favorite musical, *Annie Get Your Gun*: "My defenses are down."

She wants to help me.

Me? Helped by my mother? My mother who wished me dead, who constantly humiliated me? Are you kidding? Not possible!

Breathing is a struggle now with so much pain in my heart, hammering inside my chest. I sob, collapsing deeper into my armchair, sensing the sweetest energy surging throughout my body, moving from below my navel.

Could *I* have a mother like other people? A mother for me? My *own* mother?

I whisper the prohibited word, "Mummy." I never use that word. *I* have no mother.

I forbid her from entering my life.

But so much has changed, and my life is changing rapidly now. Now *I* am the returning one, not my mother. I am home where I belong at last. The prodigal daughter returns and is granted a huge gift: hearing the voice of her mother. And I have come home to my feelings.

I am called to action. I get up, find my cell phone, return to my armchair, and speak into it, breathlessly recording what my heart is hearing.

My Mother's Message

Hello, Wadi,

Yes, I am here. But I am not the person you knew as your mother. I am the soul of that wretched person who is connecting to your soul to complete our work, so we don't continue this in our next lives.

Where I am now, I must face the people I hurt, the opportunities I missed, and the chances for joy I turned my back on.

You must be wondering how I can help you. You might have resistance to listening to me. It's okay if we can't make this work.

But now I see a window of opportunity that maybe we can open together.

At this time in your life, you can reflect on your pain, your healing, your legacy, and the many gifts life bestowed on you. You can weave it together into something healing for others, as well as for you. Fortunately, you still have time to heal your relationships with your soul and with those you love.

I can help you look more deeply into your soul and see what parts need healing, because I am responsible for much of your pain.

You used to have a deep wound from not being loved as a child because your needs were not met. You still feel like a needy person. Many of your spiritual activities have helped, but filling that emptiness in your soul is our task now. We can weave any torn parts back together if we can communicate with respect and caring. We can do our mending by having a daily conversation where you tell me what you needed as a child, and I listen to you. We can learn the lessons we were meant to learn together.

I ask only one thing, Wadi. Please try to remember one positive thing about me and write it down. It could be my lovely skin, my beautiful red hair, or that excellent apple pie I baked once a year. It could be the way I tried to help you as you got older by sending money, writing letters, and trying to be optimistic.

Let us start today, Wadi. For my part, I remember how pretty you were. I could not believe I had a blond-haired, blue-eyed daughter when Daddy and I both had brown eyes. You were so pretty, and now I see you are a beautiful older woman.

Daddy is here. He says, "When you use our old family silverware, Wadi, remember you did come from a family that was more than the train wreck you remember. We did love you and we love you now. If you could remember that one thing, the torn place in your soul could begin to weave itself back together."

Recognizing My Mother in Suburban Landscapes

I struggle to steady myself, gripping the arms of my chair. No luck from decades of therapy, healing, and spiritual work. Could not shift my deep pain, my existential suffering. And what about all the grounding, connection, and reverence for Nature I experienced at Deep Creek? No luck then, either. Nothing could heal my estrangement from my mother.

Now I hear a different song: the voice of an adult woman, an evolved presence. She speaks with clarity and without shame. She invites me to rewrite my story and weave new emotions around an ancient, painful relationship.

Then a huge idea hits me like a bullet.

I wrap my arms around myself and rock as I embrace a gigantic realization. I grab one trembling hand to steady it. How did I miss it all these years!

Miss something *so* gigantic?

For five decades, working as a feminist activist and a community planner, repeatedly, persistently, I rededicated my life to creating better suburban environments for lonely, isolated women. Yet I never once acknowledged that my mother was one of those women.

I am blind to this reality. For fifty years!

Mary, my mother, was also a victim of the post-war suburban dream.

Now Mary invites me to consider a larger story of madness, oppression, and dispossession. *Her* story. My mother losing her moorings in a raw Canadian suburb in the 1950s and slipping into madness... My crazy mother, living in my landscape of memory.

And I blame her. I blame the victim.

I saw many things in that "gendered landscape" throughout my career, but failed to see how its "wrongness" contributed to my mother's "wrongness." My feminism and environmental politics deepened my understanding of her predicament. Yet I was closed off to this major insight!

Now, in this moment, a combination of activism, immersion in Nature and, finally, a massive, unexpected grief unravel my tightly woven and persistent hatred.

What is my professional motto, again? *Listen to all the voices.* In a 1985 conference speech about women's housing needs in suburban Sydney, I cry out to my audience:

> *There are enormous resources in Minto, requiring only the catalyst of sensitive and dependable community development intervention. The women of Minto know what they need and what their community needs. Put simply, they need help. And they need it now.*

On that occasion, I'd done a detailed study. But I always knew what I'd find before I began. I recount a tragic story of a lonely woman in the isolated suburb of "Brown Hills" a hundred times over five decades. I even sing about it. I write a story about a woman named Dulcinea (after the heroine in "Man of La Mancha"), her husband, Fred, and their two children, "1.0" and "0.6." Entitled "Planning as Women

Mattered: the Story of Brown Hills," it is published in a Vancouver feminist magazine in 1978.

I'm facing that reality every day. Yet my wounding blinds me and makes me deaf to hearing what Life keeps trying to tell me. I survive by shutting down and shutting out my feelings.

Now, I respond to Mary's invitation. A piteous, desperate poem pours from me. I jump up and grab my journal to record it:

Gone. Away. Now.

Mummy, Mummy!

Where are you, Mummy?
I'm here, Mummy!
Please love me, Mummy!

I'm good, Mummy
I need love—
I need love to live
or I will die

Some part of me is dying.
Some part of me has died
without your love.

Please don't push me away, Mummy
Oh, Mummy, that feels good.
Hold me close. Please.

The scaredy parts will go
away now
The scaredy parts:
Gone. Away. Now.

I speak the poem in a child's voice and that settles my heart. Something new and hopeful is growing here. In the scaredy parts. In the spaciousness created by Mary's invitation and my simple poem, a miracle occurs.

Now, mercifully, I hear *Mary's* voice. And I hear my whispered reply. Mary and I are nudging towards the hesitant beginnings of a conversation.

"Oh Mummy! I hear you. Thank you for saying that I was pretty and am beautiful now."

I recognize your voice, Mummy.
I hear your voice, Mummy.
I recognize you, Mummy.

Mary, I see you. I hear you.

I am having a conversation with my mother at her invitation.

I am standing now. My new eyes see so much better. Outside my window, raindrops sparkle on emerald leaves. The sky shimmers. A pale moon rises in a rainwashed sky, edging the nearby buildings in crystal. I hear better now. A dance of rain plop-plopping on my hummingbird feeder.

Now I hear a voice from that forest: the Earth Mother, who commanded my consciousness nearly three decades ago. Words that changed me forever: *Look upwards, child, and hold yourself fast.* Reconsecrated, I obey the Mother's command. I embrace the sky.

I remember Tristia's warning and voice my new reality: *Now I am at home on this whole Earth.* No longer in exile, no longer rebelling against my childhood landscape and the dark figure who dominated it. My grief is softening and my pain eases. I come to peace. I am a wounded healer. And I am living the life I was born for.

Another realization. I grasp the windowsill.

I *did* have a good mother all along. And I have one now. The Living Earth is my mother. Since my first imaginings, my earliest seconds and hours, my first hesitant days. The Earth reached out to me in visible and invisible ways. Wrapped tendrils of love and care around me, protected, comforted, and sang to me. Taught me to dream. And, finally, brought me home.

The Earth Mother I revered at Deep Creek is my mother. She addressed me as "child." But I could not accept that designation then. Because I was too deeply estranged from maternal energy. I did hear the word "consecrated"—in service. I entered Her service.

Now I have come full circle. To experience the deepest connection, I needed to hear Mary's voice. For that, I waited three more decades.

Finally, I understand. No child of this blessed Earth can *ever* be motherless.

Now I see Mary, my other mother, grounded, glowing, spiraling toward me. She beckons, and I come into the light. No longer trapped in the tiny white house with the green trim, she is everywhere: a glowing sun of spirit enlivening the dark places in the forest.

I welcome my mother into my heart.

Mary reaches out again

Two days later, Mary reaches out to me again. It's late afternoon in early autumn and shadows are deepening in my dense, inner-city neighborhood. It feels like a cocoon. I am growing a different me inside its protection. I quickly grab my phone and record what I hear. I know it's Mary from her turn of phrase. I hear my childhood name, *Wadi*, a name few people know. I sit back down, wrap her blue Shetland wool shawl around my shoulders, prop my feet up on the ottoman. And listen.

Mary is begging to be reunited:

Oh, Wadi,

I am incredibly surprised that you replied. Thank you. I know you hated me, and I understand why. Nobody could have been a worse mother!

From an early age, I knew I was not right. My mother was widowed and so busy with five children. She always treated me differently. She could not understand her daughter who was adrift. Adrift was me: my whole life. I was never good at anything. And I couldn't concentrate because of the voices in my head screaming that I was a failure.

You know what happened when your brother was born. He died, and your cousin Susan was being born to my sister-in-law in the next bed. My brother took my dead baby away. When Daddy came home on compassionate leave, the doctor told him never to talk about our baby. We never discussed Harootune's death, or said a prayer, or held a funeral, or visited a cemetery. Nothing. We never said a single word. We just swallowed our sadness and tried to get on with our lives.

On our car trip to Vancouver, I worried about how I'd manage. I wasn't good at making friends and was no good at being a mother. Daddy planned to get us established in Vancouver and then go away on the road for three months. I had to manage everything myself.

I had never managed anything.

Moving to Vancouver ruined my life. It rained all the time. And for years, we had only dirt roads, our yard was mud, the house was small, and there was nothing around. But everybody else seemed to be living a perfect domestic life. Except me. I was adrift in a sea of mud. I was lonely, I missed my friends, my Ontario family, I missed being part of a social scene there, and feeling like I belonged. I had dreams of going to fancy parties, wearing elegant cocktail dresses, beautiful shoes, lovely jewellery, and being an elegant hostess. Instead, I was stuck in the mud.

The supermarket was miles away, and I couldn't work out how to get groceries delivered. And because we didn't have a clothes dryer, wet sheets and towels were always hanging in the kitchen. It was hardly elegant!

And then I had you and you were supposed to be a picture-perfect princess, standing beside me at fancy dinner parties with a big, admiring family crowded around. Daddy did have a family, but I didn't like them because they were so "Saskatchewan." In Ontario, we would not associate with Prairie people like that. I didn't know how to be with them, and they didn't like me because I was a snob.

And I had the voices in my head.

Mothering

And I was not particularly good in the sex department. I had been hurt. I couldn't remember how. I knew I wasn't right.

It was wartime, and Daddy and I did a crazy thing and got married. I was shy and frightened, and Daddy was also shy and a bit prudish. He was just an ignorant Prairie boy. We didn't have much fun together in the sex department.

So, I wasn't any good in bed, I never learned to cook, and I hated everything about being a parent and keeping house. Of course, we had maids, a seamstress, and gardeners back in Orillia, Ontario.

When I tried to make friends with them, the Norgate women looked at me oddly because I flirted with their husbands. And I didn't like them anyway. People from the better families like ours would not normally associate with people from a suburb on the wrong side of the tracks.

And I never knew where our next money was coming from. Daddy didn't send money very regularly, and the bank manager kept phoning about the mortgage payments. Sometimes we didn't have money for food.

Things were fine before you started treating me the way you did. I called you "radar ears." You saw everything, heard everything, investigated everything, interrogated me, asked me endless questions, and blamed me for everything that was going wrong in your life. You were so bossy, organizing us, telling us what to do, pointing out my weaknesses and how badly I was managing. I was furious at you because you saw right through me. You kept telling me I should bake cookies and go to parenting classes.

I really wanted to hold you, but I didn't know how to do that, either. When I was giving you a bath, I would be overcome with desire that I couldn't understand. It was powerful, and I had a lot of trouble with it. I knew what I was doing was wrong, but I really got a kick out of it because I felt strong and powerful when I was doing those things to you in the bath. Later, in my bed, I would curl up in a ball, feeling so filthy and evil, and knowing that God hated me.

When I reached the point that God hated me, I was a goner. My daughter hated me, I was hurting my child, my husband was never home, I couldn't relate to my neighbors, and I didn't know how to do anything properly. I was a total mess.

When I was crying in my bed and feeling so evil and sick, and depressed and dirty, it never occurred to me to get a job. When your daddy had his heart attack, I did get a job. It wasn't that hard, it didn't kill me, and it certainly put food on the table.

In my lonely life, days, and weeks, and months, and years just floated by. The world changed, fashions changed, politics changed, Elvis and the Beatles came and went, everything changed, and I was just the same. But sadder, angrier, more despairing, lost, and adrift.

Leaving me was the greatest favor Daddy ever did for me. That's the God's truth. Then I had to face my life. I sold the house, got a job, rented an apartment, and had a reasonably good life for a few years until my head went sick again.

But I left a trail of destruction. I knew you hated me. I hated me. I hated every day of my life. I hated my marriage, I hated my daughter, I hated my home, I hated Vancouver, I hated the weather! No wonder you hated me because I hated everybody and everything.

Mothering

In the last few weeks, I noticed a big change in you, Wadi. Now, with your heart broken again, maybe you can understand the enormous heartbreak that was my life. Yes, I brought a lot of it on myself, but I was a wounded bird, and I didn't have any skills or abilities to heal myself.

Now, maybe, I can make a difference. You can call on me now. I can help you remember, heal your memories, and help you write a book that is healing for other people. You have been through a hard time recently. And before that, so much tragedy when you lost your beloved husband. And even though you are an old woman, you are still the tough little shit you always were.

Maybe now you can listen to me and we can share our broken hearts. Maybe something good might come of this, at last.

Can you find a place in your heart for me, Wadi?

There we were all those years ago, up to our ears in pain and suffering. And here we are now. Both of us healed! I always dreamed I could do something good for you. Maybe I could feel proud of me. It feels like a long stretch, but more miraculous things have happened.

I know firsthand that Karl reached you after he died, and together you healed your relationship's broken parts.

Maybe it's my turn now. Maybe we can do something together.

I know you want to stop everyone's pain. Maybe I can help. Maybe we can put an end to all this sadness.

Will you try to do that with me, please, Wadi?

AFTERWORD 3

I'm sitting in a different room. The energy's transformed from highly charged to peaceful. Mary has disappeared. My tiny patch of sky is black now. How quickly it darkens in this season!

I slowly untangle myself and step up to turn on the light behind my armchair. I arch my back, surprised to be breathing. Then I settle back, wrap Mary's shawl around me, and breathe…

Oh, Mary, yes. I want this suffering to end. Today! I'll try my best to do what you ask. Of course, I forgive you. Please forgive me. I'm trying hard to forgive us all.

After my years of shame, a blessing returns my mother to me. She finds me, I find her, and we find a way to reconcile. I come home from the heartbreak of exile. After all my escapes, exiles, trials, adventures and misadventures, I accept the gift of grace the Earth Mother promised so many years ago. Now, I see my mother's life and my life in a different light.

Before this moment, I could never imagine *my* voice speaking such words. Now I hear it, strong, warm, and authoritative, like a loving adult speaking to a child.

Oh, Wadi. I love you with all my heart. You are so brave, so strong, and so beautiful. I'm so proud of you. You are safe with me now. I waited all these years to take care of you, and now I will.

And now, my climate activism is calling. Time to stand up and speak out.

I must get on with it.

In the forest, they are waiting to see what I can do.

Appreciations

This book has had a long gestation and many midwives. As the central, auto-ethnographic chapter in my PhD dissertation in environmental ethics at Australia's Murdoch University (1996), its genesis was nurtured by two brilliant and caring academics, Professor Peter Newman AO and Dr. Patsy Hallen of the Institute for Sustainability and Technology Policy (ISTP). I bow in gratitude for their many hours' work, gentle direction, sensitive tutoring, and skilled advice. Both modeled an ethic of caring in the most profound sense and guided me away from foolish errors.

Patsy, in particular, *encouraged* my foolishness, echoing words I later heard in 1994 from Jungian analyst, Jean Shinoda Bolen, at a conference in Ireland: "Only by being innocent and risking being foolish will we heal those parts of us and help to heal the Earth."

Peter and Patsy respected my need to proceed in my way and to speak with my voice. They ensouled this process for me and with me. I honor the green heart in each of them.

In 1994, as I am reading Patsy an early draft of the *Creeksong* story, I look up to find her weeping. Every student dreams of such a supervisor.

For his part, Peter has been urging me to write this book for 30 years. Here it is, finally, Peter.

The astute observations and huge practical assistance of my husband and research assistant, Karl-Heinz Langheinrich, guided and supported my early research, analysis of survey materials, and writing.

I was blessed with Aidan Davison as my Murdoch office mate for four years and he is a cherished friend. I thank Aidan for decades of warm friendship and for helping me understand the relationships between cities and sustainability.

During 1992, my field research in the Northern Territory was guided by the late Professor David Lea, formerly Director of the North Australia Research Unit (NARU), Australian National University, Darwin. David's help included the logistical support required by my "Deep Creek" rural circumstances. His commitment to sustainable development and reform encouraged me during tough times. David made available NARU's excellent research support services, as well as providing astute professional guidance, and warm friendship when I dearly needed it (with his generous wife, musician and composer, the late Beverley Lea).

In the School of Architecture at the University of British Columbia, from 1995 to 1996, the late Shelagh Lindsey, philosopher and sociologist, undertook to be my overseas supervisor, supporting my research with countless acts of generosity, love, scholarship, and encouragement, reading, and providing detailed comments on drafts of several chapters. Thank you, Shelagh.

My initial research was funded for four years by an Australian Postgraduate Research Award, by the Dorothy Davidson Fellowship from the Australian Federation of University Women (AFUW), Queensland Branch, and a postgraduate student travel grant from Murdoch University, Western Australia. I thank these bodies, especially the gracious women of AFUW in Brisbane.

As I was about to commence this research, a colleague who was completing her PhD advised me that I must forego my former (and naïve) collaborative ways to ensure that nobody stole my ideas. I completely ignored her advice. How glad I am for that. Throughout my dissertation and this book are woven strands of information, insight, wisdom, and encouragement from scores of friends and colleagues who have read this work in progress or contributed in other ways. I acknowledge all those people with deepest thanks.

I acknowledge individually some to whom I am incredibly grateful: the professional and administrative staff of the North Australia Research Unit (NARU), especially Colleen Pyne and Sally Roberts Bailey of the incomparably cool NARU Library; the adults and children of the "Deep Creek" community at Humpty Doo; and these friends, scholars, and supporters: Juergen Schmidt, Ann Cross, Susan Ball, Evelyn Martin, Dr. Timothy Beatley, Dr. Leonie Sandercock, Dr. Ann Forsyth, Professor Emerita Clare Cooper Marcus, the late Professor Robert Zehner, Dr. Jean Hillier, Dr. Aidan Davison, Joc Schmiechen, Paul Josif, Henry Koops, Owen

Peake, Helen Buchanan, Jenny Longley, Susan Davidson, Roselina Stone, Jan Kapetas, Dr. Vanda Rounsefell, Karen Assumption, Bonnie Schoenberger, Rae Fry, Linda Wirf, Wolfgang Wirf, Amanda Rutherford, Carol Bacci Hartley, Kelvin Walsh, Kristin Stewart, Anna Puttner, Brian Richards, Dr Andrea Cook, Linda Butcher, Christine Jones, Dr. David Wilmoth, Dr. Don Perlgut, Dr. Chamlong Poboon, Che Poboon, and Dr. Sandra Taylor.

The five jewels of my Adelaide-based Accountability Group brightened this process with their love, encouragement, practical assistance, professional wisdom, and good humor. They read every word of my thesis and commented on it. What a blessing! I honor the memory of the late Malcolm Challen and extend warmest thanks to Shelagh Noble, Janet Gould, Angela Hazebroek OAM, LFPIA, and Dr. Iris Iwanicki LFPIA.

I thank my friends who visited me at Humpty Doo and supported me there: Susan Ball, Dr. Vanda Rounsefell, Shelagh Noble, Janet Gould, Joc Schmiechen, Clare Cooper Marcus, Lucy Marcus, and my late, marvelous friend, Barbara Boden (*B2*). I also thank Barbara for many generous interludes of hospitality in Darwin, for helping me concrete my "office" floor, and for supporting me to develop an unswerving devotion to Merlot.

I thank the late Roy Pallant of North Vancouver for valuable insights into the early history of Norgate Park.

I bow in gratitude to my great friend and teacher, talented healer and clairvoyant, the late Carol Bacci Hartley, and I thank her and her husband, Grant Hartley, for their love, hospitality, support, and healing.

In a similar vein, my new Canadian friend, Sandra Wagman, of Unique Insight: Readings with a Twist, helped me on several occasions to delve more deeply into family dynamics by journeying with me into my past. My childhood reminiscences were enormously strengthened by my close collaboration with this skilled intuitive psychic medium. Thank you, Sandra. To learn about Sandra, see: https://www.uniqueinsightreadings.com/

Through Sandra, I also bless the memory and deeply thank Rachel Harutine Sarkissian and Hosannah Harutine Sarkissian.

I am exceptionally grateful to my dear friend of 68 years, Canadian artist, writer, and broadcaster, Carol Munro, for permission to use the beautiful encaustic painting, "Root and Blossom," which graces this book. Carol also spent many hours editing earlier versions of this book and providing warm hospitality, a shoulder to cry on, and astute editorial guidance. Carol's spectacular artwork can be found at carolmunro.ca. Thank you again, Carol.

Carol's granddaughter, my excellent friend, Molly Rose Vincent, can read very well and also read parts of this story. I bless this glorious eight-year-old for her generous feedback. Thank you, Molly!

I thank another dear friend of 68 years, esteemed Canadian poet, Dr. Jane Munro, for permission to use her beautiful poem, "Flax," and for decades of deep and nourishing friendship.

I thank my friend Jennifer Matthews and bless our friendship and her patient reading of my manuscript over several years.

I thank Dr. Julian Louey of Vancouver for his generous gift of a writer's retreat in March 2021.

I thank my cousin, Raffi R. Berberian, for his generous help and gifts over many years, and his sister, my cousin, Dr. Cynthia Berberian Hale, for a huge amount of archival assistance most generously and graciously offered to help me better understand my Armenian heritage and its effects on my life and work.

I am indebted to musician, composer, singer and engagement practitioner, Rachel Colella of South Australia, for arranging, playing, and singing my composition, "My Creeksong." (And for encouraging me that it *was* a song.) I wrote that song 30 years ago! Rachel also prepared an instrumental version of "My Creeksong" and shared some of her other compositions that we are using in the *Creeksong* audiobook. Our collaboration, extending far beyond our shared identities as community engagement practitioners, has been richly rewarding. Thank you so much, Rachel! You brought my song to life.

For more about Rachel Colella and her music, please visit: https://www.reverbnation.com/ravenk8/ and https://myspace.com/ravenk8/

I am very grateful to gifted voice coach and master teacher of vocal technique, Spencer Welch, Vancouver, for helping me to turn my lyrics and a tune that had been rattling around in my head for 26 years into music that Rachel could work with and produce "My Creeksong." See: https://spencerwelch.com/

The other song in the audiobook is by Melbourne singer, songwriter and guitarist, Dominic (Dom) Brinkley. It's called "Climate Blues." Written in 2020, it's cry of despair and a call to action to Australians—and their right-wing federal government—regarding climate change issues. Dom generously provided his song to support this book (and its messages). You can also hear his instrumental version throughout the audiobook. Thank you, again, Dom!

You can listen to Dom's song on Spotify: https://tinyurl.com/2n8nh92d/

And here is a link to his website: https://dombrinkleymusic.bandcamp.com/

For great audio recording assistance to me and Chris Baudat, I thank Rajesh Gunaskaran.

I thank the indomitable Brett Nielsen of Big Toe Productions for his generosity and for explaining the exigencies of recording and mastering bush sounds. Especially decades ago. And with no hands! See: https://brettnielsen.com/breakfast-at-kakadu/

Over the past three decades, many friends and colleagues have read, edited, and commented on this book in its many forms. I acknowledged a joyful debt of gratitude to them:

Sharon Butala, Dr. Aidan Davison, Dr. Andrea Cook, Andrew Curthoys, Angela Hazebroek OAM LFPIA, Anna Brassard, Anne Dunn AM, Anne Gorman, Barry Murphy, Becky Hirst, Brendan Hurley, Brian Hinton, Carol Munro, Prof. Emerita Clare Cooper Marcus, Colette Meunier, Cynthia Berberian Hale, David Dacus, David Hunter, David Vaisbord, Dr. David Wilmoth, Desley Renton, the late Douglas Coomes, Heather Webster, Howard Bartlett, Dr. James O'Callaghan, Dr. Jane Munro, Jean Millar, Jennifer Matthews, Jenny Bennett, Joc Schmiechen, John Bevelander, Justin Ray, Dr Leonie Sandercock, Leonie Shore, Dr. Lori Mooren, Margaret Wilson, Maxine Schleger, Michael Collie, Michael Kerry, Dr. Mike Mouritz, Molly Rose Vincent, Monica Sidhu, Dr. Noel Wilson, Dr. Norman Etherington, AO, D. Patrick Miller, Dr. Peter Hayes, Peter Leask KC, Prof. Peter Newman AO, Petrea King, Wendie Batho, Phil Durston, Rachel Colella, Raffi Berberian, Dr. Rebecca Bateman, Robyn Schmiechen, Steph Vajda, Tammi Mann, Tandy Solomon, Dr. Vanda Rounsefell, Wiwik Bunjamin-Mau, and Yollana Shore.

I single out for gratitude my precious friend of 44 years, Colette Meunier, also an urban planner. I marvel again at her incredibly insightful and precise editing assistance, and delight in her loving care. Thank you, again, Colette.

In that vein, I extend my deep gratitude to two former PhD students who studied with me at Murdoch University in the 1990s. I thank Dr. Mike Mouritz, of Curtin University, Perth, for many blessings, including reviewing almost every page of this manuscript. Dr. Aidan Davison of the University of Tasmania has similarly helped me by generously reading and commenting on almost every page of this book. Both these collaborations have enriched me personally, as well as improving this book.

I bless my dear friend of 60 years, Peter Leask KC, for his unswerving support of the *Creeksong* project and his generous gift of structural editing advice on this, our second book together.

As I was completing this book, I found the world's best editor, Anderson S. García. In Venezuela! Anderson is a skilled professional editor *and* a psychologist. His psychological insights now permeate this book. What a blessing to receive this remarkable help in the last stages of book production. Thank you, again, Anderson!

I thank my editor, Erin Stalcup, for her challenging, generous, perceptive, and thoughtful editing and support. This book is so much better for Erin's astute editing.

Christopher Baudat and I acknowledge the generous and warm support and assistance of Carl Craig and Carlyn Craig of Post Hypnotic Press in Vancouver, in the design and production of the *Creeksong* audiobook.

I have been a huge fan of Chellis Glendinning's writing for many decades. I am honored that she agreed to write the Foreword to this book, and I thank her for her generous contribution.

I thank my great friend, Doug Swanson, who died many years ago, for encouraging me to visit Camp Concern in 1976. I honor Doug's dream of the "subversive science" of ecology in this, my book about ecology.

I honor the memory of my indefatigable friend, "Mica," the *Green Man*, who graciously agreed for me to build a house and live for a year on his "Deep Creek" property in Australia's Northern Territory at Humpty Doo. I offer gratitude for your deep green heart, your prodigious mind, your wild literacy, spacious generosity, our long friendship, your passionate loving, and your brilliant mentoring. I also offer my sincere respect for your privacy. While I know that you disagreed strongly with many of my characterizations and interpretations in earlier versions, you also generously helped me in innumerable ways: logistical, philosophical, educational, spiritual, and personal. You have guided me in recent years to present a balanced version of our shared story.

In January 1991, Mica told me, "You have me for life as a friend." Now I remind you, Mica, that you have *me* forever—through all lives—as your friend. You know better than anyone that I would not be the "green" and philosophical activist I am today without your fierce commitment to my conscientization, my education, and the strengthening of my courage. "Mica" died at Humpty Doo surrounded by those who loved him in December 2015. I bless your memory. I feel your love and support as I write about the many dimensions of our shared journey.

Here is my book about ecology, Mica.

My late husband, Karl-Heinz Langheinrich, a passionate deep ecologist, who died suddenly on 6 February 2016, was this book's first cheerleader. From 1993 to 2016, he read every word and brought to this project the fire and insight of a man with his manhood, gender politics and environmental politics intact. How Karl loved the Earth! Karl's partnership, love, and unconditional support nourished and uplifted my spirits over 23 years (and beyond). His wild philosophical mind, great cooking, tireless welding, subtle humor, patient proofreading, and tough fearlessness made creating this book with him glorious, even during the tough times.

It would be an understatement to say that this writing project has had a life of its own. Many lives, actually. It's invited many wonderful people into my life over more than three decades. My partner, Christopher André Baudat, is a recent and most welcome contributor to this book—and to my life. He has read every word and provided detailed editorial advice and insights, as well as photographs and generous support in innumerable ways over 18 months. Chris is also the producer of the *Creeksong* audiobook.

I bless Chris for his generosity, kindness, unconditional support, editing, proofreading, persistence, photography, *shiatsu*, gelati, technical support, and everything else. I thank him for learning how to create an inspirational audiobook and persisting with it. Mostly, I thank him *for making a home for this book in his heart*.

I honor the memory of my parents. I offer huge respect and gratitude to Mary Tudhope Cooke Sarkissian Miles, my mother (known as "Tud" to her family and friends). Now you are the blessing of a soothing, refreshing stream at the culmination of a long pilgrimage. Thank you for your invitation to our astonishing new conversation.

I honor Gordon Samuel Alexander Sarkissian, my father, *puer aeternus*, for your boundless, boyish enthusiasm and for teaching me to sing the brave songs that live in my heart. And for the one song you wrote:

It's you
Every beat of my heart's
For you, only you
All the stars up above
Whisper sweetly
It's love, it's love...

I bless the gift of flowing water: the Capilano River in North Vancouver, Horns Creek at Humpty Doo, and the Tweed River in Uki, Australia, that returned my life to me.

I bless the gift of trees. Honoring above all the abundant blessings and lessons that trees continue to shower upon me, I kneel in humility and gratitude before *Tristia* and the spirit of *Alba*, the White Gum. I bless my Nimbin tree with its colony of laughing kookaburras, and the remnant temperate coastal forests of Vancouver.

I bless the Earth. To Gaia, the Earth Mother, *my* Mother, protector, and guide: I bow deeply to reaffirm my servitude.

I continue to hold fast to the Mother.

Previously Published Stories by Wendy Sarkissian

Sarkissian, Wendy (1993). "Watching the Fire," *Northern Perspective 16*(2), December: 109-115.

Sarkissian, Wendy (1994a). "Counting," *Northern Perspective 7*(1), August: 40-43.

Sarkissian, Wendy (1978). "Planning as if Women Mattered: The Story of Brown Hills," *Makara, 3*(3) (September): 10-13.

Permissions

Jane Munro: Jane Munro's poem, "Flax" from her 2006 book of poems, *Point No Point*, is reprinted with permission of Jane Munro and her publisher, McClelland & Stewart, Toronto.

Carol Munro: Cover art by permission of the artist, Carol Munro: "Root and Blossom" 16" x 12," encaustic on canvas, undated. www.carolmunro.ca.

Dominic Brinkley: Lyrics from the song "Climate Blues" by Dominic Brinkley, are reproduced by permission of Dominic Brinkley.

Credits: Released February 16, 2020. Music and lyrics by Dominic Brinkley. Performed by Dom Brinkley (vocals, guitar). Artwork by Dan Blitzman. Artwork reproduced by permission of Dan Blitzman.

Brett Nielsen: *Breakfast at Kakadu*. Brett Nielsen of Big Toe Productions, Australia, has granted permission to use this soundscape in the audiobook. See: https://brettnielsen.com/breakfast-at- kakadu/

Rachel Colella: permission to reproduce the sung and instrumental versions of "My Creeksong" and other compositions. *My Creeksong* words and music by Wendy Sarkissian. Arranged and performed by Rachel Colella, Adelaide, South Australia, 7 November 2022.

The Michael Leunig Studio, Melbourne Australia: permission to reproduce in its entirety the *Prayer* by Michael Leunig on page xx.

Cover design by Matthew Fielder.

Cover design by Gerardo Basilio

Cover art is based on artwork by Augustine Wong (Dubai), https://unspash.com/

All photographs are by the author unless otherwise attributed.

Specific Image Attributions

page xx: Chellis Glendinning by Anton Brkic, Pixel Images, Santa Fe, NM. Used with permission.

page xxi: Wendy Sarkissian: Susan Ball, 1992.

page 2: Dominic Brinkley: Raphael Love.

page 54: Plan of Norgate Park, 1952 drawn by Samaneh Arasteh PhD, 2022.

page 55: Collage of Norgate Park houses: Christopher Baudat, 2022.

page 68: Dreamstime: Little Girl Lost in Forest Walking Alone. Royalty-Free Stock Photo.
ID 109286249 © Stefan Ugljevarevic.

page 80: 1940s Lumber Industry Logging Truck With Full Load Driving Down Dirt Road © Panoramic Images / Classicstock. Used with permission.

page 218: *Feng shui* / Geomancy map by Juergen Schmidt.

page 256: Wendy Sarkissian: Susan Ball, 1992.

page 257: Wendy Sarkissian: Vanda Rounsefell, 1992.

page 311: Wendy Sarkissian: Joc Schmiechen, 1992.

page 375: Sketch by Shelagh Noble, 1992.

page 511: Wendy Sarkissian: Christopher Baudat.

Back cover photo: Joc Schmiechen, 1992.

Back cover photo of Wendy Sarkissian: Christopher Baudat, 2022.

Notes and Acknowledgement of Quotations

NORGATE PARK
Reference: Snyder, Gary (1990). *The Practice of the Wild: Essays*. San Francisco: North Point Press.

LOST IN THE FOREST
Reference: Wagoner, David (1994). "Lost," in *The Heart Aroused: Poetry and the Preservation of the Soul in Corporate America*, ed. David Whyte. New York: Doubleday: 259-261.

STARVING FOR SOMETHING ELSE
Reference: https://mamasaynamaste.com/

SINGING THE BLUES
References:
Smith, Betty (1998). *A Tree Grows in Brooklyn*. New York: Perennial Classics, Book 2, Chapter 5.
"Singing the Blues" written by Melvin Endsley and published in 1956. The song was first recorded and released by **Marty Robbins** in 1956. https://www.musixmatch.com/

ESCAPE FROM NORGATE PARK
My Heart Stood Still, 1927 by Richard Rogers and Lorenz Hart.
Reference: www.songmeaning.com/

CAMP CONCERN
References:
Kohàk, Erazim (1984). *The Embers and the Stars: A Philosophical Inquiry into the Moral Sense of Nature.* Chicago: University of Chicago Press.
Eagles: https://www.azlyrics.com/lyrics/eagles/desperado. html
Hammond, Catherine, ed. (1991). *Creation Spirituality and the Dreamtime.* Sydney: Millennium Books: xiii.

PART 4: A MIDLIFE JOURNEY
Reference: Halifax, Joan (1993). *The Fruitful Darkness: Reconnecting with the Body of the Earth.* San Francisco: HarperSanFrancisco: 18-19

1. THE YEARNING
Reference: Houston, Jean (1992). *The Hero and the Goddess: the* Odyssey *as Mystery and Initiation.* London: Aquarian Thorsons.

DRINKING THE TEARS OF THE EARTH
Reference: Munro, Jane (2006). "Flax," *Point No Point.* Toronto: McClelland & Stewart: 25.

I AM BEING DRAGGED ALONG
References:
Bolen, Jean Shinoda (1994a). *Crossing to Avalon: A Woman's Midlife Pilgrimage.* San Francisco: HarperSanFrancisco.
Achterberg, Jean (1988). "The Wounded Healer: Transformational Journeys in Modern Medicine," in Gary

Doore, ed. *Shaman's Path: Healing, Personal Growth, & Empowerment.* Boston and London: Shambhala: 115-125.

Fox, Matthew (1993). *Creation Spirituality: Liberating Gifts for the Peoples of the Earth.* San Francisco: HarperSanFrancisco.

MY PLAN TO LEARN ABOUT ECOLOGY

Reference: Starhawk (1982) *Dreaming the Dark: Magic, Sex & Politics.* Boston: Beacon Press.

MY HIPPIE LOVER

References:

Halifax, Joan (1993). *The Fruitful Darkness: Reconnecting with the Body of the Earth.* San Francisco: HarperSanFrancisco.

Hite, Shere (1976). *The Hite Report: A Nationwide Study of Female Sexuality.* New York, Seven Stories Press.

WHERE ARE YOUR BOOKS ON ECOLOGY, WENDY?

Reference: Grof, Christina (1993). *The Thirst for Wholeness: Attachment, Addiction, and the Spiritual Path.* San Francisco: HarperSanFrancisco.

INSIDE THE INSIDE

Reference: Bolen, Jean Shinoda (1994a). *Crossing to Avalon: A Woman's Midlife Pilgrimage.* San Francisco: HarperSanFrancisco.

CHRISTMAS PRESENT

Reference: Bly, Robert (1990). *Iron John: A Book about Men.* Shaftesbury, Dorset: Element.

A VISIT FROM A KOOKABURRA

References:

Halifax, Joan (1993). *The Fruitful Darkness: Reconnecting with the Body of the Earth.* San Francisco: HarperSanFrancisco.

Snyder, Gary (1990). *The Practice of the Wild: Essays*. San Francisco: North Point Press.

Dillard, Annie (1974). *Pilgrim at Tinker Creek*. New York: HarperCollins.

Ehrlich, Gretel (1985). *The Solace of Open Spaces*. New York: Viking.

Oliver, Mary (2020). "The Gift," in *Devotions: The Selected Poems of Mary Oliver*. New York: Penguin Books: 14.

Murdock, Maureen (1990). *The Heroine's Journey*. Boston and London: Shambhala.

Debussy, Achille Claude. https://blog.imagesmusicales.be/debussys-controversial- golliwog/ See also: https://www.amazon.com/Golliwoggs-Cakewalk-Sheet-Alfred-Masterwork/dp/0739016415.

THE ONLY BEING THAT DOES NOT KNOW ITS PLACE

Reference: Reference: Halifax, Joan (1993). *The Fruitful Darkness: Reconnecting with the Body of the Earth*. San Francisco: HarperSanFrancisco.

CREEKSONG

References:

Rolston, Holmes III (1981). "The River of Life: Past, Present, and Future," in Ernest Partridge, ed. *Responsibilities to Future Generations*. Buffalo. NY: Prometheus Books: 130.

Ehrlich, Gretel (1985). *The Solace of Open Spaces*. New York: Viking: 75.

Griffin, Susan (1978). *Woman and Nature: The Roaring Inside Her*. New York: Harper and Row: 186.

RETREATING FROM MY RETREAT

References:

Halifax, Joan (1993). *The Fruitful Darkness: Reconnecting with the Body of the Earth*. San Francisco: HarperSanFrancisco.

Durack, Mary (1975). *Keep Him My Country*. Adelaide: Seal Books.

Modjeska, Drusilla (1990). *Poppy*. Melbourne: McPhee Gribble Australia

WHAT IT MEANS TO KILL A TREE

References:

Rose, Deborah Bird (1988). "Exploring an Aboriginal Land Ethic," *Meanjin* 47 (3): 380.

Antler, untitled poem, in Elizabeth Roberts and Elias Amidon, eds. (1993). *Earth Prayers from Around the World*. New York: HarperSanFrancisco: 322.

LIVING WITH SMALL NATIVE ANIMALS

Reference: Ehrlich, Gretel (1985). *The Solace of Open Spaces*. New York: Viking.

THE BUSINESS OF SUSTAINABILITY

References:

Starhawk (1989) *The Spiral Dance: The Rebirth of the Ancient Religion of the Great Goddess*. San Francisco: Harper and Row.

Coombs, H.C. (1990). *The Return of Scarcity: Strategies for an Economic Future*. Cambridge: Cambridge University Press and Canberra: Centre for Environmental Studies, Australian National University.

Coombs, H.C. (1992). "Coombs: Australian Society Being Corrupted," *ANU Reporter* 23 (20), 9 December: 1, 5.

FEELING CRAZY, UNSTUCK

Reference: Hale, Carl S. (1992). "Psychocatabolism and the Dark Night of the Self," *Journal of Humanistic Psychology* 32 (1), Winter: 65-89.

FINDING MY PURPOSE

Reference: Snyder, Gary (1990). *The Practice of the Wild: Essays*. San Francisco: North Point Press.

REMEMBERING LAST YEAR'S BUSHFIRE
References:

Bolen, Jean Shinoda (1994a). *Crossing to Avalon: A Woman's Midlife Pilgrimage*. San Francisco: HarperSanFrancisco.

Ehrlich, Gretel (1985). *The Solace of Open Spaces*. New York: Viking.

Watts, Alan (1973). *THE BOOK: On the Taboo Against Knowing Who You Are*. London: Abacus.

NO BOUNDARY
References:

Griffin, Susan (1978). *Woman and Nature: The Roaring Inside Her*. New York: Harper and Row.

Wilber, Ken (1985). *No Boundary: Eastern and Western Approaches to Personal Growth*. Boston: Shambhala.

FIRE ECOLOGY, ACCORDING TO ALAN
Reference: Seed, John (1996). "The Bradley Method of Bush Regeneration," in Michael Tobias and Georgianne Cowan, eds. *The Soul of Nature*. New York: Plume-Penguin: 287- 290.

LISTENING TO TRISTIA
References:

Thoreau, Henry (1906). *The Writings of Henry David Thoreau*. Boston: Houghton Mifflin.

Browning, Elizabeth Barrett (2012). "Aurora Leigh" (1857), in Nicholson, D.H.S. and A.H.E. Lee, eds. *The Oxford Book of English Mystical Verse*. Berkeley, CA: Apocryphile Press.

4. THE RETURN
References:

CREEKSONG

Halifax, Joan (1993). *The Fruitful Darkness: Reconnecting with the Body of the Earth*. San Francisco: HarperSanFrancisco.

Grof, Christina (1993). *The Thirst for Wholeness: Attachment, Addiction, and the Spiritual Path*. San Francisco: HarperSanFrancisco: 124.

Bolen, Jean Shinoda (1994a). *Crossing to Avalon*: *A Woman's Midlife Pilgrimage*. San Francisco: HarperSanFrancisco.

CONSECRATION: THE KISS OF KNOWLEDGE

Reference: Oelschlaeger, Max (1991). T*he Idea of Wilderness: From Prehistory to the Age of Ecology*. New Haven: Yale.

MY CREEKSONG

Words and music © Wendy Sarkissian, 2022. Arranged and performed by Rachel Colella, 2022.

AFTERWORD 3

References:

Williamson, Marianne (1992). *A Return to Love: Reflections on the Principles of A Course in Miracles*. New York: HarperCollins: 150

Sarkissian, Wendy (1985). *On Their Own: Social Needs and Behaviour of Tenants in an Outer- Suburban Public Housing Estate*. Paper presented to the Australian National Housing Conference, Sydney, May.

Sarkissian, Wendy (1978). "Planning as if Women Mattered: The Story of Brown Hills," *Makara, 3*(3) (September): 10-13.

APPRECIATIONS

Reference:

Bolen, Jean Shinoda (1994b). "Crossing to Avalon", paper to International Transpersonal Association, 13th International Conference, Killarney, Ireland, 23 May. Audiotape from Conference Recording Service, Berkeley, California, Tape 005.

References

Achterberg, Jean (1988). "The Wounded Healer: Transformational Journeys in Modern Medicine," in Gary Doore, ed. *Shaman's Path: Healing, Personal Growth, & Empowerment*. Boston and London: Shambhala: 115–125.

Aitken, Robert (1982). *Taking the Path of Zen*. New York: North Point Press.

Antler, untitled poem, in Elizabeth Roberts and Elias Amidon, eds. (1993). *Earth Prayers from Around the World*. New York: HarperSanFrancisco: 322.

Australia, Bureau of Meteorology (1991). *Surviving Cyclones*. Canberra: Australian Bureau of Meteorology.

Australia, Bureau of Meteorology (1992). *Monthly Weather Review, Northern Territory*. Darwin: Bureau of Meteorology, April.

Australia, Ecologically Sustainable Development Steering Committee (1992a). *Draft National Strategy for Ecologically Sustainable Development: A Discussion Paper*. Canberra: AGPS.

Australia, Ecologically Sustainable Development Steering Committee (1992b). *Final Report: Executive Summary*. Canberra: AGPS.

Australian Parks and Wildlife Service (1980). *Kakadu National Park Plan of Management*. Canberra: ANPWS.

Beatley, Timothy (1989). "Environmental Ethics and Planning Theory," *Journal of Planning Literature* 4(1), Winter: 1-32.

Blum, Ralph H. (1985). *The Book of Runes: A Handbook for the Use of an Ancient Oracle: The Viking Runes.* Sydney: Angus & Robertson Publishers.

Bly, Robert (1990). *Iron John: A Book about Men.* Shaftesbury, Dorset: Element.

Bolen, Jean Shinoda (1994a). *Crossing to Avalon: A Woman's Midlife Pilgrimage.* San Francisco: HarperSanFrancisco.

Bolen, Jean Shinoda (1994b). "Crossing to Avalon", paper to International Transpersonal Association, 13th International Conference, Killarney, Ireland, 23 May. Audiotape from Conference Recording Service, Berkeley, California, Tape 005.

Bolen, Jean Shinoda (2011). *Like a Tree: How Trees, Women, and Tree People Can Save the Planet.* San Francisco: Conari Press.

Bolen, Jean Shinoda (2003). *Crones Don't Whine: Concentrated Wisdom for Juicy Women.* Boston: Conari Press.

Bradshaw, John (1995). *Family Secrets: What You Don't Know Can Hurt You.* New York: Bantam.

Brinkley, Dominic (2020). "Climate Blues." Spotify: https://open.spotify.com/album/1a70sxOKGelfgWDrKTEzVq/

Browning, Elizabeth Barrett (2012). "Aurora Leigh" (1857), in Nicholson, D.H.S. and A.H.E. Lee, eds. *The Oxford Book of English Mystical Verse.* Berkeley, CA: Apocryphile Press.

Cadman, David (1994). "Voice of the Land," *Resurgence,* Issue 162, January/February: 24-25.

Casarjian, Robin (1992). *Forgiveness: A Bold Choice for a Peaceful Heart.* New York: Bantam.

Coombs, H.C. (1992). "Coombs: Australian Society Being Corrupted," *ANU Reporter* 23(20), 9 December: 1, 5.

Coombs, H.C. (1990). *The Return of Scarcity: Strategies for an Economic Future.* Cambridge: Cambridge University Press and Canberra: Centre for Environmental Studies, Australian National University.

Debussy, Achille Claude. https://blog.imagesmusicales.be/debussys-controversial-golliwog/ See also: https://www.amazon.com/Golliwoggs-Cakewalk-Sheet-Alfred-Masterwork/dp/0739016415.

Dillard, Annie (1974). *Pilgrim at Tinker Creek.* New York: HarperCollins.

Doore, Gary ed. (1988). *Shaman's Path: Healing, Personal Growth, & Empowerment.* Boston and London: Shambhala.

Durack, Mary (1975). *Keep Him My Country.* Adelaide: Seal Books.

Egar, Ruth and Wendy Sarkissian (1985). "Reviewing the Australian Suburban Dream,: A Unique Approach to Neighborhood Change with the Family Support Scheme," in Marilyn Safir *et al.,* eds. *Women's Worlds: From the New Scholarship.* New York: Praeger: 270-279.

Ehrlich, Gretel (1994). *A Match to the Heart.* New York: Penguin.

Ehrlich, Gretel (1985). *The Solace of Open Spaces.* New York: Viking.

Environment Australia (2003). *Kakadu National Park: Visitor Guide and Maps.* Darwin: Commonwealth of Australia.

Evernden, Neil (1985). *The Natural Alien: Humankind and Environment.* Toronto: University of Toronto Press.

Fox, Warwick (1990). *Toward a Transpersonal Ecology: Developing New Foundations for Environmentalism.* Boston and London: Shambhala.

Fox, Matthew (1993). *Creation Spirituality: Liberating Gifts for the Peoples of the Earth.* San Francisco: HarperSanFrancisco.

Glendinning, Chellis (2019). *In the Company of Rebels: A Generational Memoir of Bohemians, Deep Heads, and History Makers.* New York: New Village Press.

Glendinning, Chellis (2008).*Objectos.* La Paz, Bolivia: Editorial 3600.

Glendinning, Chellis (1994). *My Name is Chellis & I'm in Recovery from Western Civilization.* Boston: Shambhala.

Griffin, Susan (1982). *Made from this Earth: Selections from Her Writing,* 1967-1982. London: The Women's Press.

Griffin, Susan (1978). *Woman and Nature: The Roaring Inside Her.* New York: Harper and Row.

Grof, Christina (1993). T*he Thirst for Wholeness: Attachment, Addiction, and the Spiritual Path.* San Francisco: HarperSanFrancisco.

Hale, Carl S. (1992). "Psychocatabolism and the Dark Night of the Self," *Journal of Humanistic Psychology* 32(1), Winter: 65-89.

Halifax, Joan (1993). *The Fruitful Darkness: Reconnecting with the Body of the Earth.* San Francisco: HarperSanFrancisco.

Hallen, Patsy (1987). "Making Peace with the Environment: Why Ecology Needs Feminism," *The Trumpeter* 4: 3-14.

Hammond, Catherine, ed. (1991). *Creation Spirituality and the Dreamtime.* Sydney: Millennium Books.

Hayes, Peter and Strider (1974). *A Slow Burn.* Carlton, Victoria: Friends of the Earth, September. Supplement to Australian Conservation Foundation newsletter.

Hite, Shere (1976). *The Hite Report: A Nationwide Study of Female Sexuality.* New York, Seven Stories Press.

Houston, Jean (1992). *The Hero and the Goddess: The Odyssey as Mystery and Initiation.* London: Aquarian Thorsons.

Houston, Jean (1987). *The Search for the Beloved: Journeys in Sacred Psychology.* Los Angeles: Jeremy P. Tarcher.

Houston, Jean (1982). *The Possible Human.* Los Angeles: J.P. Tarcher.

Injalak Arts and Crafts Association (1993). *Kunwinkju Seasonal Calendar 1994.* Oenpelli, N.T.: Injalak Arts and Crafts Association.

"Insult to Women: Hudson Accused," *Adelaide Advertiser*, 20 December 1977.

Johnson, Robert A. (1991). *Owning Your Own Shadow: Understanding the Dark Side of the Psyche.* San Francisco: HarperSanFrancisco.

Jung, Carl quotations. https://mamasaynamaste.com/

Kaza, Stephanie (1994). *The Attentive Heart: Conversations with Trees.* New York: Fawcett Columbine.

Kohák, Erazim (1984). *The Embers and the Stars: A Philosophical Inquiry into the Moral Sense of Nature.* Chicago: University of Chicago Press.

Kornfield, Jack (1993). *A Path With Heart: A Guide through the Perils and Promises of Spiritual Life.* New York: Bantam Doubleday Dell.

Kornfield, Jack and Breiter, eds. (1985). *A Still Forest Pool: The Insight Meditation of Achaan Chah.* London: Theosophical Publishing House.

Leunig, Michael (1993). "Prayer" in *A Common Prayer Collection.* Melbourne. Collins Dove.

Lorenz, Konrad (1961). *King Solomon's Ring.* Translated by Marjorie Kerr Wilson. London: Methuen.

Louv, Richard (2005). *Last Child in the Woods: Saving Our Children from Nature-deficit Disorder.* Chapel Hill, NC: Algonquin Books of Chapel Hill.

Lovelock, James E. (1979). *GAIA: A New Look at Life on Earth. New York*: Oxford University Press.

Lovelock, James (1988). *The Ages of Gaia.* New York: W.W. Norton.

Macy, Joanna (1993). *World as Lover, World as Self.* London: Rider.

Macy, Joanna (1991). "Waking Up in the Dreamtime," in Catherine Hammond, ed. *Creation Spirituality and the Dreamtime*. Sydney: Millennium Books: 21-34.

Macy, Joanna (1983). *Despair and Personal Power in the Nuclear Age*. Philadelphia: New Society Publishers.

Macy, Joanna and Chris Johnstone (2022). *Active Hope: How to Face the Mess We're in with Unexpected Resilience and Creative Power*. Second edition. Novato, CA: New World Library.

Marcus, Clare Cooper (1995). *House as a Mirror of Self: Exploring the Deeper Meaning of Home*. Berkeley: Conari Press.

Marcus, Clare Cooper (1987). "Alternative Landscapes: Ley-Lines, Feng-Shui and the Gaia Hypothesis," *Landscape 29*(3): 1-10.

Marcus, Clare Cooper and Wendy Sarkissian (1986). *Housing as if People Mattered: Illustrated Site-Design Guidelines for Density Family Housing*. Berkeley: University of California Press.

Mariechild, Diane (1981). *Mother Wit: A Feminist Guide to Psychic Development*. Trumansburg, NY: The Crossing Press

Mathews, Freya (1991). *The Ecological Self*. London: Routledge.

Meadows, Donella H., Jorgen Randers, Dennis L. Meadows, and William W. Behrens (1972). *The Limits to Growth: A Report for the Club of Rome's Project on the Predicament of Mankind*. New York: Universe Books.

Modjeska, Drusilla (1990). *Poppy*. Melbourne: McPhee Gribble Australia.

Munro, Jane (2006). "Flax," *Point No Point*. Toronto: McClelland & Stewart: 25.

Murdock, Maureen (1990). *The Heroine's Journey*. Boston and London: Shambhala.

Naess, Arne (1993). "The Deep Ecological Movement: Some Philosophical Aspects," in Armstrong, Susan J. and

Richard G. Botzler, eds. *Environmental Ethics: Divergence and Convergence.* New York: McGraw-Hill: 411–421.

Naess, Arne (1989). *Ecology, Community and Lifestyle: Outline of an Ecosophy.* Translated and revised by David Rothenberg. Cambridge: Cambridge University Press.

Nash, Roderick Frazier (1989). *The Rights of Nature: A History of Environmental Ethics.* Madison: University of Wisconsin Press.

Nash, Roderick Frazier (1970). *Wilderness and the American Mind.* New Haven: Yale.

Nielsen, Brett (1992). *Breakfast at Kakadu.* CD of natural sounds (including birdsong) from Kakadu National Park in the Northern Territory of Australia. With David Howell on didgeridoo click sticks. Darwin: Big Toe Productions.

Nuclear risks. https://nuclear-risks.org

O'Donohue, John (2000). *Eternal Echoes: Celtic Reflections on Our Yearning to Belong.* New York: Harper Perennial.

Oelschlaeger, Max (1991). *The Idea of Wilderness: From Prehistory to the Age of Ecology.* New Haven: Yale.

Oliver, Mary (2020). "The Gift," in *Devotions: The Selected Poems of Mary Oliver.* New York: Penguin Books: 14.

Press, Tony, David Lea, Ann Webb and Alistair Graham, eds. (1995). *Kakadu: Natural and Cultural Heritage and Management.* Darwin: Australian Nature Conservation Agency and the North Australia Research Unit, Australian National University.

Rolston, Holmes III (1981). "The River of Life: Past, Present, and Future," in Ernest Partridge, ed. *Responsibilities to Future Generations.* Buffalo. NY: Prometheus Books: 123-133.

Rose, Deborah Bird, ed. (1995). *Country in Flames: Proceedings of the 1994 Symposium on Fire and Biodiversity in North Australia.* Biodiversity Series, Paper No. 3, Biodiversity Unit. Canberra and Darwin: Biodiversity Unit,

Department of the Environment, Sport and Territories and the North Australia Research Unit, Australian National University.

Rose, Deborah Bird (1994). "Flesh. and Blood, and Deep Colonising," in Morny Joy and Penelope Magee, eds. *Claiming the Rites: Studies in Religion by Australian Women Scholars*. Adelaide: The Australian Association for the Study of Religions: 327-341.

Rose, Deborah Bird (1992a). "Breathing and Seeing Country," *The Olive Pink Society Bulletin 4* (1): 22-27.

Rose, Deborah Bird (1992b). *Dingo Makes Us Human: Life and Land in an Australian Aboriginal Culture*. Sydney: Cambridge University Press.

Rose, Deborah Bird (1988). "Exploring an Aboriginal Land Ethic," *Meanjin 47*(3): 378-387.

Rose, Deborah Bird (1987). "Consciousness and Responsibility in Aboriginal Religion," in W.H. Edwards, ed. *Traditional Aboriginal Society: A Reader*. Melbourne: Macmillan: 257-269.

Sarkissian, Wendy (2020). *Stay Close: How to Heal from Grief and Keep Connected with One Who Has Died*. Napa, CA: Fearless Literary. Ebook: https://amzn.to/2CR6q29. See www.stay- close.com/

Sarkissian. Wendy (1996). *With a Whole Heart: Nurturing an Ethic of Caring for Nature in the Education of Australian Planners*. Unpublished PhD dissertation. Perth: Murdoch University.

Sarkissian, Wendy (1994). "Counting," *Northern Perspective 17*(1), August: 40-43.

Sarkissian, Wendy (1993). "Watching the Fire," *Northern Perspective 16*(2), December: 109-115.

Sarkissian, Wendy (1992). "Ecological Literacy and Urban Planning and Development," Paper to Royal Australian Planning Institute Biennial Congress, Canberra, May.

Sarkissian, Wendy (1991). "At the Crossroads: A Personal Project in Environmental Education," 1991 Greenhouse Conference, Adelaide, South Australia, 31 August.

Sarkissian, Wendy (1985). On Their Own: Social Needs and Behaviour of Tenants in an Outer-Suburban Public Housing Estate. Paper presented to the Australian National Housing Conference, Sydney, May.

Sarkissian, Wendy (1978). "Planning as if Women Mattered: The Story of Brown Hills," *Makara, 3*(3) (September): 10-13.

Sarkissian, Wendy and Dianna Hurford with Christine Wenman (2010). *Creative Community Engagement: Transformative Engagement Methods for Working at the Edge.* London: Earthscan/Routledge.

Sarkissian, Wendy with Nancy Hofer, Yollana Shore, Steph Vajda and Cathy Wilkinson (2009). *Kitchen Table Sustainability: Practical Recipes for Community Engagement with Sustainability.* London: Earthscan/Routledge.

Schmidt, Juergen (2006). *The Hidden Forces of Nature: An Exploration of Energy, Life and Time.* Balhannah, South Australia: Energy Ecology Publishers.

Schumacher, E.F. (1977). *A Guide for the Perplexed.* New York: Harper and Row.

Seed, John (1993). "We Call Upon the Spirit of Evolution..." in Elizabeth Roberts and Elias Amidon, eds. (1993). *Earth Prayers from Around the World.* New York: HarperSanFrancisco: 34-35.

Seed, John (1996). "The Bradley Method of Bush Regeneration," in Michael Tobias and Georgianne Cowan, eds. *The Soul of Nature.* New York: Plume-Penguin: 287-290.

Seed, John, Joanna Macy, Pat Fleming and Arne Naess (1988). *Thinking Like a Mountain: Towards a Council of All Beings.* Philadelphia and Santa Cruz, California: New Society.

Sivaraksa, Sulak (1992). *Seeds of Peace: A Buddhist Vision for Renewing Society.* Berkeley: Parallax Press.

Smith, Betty (1998). *A Tree Grows in Brooklyn.* New York: Perennial Classics.

Snyder, Gary (1990). *The Practice of the Wild: Essays.* San Francisco: North Point Press.

Snyder, Gary (1993). "Understanding the Commons," in Susan J. Armstrong and Richard G. Bottler, eds. *Environmental Ethics: Divergence and Convergence.* New York: McGraw-Hill: 227-231.

Snyder, Gary (1992). *No Nature: New and Selected Poems.* New York: Pantheon.

Starhawk (1989a). "A Story of Beginnings," in Judith Plant, ed. *Healing the Wounds: The Promise of Ecofeminism.* London: Green Print. 115-117.

Starhawk (1989b). "Feminist, Earth-based Spirituality and Eco-feminism," in Judith Plant, ed. *Healing the Wounds: The Promise of Ecofeminism.* London: Green Print: 174-185.

Starhawk (1989c) The Spiral Dance: *The Rebirth of the Ancient Religion of the Great Goddess.* San Francisco: Harper and Row.

Starhawk (1982) *Dreaming the Dark: Magic, Sex & Politics.* Boston: Beacon Press.

Suzuki, David (1993). "How Much Time Do We Have Left?" public lecture, University of Western Australia, Perth, 20 November.

Thoreau, Henry (1906). *The Writings of Henry David Thoreau.* Boston: Houghton Mifflin.

Wagoner, David (1994). "Lost," in *The Heart Aroused: Poetry and the Preservation of the Soul in Corporate America*, ed. David Whyte. New York: Doubleday: 259-261.

Watts, Alan (1973). *THE BOOK: On the Taboo Against Knowing Who You Are.* London: Abacus.

CREEKSONG

Whyte, David (ed.) (1994). The Heart Aroused: Poetry and the Preservation of the Soul in Corporate America. New York: Doubleday.

Wilber, Ken (1996). *A Brief History of Everything.* Boston and London: Shambhala.

Wilber, Ken (1995). *Sex, Ecology, Spirituality: The Spirit of Evolution.* Boston and London: Shambhala.

Wilber, Ken (1991). "Taking Responsibility for Your Shadow," in Connie Zweig and Jeremiah Abrams, eds. *Meeting the Shadow: The Hidden Power of the Dark Side of Human Nature.* New York: Tarcher: 279-280.

Wilber, Ken (1985). *No Boundary: Eastern and Western Approaches to Personal Growth.* Boston: Shambhala.

Wilber, Ken (1983). *Up From Eden: A Transpersonal View of Human Evolution.* London: Routledge and Kegan Paul.

Williamson, Marianne (1992). *A Return to Love: Reflections on the Principles of A Course in Miracles.* New York: HarperCollins.

World Council on Economic Development (WCED) (1987). *Our Common Future. The Report of the World Commission on Environment and Development.* Oxford: Oxford University Press.

Index

About the Author

*W*endy Sarkissian is a feminist, award-winning community planner and author, environmental ethicist and activist. She holds a Masters in Literature from Connecticut College, a Masters of Town Planning from Adelaide University, and a PhD in environmental ethics and planning from Murdoch University, Western Australia. She is a Life Fellow of the Planning Institute of Australia.

Wendy is co-author of numerous professional books on planning, community engagement, and housing. Canadian-born, she spent a lifetime living and working many Australian cities and towns. Since 2017, she's made her home in downtown Vancouver, Canada.

For more information about Wendy's writing, the *Creeksong* audiobook, and the *Creeksong* blog, please visit www.creeksong.net/

For Wendy's professional work and other writing, please see: www.sarkissian.com.au/